Robert Mallet

Great Neapolitan Earthquake of 1857 The First Principles of Observational Seismology as Developed

Robert Mallet

Great Neapolitan Earthquake of 1857 The First Principles of Observational Seismology as Developed

ISBN/EAN: 9783741173455

Manufactured in Europe, USA, Canada, Australia, Japa

Cover: Foto ©ninafisch / pixelio.de

Manufactured and distributed by brebook publishing software (www.brebook.com)

Robert Mallet

Great Neapolitan Earthquake of 1857 The First Principles of Observational Seismology as Developed

GREAT NEAPOLITAN EARTHQUAKE OF 1857.

GREAT NEAPOLITAN EARTHQUAKE OF 1857.

THE FIRST PRINCIPLES

OF

OBSERVATIONAL SEISMOLOGY

AS DEVELOPED IN THE

REPORT TO THE ROYAL SOCIETY OF LONDON
OF THE EXPEDITION MADE BY COMMAND OF THE SOCIETY INTO
THE INTERIOR OF THE KINGDOM OF NAPLES,

TO INVESTIGATE THE CIRCUMSTANCES OF THE GREAT
EARTHQUAKE OF DECEMBER 1857.

BY

ROBERT MALLET, C.E., F.R.S., F.G.S., M.R.I.A.,
&c., &c.

"Nam *fingendum* est *excogitandum* sed inveniendum quid *natura faciat* aut *ferat*."

USED BY THE AUTHORITY AND WITH THE AID OF THE
ROYAL SOCIETY OF LONDON.

IN TWO VOLUMES—VOL. II.

CHAPMAN AND HALL, LONDON.
1862.
[*The Right of Translation is reserved.*]

LIST OF ILLUSTRATIONS

USED OR REFERRED TO

IN THE SECOND VOLUME.

NOTE.—In the following LIST OF ILLUSTRATIONS, and in the text, wherever the reference is made in the words, "*Collection of the Royal Society,*" or "*Coll. Roy. Soc.*," it is to be understood that such Illustrations have been necessarily omitted from this work, in order to limit the expense of reproducing so great a number of Photographs or Sketches, and that the originals of all such as are so omitted are to be found in the possession of the *Royal Society of London.*

MAPS A. B. C. D. E.

Seismic Map A, with Wave-paths and Isoseismal Curves, for the Neapolitan Earthquake of December 16, 1857	*V. Brooks, left-hand pocket.*	
Report to Royal Society of London, Map B, showing the Physical Features of the Neapolitan Earthquake of December 16, 1857	" *right-hand pocket.*	
		Page.
Approximate Comparison of Seismal Areas, Neapolitan Earthquake of December, 1857, Map C	*to face*	253
Comparative Map, D, of the Seismic Bands of the Mediterranean	" "	370
Earthquake of December 16, 1857—Map E. No. 1. Diagram of observed Maxima and Minima Wave Emergences, and Resulting Depth of Focus. No. 2. Diagram of Mean Wave Emergences, and Deduced Mean Focal Depth	" "	246

LIST OF ILLUSTRATIONS USED OR REFERRED TO IN THE SECOND VOLUME.

Number.		Page.
	Montemurro.—See No. 262 . . . *V. Brooks, Frontispiece.*	
259.	Montemurro . . . . „ *to face*	2
260.	Collection of the Royal Society	1
261.		
262.	Montemurro.—*See Frontispiece* . . . *V. Brooks.*	
263.	Collection of the Royal Society	5
264.	Woodcut . . . . *Dalziel Bros.*	6
265.	Montemurro, Palace of Don Andrea Fino . *V. Brooks, to face*	7
266.	Collection of the Royal Society	9
267.	„ „	5
268.	„ „	8
269.	Montemurro, Column and Cross uninjured . *V. Brooks, to face*	10
270.	Viggiano . . . . . . „	13
271.	Viggiano . . . . . . „	13
272.	Collection of the Royal Society	14
273.	„ „	15
274.	Great landslips and fissures in the Piano of Mettine, on the River Agri, near Viggiano—Eye sketch . . . . *V. Brooks, to face*	14
275.	Collection of the Royal Society	16
276.	„ „	18
277.	„ „	19
278.	„ „	20
279.	Woodcut . . . . . . *Dalziel Bros.*	22
280.	Collection of the Royal Society	23
281.	„ „	24
282.	Woodcut . . . . . . *Dalziel Bros.*	20
282 *bis.*	The Chigna Madre, Tramutola . . *V. Brooks.*	23
283.	Collection of the Royal Society	25
284.	„ „	29
285.	„ „	29
286.	„ „	29
287.	„ „	29
288.	„ „	29

LIST OF ILLUSTRATIONS.

Number.			Page.
289. Oriessa		V. Brooks, to face	34
290. Salvitello		"	35
291. Woodcut		Dalziel Bro.	36
292. Collection of the Royal Society			37
293.	"	"	38
294.	"	"	38
295. Little Monument at Vietri di Potenza, &c.		V. Brooks.	29
296. Collection of the Royal Society			41
297.	"	"	53
298.	"	"	53
299.	"	"	52
300.	"	"	53
301.	"	"	58
302.	"	"	59
303.	"	"	59
304.	"	"	59
305.	"	"	59
306.	"	"	59
307.	"	"	60
308. Woodcut		Dalziel Bro.	60
309. Collection of the Royal Society			61
310. Woodcut		Dalziel Bro.	61
311. "		"	64
312. "		"	67
313. Cathedral of Potenza		V. Brooks, to face	68
314. Collection of the Royal Society			71
315.	"	"	71
316. Fog Frosted Stubble.—See page 35, vol. ii.		V. Brooks.	
317. Erosion, Valley of the Aritello, near Potenza.—See page 35, vol. ii.		"	
318. Atella, and part of the Vulture Range		"	86
319. Lombardic Church at Atella		"	68
320. Woodcut		Dalziel Bro.	88
" Figs. 2 & 3, Collection of the Royal Society			88
321. Monte Vulture, near Rionero		V. Brooks, to face	92
322. Collection of the Royal Society			94
323.	"	"	93 & 94
324. S.W. Shoulder of Monte Vulture		V. Brooks, to face	96
325. Torrent, Monte Vulture		"	97
326. Collection of the Royal Society			100
327. The Great Crater of Vulture, with Monticchio Monastery		V. Brooks, to face	100

LIST OF ILLUSTRATIONS.

Number.		Page.
328. North End, Monticchio.—See page 96, vol. ii.	V. Brooks	
329. Collection of the Royal Society	.	105
330. " "	.	105
331. Barletta, part of a heavy wall outside the town.—See page 7, vol. ii.	V. Brooks	
332. Collection of the Royal Society	.	112
333. " "	.	112
334. Muro, Monte Croce in the distance	V. Brooks, to face	124
335. Collection of the Royal Society	.	125
336. Woodcut	Dalziel Brs.	126
337. Figures 1, 2, 3, Bella—Bella. View near the north end of the Gorge, and Muro	V. Brooks, to face	127
338. Fissures in the ground, three miles from Bella.—See page 86, vol. ii.	V. Brooks	
339. Collection of the Royal Society	.	130
340. Polverchara of Cataldo	V. Brooks, to face	133
341. Slipping Rocks, Valley of the Maldo	"	133

ERRATA.

Vol. II., page 274, line 1, after "curve" add (— · — · — ·).
  "   " 275 " 10, for (— · · · — · · · —) read (— · · — · · —).
  "   " 281 " 28, for "Toura" read "Tauria."
  "   " 308 " 5, omit comma after close.
  "   " 308 " 4, read √s.
  "   " 328 " 3, for "truth" read "trath."
  "   " 334 " 14, after "that" omit the word "and."

PART II.
(CONTINUED.)

CHAPTER XXIII.

MONTEMURRO.

It was after the sullen sunset, of a wet and wild day, before we were able to reach the bottom of the ravine beneath Montemurro. We had mistaken the way in the rapidly-gathering darkness, and had to cross the stream, here small and shallow, again, and to urge the mules, jaded with the long day's march and the fatigues of the continuous ascent and sticky mire of the last three or four miles, up the steep clay bank, beyond A (Photog. No. 259), and beneath the town (Photog. No. 262), where the deep clays into which they sank to the knees, were encumbered by the stones and ruin of the houses above, that had pitched out over and shot down the bank. It was with much difficulty that the laden animals were got to the summit, which brought us almost directly, on to the plateau of ruins, and in a few yards more we stood in front of the great monastery of St. Francisco, on what had been, a Piazza or Largo, and comparatively unencumbered with rubbish (Photog. No. 260, Coll. Roy. Soc.).

A few persons, with a gendarme and two or three monks, were approaching, the men bearing on their shoulders a large sort of deep wooden tray, of some 7 feet by 4, with one or two lights. I guessed what it meant, and as they passed I stood in the stirrups, and more senses than sight told, that three mangled and ghastly corpses formed their burden. It was the last of the day's task, to one of the labouring parties, occupied still in exhuming from the ruins and interring, the five thousand human beings that had suddenly found their fate beneath their own roof-trees, in this the most tremendously visited, of the earthquake cities.

I addressed one of the monks and handed him Cardinal Wiseman's letter; but scarce glancing at it in the twilight, he sullenly turned away, with merely "Abbiami di che," and we soon found ourselves alone, amidst darkness and a labyrinth of uninhabited ruins. After wandering about for some time on foot, we found a hut, in which a man (Giuseppe), his wife, and her mother were living, and with some entreaty and liberal promises got sheltered, sitting up, however, all night, as the hut, which was not above 12 feet by 10, did not afford room for more than the women to lie down.

Three of my muleteers passed the night round the fire of shattered house-timber that we kept up outside, the others, with the mules, in the ruins of a large church not far off. The rain poured in through the wretched improvised roof of reeds and boards, and the night passed in weary discomfort, relieved only after some broken sleep, by Giuseppe's account of the terrible night of the earthquake here, now just eight weeks past. With the first cold grey

of swiftly-coming dawn, I gladly sallied forth. The rain had ceased, the cold and air felt freshening, the stars had shone brightly in the dark sky when I had looked out before, and now shapeless masses of ruin rose still blacker against it wherever I could see. Crossing a space encumbered with beams and fragments, with deep mud and water from ponded drainage, I clambered up a huge heap, beside the tower of a fallen church, and from the vantage-point, looked over the desolation of the prostrate city. Alone, and at that cold and silent hour, the impression was one never to be forgotten. I descended at the opposite side, over the massive walls broken into steps, between huge fragments, and on slopes of rubbish; as I reached the level of the interior, something caught my foot—I stooped and found it was a long and broad piece of ancient-looking lace, that had decked some crushed altar. While I looked at it, a large piece of wall came toppling from the still standing part of the tower above, and crushed into fragments upon the talus of rubble down which I had just come, and over which I had again to make my way back to our head-quarters.

CHAPTER XXIV.

MONTEMURRO—THE CITY OF THE DEAD.

MONTEMURRO—a Saracen settlement originally—was a place of great antiquity:

> "Urbes constituit ætas, hora dissolvit." *

It stood upon a tolerably level plateau, surrounded on every side by deep ravines, in some places 700 or 750 feet in total depth, with precipitous sides of clay, and torrents in the bottom, falling into the Laderana. The plateau is also intersected in several places by smaller "nullahs," with abrupt banks; and the city had extended, until its buildings occupied the whole surface, out to and even beyond the very edges of banks above these surrounding ravines.

To the north and east, the elevated and rolling piano slopes back a long way, covered everywhere with deep clays, similarly cut into, by watercourses, and covered with oak forests and olives. Beyond this the Serra di Armento, seen in the horizon of Photog. No. 262, rises, and to the N.W. beyond this Monte Agresto; while high and far beyond both, the summits of Il Santo Spirito are capped with snow. Montemurro, therefore, stood at the southern and south-eastern verge, and upon the outlying

* SENECA.

brow, of an extensive table-land, sloping up to lofty mountain-masses extending for more than 16 miles to the north and N. W. From the high lands above the town, I could see three great river-beds—the Agri, the Moglia, and the Racanello that sweeps past Castel Saraceno, and which fall into the Agri much lower down; and looking N.E., the upper forks of the Sauro were visible, all running in deep beds, through a clay country, lofty and rolling in surface.

The mass of the plateau of Montemurro, seems at first to be nothing but clay; but upon the highest points of the town, and a little beyond it to the north and N. E., the soft, crumbly, yellow, calcareous sandstone, a half-compacted rock, comes bare up to the surface, and obviously forms a great cone, upon and around which, the immense clay deposits are heaped up.

The beds, here thick and ill-defined, run in strike nearly east and west, and dip rapidly to the south at 50°. They show themselves here and there, intercalated with some harder argillaceous shaly rock. (See Geological Section, Diagram No. 241.)

At Giuseppe's "cabane," which is nearly on the same level as the base of the great tower of the Chiese Madre, and the Franciscan Monastery (Photog. Nos. 203 and 207, Coll. Roy. Soc.), and about the mean level of the plateau of the town, the barometer stood (18th of February), at 9·30 A.M., Naples time, at 27·10 inches, thermo., 64°. The elevation above the sea is therefore 2695·8 feet, and about 2000 feet above the bed of the Agri, opposite, the whole of which fall, the torrent of the Laderana has within four or five miles. Its effects upon the clay banks may thence be understood.

The eye sketch (Fig. 264) shows the general position of Montemurro, which stood upon a nob or tongue of flat-

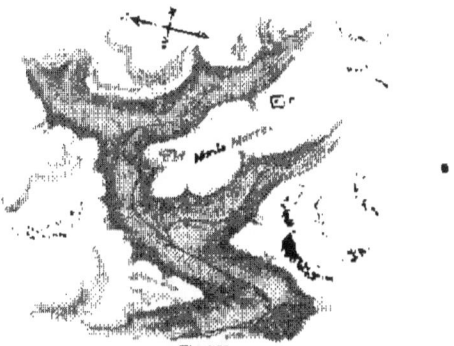

Fig. 264.

topped land, between two precipitous ravines, of immense depth, cut laterally by many minor ones, the clay banks continually shedding down, and the toes of the slopes washed away by the torrents. It occupied the whole surface of the tongue, which was built upon, out to the very edges, and even beyond the tops of the slopes.

The whole town is one vast heap of rubbish, and about an equal proportion, of the houses, &c., that stood at the extreme verges of the N. E. and S. W. banks, have been shot over in falling, so that streams of loose stone and rubbish, now whiten the slopes at both sides of the place.

The great mass of the place is, of course, beyond reach of exact examination; the remains of four of the most important buildings, however, afforded all the indications I needed. Of these, *a* (Fig. 264) is the Palazzo Fino, a modern and large, well-built, cardinal mansion, standing right across the head of one of the deep ravines. It is

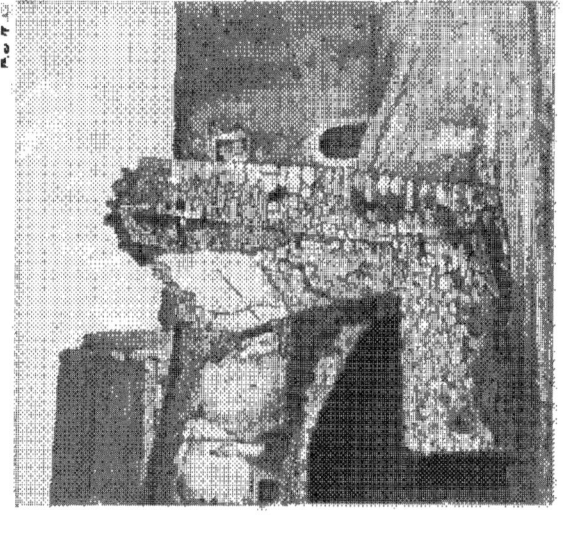

three stories above the ground, and the principal floor had vaulted ceilings, of hollow pottery (Photog. No. 265). It is fissured from base to roof, in all the walls; several fissures are open 2½ inches at top, and give excellent measures of wave-path, which averages 143° E. of north to south. The N.W. and S.E. quoins, have suffered by far the most severely, and at these places, the roof and floors are down. The building is of great length, at least 150 feet. The fissures about these quoins are diagonal, and indicate emergence from the north, but uncertainly, $e = 15°$ to $20°$. The fissures in the middle of the front and back walls, are much more nearly vertical, as are also some in the south end wall, and internal cross walls.

The unfortunate owner, Don Andrea del Fino, on the night of the earthquake, was with his wife in bed, his daughter sleeping in the adjoining chamber on the principal floor. At the first shock, his wife who was awake, leaped from bed, and at the instant after, a mass of the vaulting above, came down and buried her husband sleeping in his bed. At the same moment, the vault above their daughter's room fell in upon her; from the light and hollow construction of the vaults, neither were at once killed. The signora escaped by leaping from the front window, she almost knew not how. For more than two hours, she wandered beseechingly, but unnoticed, amongst the mass of terrified survivors in the streets without, before frantic confusion, permitted her to obtain aid from her own tenants and dependents, to extricate her husband. They got him out after more than eighteen hours' entombment, alive, indeed, but maimed and lame for life. His daughter was dead. As he despairingly had longed for release, from the compressing rubbish, which the second shock of an hour after the first, had so shaken and closed in round him, that he could scarce breathe, he heard but a few feet off, her agonizing cries and groans, grow fainter, and fainter, and end in death. The lady, to whose faithful devotion his own life was owing, had escaped without a scratch. This one episode, from the innumerable relations given me, of personal peril and sad adventure, will scarce be deemed out of place, as affording a vivid picture of the terrors of an earthquake night.

> μεσονύκτιος ἀλλύμαν,
> ἦμος ἐκ δείπνων ὕπνος
> ἡδὺς ἐπ ὄσσοις εἴσαται.
>
> Σαβϕη, 903.

This palazzo is *the only* building here, that has not been prostrated, or gutted of floors and roof, &c ; the only lofty fragments standing anywhere, are fragments of the towers of the churches at *c, d,* and *b*.

At *b* (Fig. 264) was the great monastery of St. Dominica (Photog. No. 268, Coll. Roy. Soc.), the great tower of which was shorn off, and an acutely-pointed aiguille alone left standing, as already alluded to (Part I.), sketched by me from the balcony of Palazzo Fino. This is not seen in any of the photographs. I am by no means certain that the acuteness of fracture *in this instance*, may be relied upon as indicating any shock having come up at an extremely sharp emergence at Montemurro; for although the fracture of the tower offered every characteristic of such, I could not corroborate it, by appeal to any other similar case here. There were very few buildings standing at all, and these indicated emergences, at angles that might be anything between 15° and 20°, and also horizontal movements; the latter with the largest velocity.

It is possible, therefore, that the sharp shearing off of *this* tower, may have arisen from some peculiarity of support that had disappeared, or other unnoticed cause. If it be concluded, that it had its origin in a wave of very acute emergence, then it would follow as most probable, that this had been delivered, upwards from the limestones, beneath the shales and other argillaceous formations of this region, as a lateral wave of dispersion, and an instant after the overthrow of the tower had been commenced by the primary wave. This might have been so, and yet from the total destruction round, no trace of the fact be discernible.

The Chiesa Madre (c), Fig. 264, (Photog. No. 266, Coll. Roy. Soc.), gave from fractures—not fissures, and therefore less trustworthy—a wave-path, 134° 30' E. of north, and of emergence from 20° to apparently horizontal, and the monastery of St. Francisco (Photog. No. 267, Coll. Roy. Soc.), at *d* (Fig. 264) one not more than 7° or 8° from north to south, and west of north.

It seemed evident upon the whole, that the general path of the primary wave, had been very close to 38° W. of north toward the south, and with an emergence of something between 15° and 20° from the north; that the whole mass of the nob or tongue of insulated land and its rock core, upon which the city stood, had been put in motion and oscillated forward and back, both in the direction of the wave, and transverse to it, the latter being the direction of the narrow diameter of the tongue. These latter movements were, quam prox. horizontal, and hence the complication of fissures, &c. To this *may* have been added, a secondary shock from the subjacent limestones in a direction not many degrees removed from vertical. We have thus the following conditions, all conspiring to produce that total destruction, for which Montemurro is pre-eminent.

    1st. A city of great antiquity, and generally ill built.

    2nd. Its position like that of Saponara, such that its solid base oscillated beneath its buildings, and added its pendulous velocity, to that of the wave.

    3rd. Orthogonal oscillations of the tongue of land, due to its form and direction.

The total velocity of movement impressed, must have been, I judged, about the same as at Saponara. There were several walls, &c., by which I might have attempted its calculation, but none sufficiently uncucumbered, or free from disturbance, to give trustworthy results. Thrown church bells or such like, there were none, all were buried; and whatever of displaced furniture, or other objects, had escaped destruction in the Palazzo Fino, had been removed.

The only *uninjured* (Photog. No. 269) object, was one of two small stone crosses, surmounting Corinthian columns, of about 15 feet in total height, mounted upon triple-stepped bases and plinths, of the same character and size as that referred to at Padula.

This was pointed out to me by one of the gendarmes, who were the sole authorities remaining at the ruined city, as a proof of its sacred character. It obviously owed its stability to the causes already explained. The other column near the Palazzo Fino, was overthrown and broken about the *middle* of the shaft; but it appeared more than probable, that it had been knocked down, by the fall of a

MONTENERO.

CAMINE, PALAZZO PALMIERI, POLLA.

beam against it—a view strongly favoured by the place of the fracture. To have been overturned simply by inertia, would have required a horizontal velocity of nearly 20 feet per second, and the total velocity here was certainly a good deal within that, which could not have left a stone standing of the four buildings to which reference has been made.

From the upper part of the Palazzo Fino, I obtained several compass bearings to correct for declination by, as for some days and until now, I had not seen the sun. I found

Viggiano bears . . . 50° W. of north.
Saponara ,, . . . 85° W. of north.
Moliterno ,, . . . 110° W. of north.
Spinosa ,, . . . 145° W. of north.

All these, when reduced by Zannoni's great map, give a declination between 13° and 14° west of north. That map was produced about 1810–1812, and having all been laid down from triangulation, and upon so great a scale, the positions marked upon it, are extremely accurate in general.

Montemurro is to this earthquake, what Oppido was to the Calabrian earthquake of 1783. The similarity as to position, and also in the frightful proportion of the deaths to the population, are stated by Grimaldi, in his excellent account of that catastrophe, pp. 19, 20 :—" Oppido. Citta de' tempi di mezzo : si vuoli edificata sulle rovine dell' antico Mamerto. . . . Popolazione, 2371 ; morti, 1813. La citta era situata sopra di una collina circondata da due fiumi : la sua altezza era de cinquecento passi in circa. . . . Questa collina si diviso in due parti : le sue rovine impedirono il corso ai fiumi, che la circondavano e si formarono ivi due gran laghi dalle acque ingurgitate."

At Montemurro I found no better witness of the events of the shock, than my host of the "cabane," Giuseppe, who was, I believe, a contrabandista, and had come to prey upon the ruins of the place, with probably a good understanding with the gendarmes in charge. He was not able to add any very material fact.

The time precisely of the first shock, no one knew anything about; the second was about an hour after the first. The movement, Giuseppe thought, was in a direction, that when pointed out with the hand, turned out to be from S. E. to N. W. He was thus not far astray as to path, but reverse to the real direction; but "there was movement every way, and he was alarmed." The sound was "very distinct and terrible;" he heard it and felt the first movement at the same instant, but "it continued after he had got into the street, he thought, a good while, but was not sure, for the noise of the falling city overpowered him."

VIGGIANO.

GRAND CERTOSA, PAVIA.
Interior of the Gallery of the Grand Court

CHAPTER XXV.

MONTEMURRO TO TRAMUTOLA.

On leaving, I rode along the north brow of the ravines for some way, and then struck over the southern slopes of the Piano Valloni, to Viggiano—a mediæval town, about five miles north west.

Viggiano is perched on the very summit of a mass of limestone, rising abruptly from beneath the deep clays of the valley of the Agri. (See Geological Section, Diagram No. 241, Fig. 2).

Its lofty, and, in places almost mural colline, is well buttressed to the north and round to the east, by other higher hills, of which Monte Calvario is the most conspicuous, also of limestone, showing no clear bedding to telescope; far beyond this, the lofty peaks of Monte Capodallo are visible, capped with snow. (See Sketch No. 270, and Photog. No. 271.) It is free from contact of other hills, upon the N. W. and west, and to this, no doubt, owes its comparative escape from destruction. It has, however, suffered very sadly, and very many of its population, almost all of whom are hereditary travelling musicians, have been killed and wounded. The wave-path, from fissures here, in houses below the town, gave 136° E. of north towards the south. It was too near to towns already examined, to make minute inquiry valuable. The comparative scale of its injury may be gathered from the Photog. No. 272 (Coll. Roy. Soc.), taken at near the centre of the town. I met here Mr. Major, an Englishman, who had been thus far into the earthquake regions with his staff, to distribute the British alms from Naples, and we rode some miles together, towards Tramutola to which I was bound, while he returned to Viggiano.

The Fiume Casale comes down here from the snowy summits far behind Viggiano, by a lateral ravine, and separates where it falls into the Agri, the argillaceous and sandy rocks, from the limestone, and, with the Agri, appears to be the separation from all the formations further west and south, in the limestone country. (See Geological Section, Spinosa to Viggiano, Fig. 2, Diagram No. 241.)

Passing along the Piano Mattine below Viggiano, and further northward, I found several most remarkable landslips, at the steep banks of the Agri; one of these is figured from eye-sketch in Diagram No. 274. It occurred at the salient boss, of a curve of the river, where the bed was about 400 feet, below the level of the surface of the piano. The surface of loamy clay land which had slipped, had been covered with coarse grass, now formed into many concentric curved fissures, and not less by the eye than 50 acres English had descended, and the topmost terrace of the slip, was about 50 feet below the level of the still standing land of the piano above it. The toe had protruded and greatly obstructed, the bed of the Agri, which was fast sweeping it away. It had ponded up at its fall the small stream, without a name, that came in from the east, and this had obviously recently made a debacle, of a vast mass of mud, from its base, round and over which, it now found its way to the Agri, by channels momentarily altering. It appeared to me that in three or four winters the greater part, if not the whole of this vast mass would be clean gone and deposited in the Adriatic. After crossing the little Fiume Galli, that comes down from Mount Capodallo, I passed the hamlets of Casa Rossa, and a solitary mansion in the midst of rich olive gardens, that seemed only known as "Il Palazzo," most of them in ruin. The houses at Casa Rossa, lay close beneath the mountain mass to the N. W., upon which Marsico Vetico stands, and as thus on an outlying stratum, and had suffered severely. Il Palazzo (Photog. No. 273, Coll. Roy. Soc.), as also a large mass that seemed, by its only remaining tower and the thickness of its walls, to have been some sort of mediæval strong house, or perhaps a convent (there was no one to be found), both gave wavepaths, generally coinciding with what I had obtained for all this region around.

The Palazzo showed also evidences of an orthogonal shake, derived from the limestone mountain-mass to the east of it, that of Marsico Vetico. Both these large buildings, stood upon the deep clays of the piano—the hamlets where these got shallow, at the junction with the limestone.

This piano, seems to be usually called that of Viscolione, or the Forest of Saponara—*i.e.*, all the upper end of the Piano of Mattine; but names of places are very loose affairs here. At the eastern end of this smaller valley, and before commencing to ascend it towards Tramutola, I found the barometer stood at 27·98 inches, thermometer 44° Fahr. (18th February at 3ʰ 3ᵐ Naples mean time), which gave the elevation 1820·3 feet above the sea level.

The fall of the river Agri, is therefore 1171 feet within about 10 miles, or upwards of 100 feet per mile—a tremendous rush for denudation, with such a volume of winter water. Just at the entrance to this piano, I passed the ruins of a beautiful church, Santa Clementina, of the eighteenth century, that had stood isolated and in the midst of grass land and forest oaks. Its fine stuccoes were a sad spectacle of ruin; it had been brick vaulted (Photog. No. 275, Coll. Roy. Soc.), and gave unmistakable proof of the direction of wave-path. The whole of the north flank and west end walls are down—direction, 139° E. of north to south.

The necessity of reaching Tramutola before dark, prevented my obtaining measures of emergence, that this building would have given. We had turned to the S. W. to ascend the piano, passing along the right bank of a small stream, the Capo d'Aqua, beneath the steep slopes of the hill of Monticello, to the S. E. for about half a mile, where we passed some farmhouses, or a small hamlet, now tenantless, which presented, by their walls, thrown outwards in all directions, evidences, not only of the direct or normal wave, but of a reflected earthquake echo, sent back to them from the flank of Monticello, which lay almost transverse to the wave-path; the echo reached them in a direction about 120° W. of north. It would have taken a day, however, to have investigated the phenomena perfectly, and involved an ascent to the top of Monticello, to get its direction precisely.

I reached Tramutola just at sunset, and having ridden

through its main street, encumbered with rubbish and stooping under props, was about to seek a night's lodging in some possible convent, when I was accosted by Don Antonio Georgio Mornno, a lawyer of the place, whose palazzo had been wholly destroyed, and who invited me to the hospitalities of his temporary home. From that gentleman and from his amiable wife, I received at the lodging which they occupied, in a shattered building in the town, the most gracious and cordially given hospitality, and from the signor, much valuable information.

CHAPTER XXVI.

TRAMUTOLA.

TRAMUTOLA, lies upon the north end of a low tongue of hills that come down the west side of the valley of Viscolione, and is surrounded by rather lofty mountains, both on the west and north. The town is built upon the white shattery limestone, upon a very gentle slope, dipping to the east and S.E. It is overhung by, and in part climbs the roots, of steep but low hills of limestone, to the west and south of it. The beds run nearly north and south, and dip 60° to 70° to the east.

The bottom of the narrow valley is deep clay and loam, and the hills at the east side opposite the town, appear to consist of hard, cherty, red and green stone, apparently metamorphic argillaceous rocks, in well-marked beds, running north and south, and dipping 50° W.

The town (Photog. No. 276, Coll. Roy. Soc.) is comparatively modern, and generally better built than usual; fissured and thrown-down houses occur in every part, but the greatest damage is found in the south and east districts of the town, where the oldest and worst-built houses existed. Signor Morano, and one or two of his friends of the better class of inhabitants, accompanied me on my examination.

The Capelluccio, della Madonna Maria dell' Pieta, a

small octagonal building, whose faces are cardinal, had two blocks projected from its walls. Assuming the wave velocity, the same here as at Polla, Padula, &c., viz., 13 feet per second, one of these gave for the $e = 0.273$; the other, $\tan e = 0.332$: both had descended from a height of 21 feet, and the latter had been thrown horizontally 15·75 feet, giving for the emergence an angle between 15° 16' for the one, and 18° 22' for the other, the latter being, in fact, the angle of maximum range. The former block had possibly, touched in its fall; the latter appeared unexceptionable, and, allowing for a very slight adherence in the block of stone, the value of e, may be taken here at 17° to 18°, and from the N. W.

The two blocks were thrown very nearly in the same direction at B B (Fig. 277, Coll. Roy. Soc.), and gave a wave-path 150° E. of north to south, which coincided with the deductions, from two pairs of large fissures, ff and $f'f'$ in a dwelling-house of two stories (C) close beside. The ground on which these are built slopes slightly to the east.

The house in which I slept, and in which Don Antonio Morano and his wife were lodging, a very large and heavily-built old one, had fissures open at the quoins, and in other places, 4 to 4½ inches wide at the wall plates (two high stories). These gave a rough estimation of the amplitude of the wave, the walls being very thick and inelastic; but the fissures were too perplexed by other adjoining buildings for calculation as to direction.

The mansion that Don Antonio lived in at the time of the earthquake, is almost wholly destroyed: it is at the extreme east side of the town, at the opposite side of the street to the Palazzo Marotta. (See Diagram No. 282, Fig. 2.) The longer axis of Don Antonio's house, stood

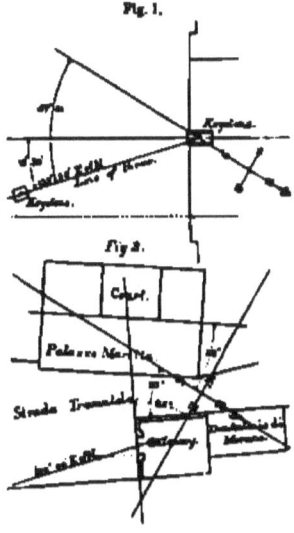

35° W. of north and south, and the S.E. gable and courtyard, with its demolished gateway, are seen in Photog. No. 278, (Coll. Roy. Soc.)* The east pier and all the blocks of stone of the elliptic arch above, had been thrown down, and lay as they fell. The general direction of wave-path that they gave, and more especially that given by the key block which had fallen, the most unperturbed in its course, was

* The key block here is that marked e. The raised timber visible had been piled upon it, between the time of my examination, and that of the photograph being taken; and several of the other blocks appear to have been disturbed in the interval.

163° 30′ E. of north to south. The wall was, therefore, nearly transverse to the wave.

This block had been thrown a distance horizontally of 9 feet, and its centre of gravity, when in place, had been 11 feet above the ground.

Adopting for the angle of emergence that given by the block at the Capelluccio, we have to satisfy the equation

$$V^2 = \frac{a^2 g}{2 \cos^2 e \, (b + a \tan e)}$$

$$a = 9: b = 11. \quad e = 18° 22',$$

and $V^2 = 218 \therefore V = 14.765$ feet per second,

or a little more than a foot and a half per second above what we assumed for V at the Capelluccio. This would not alter the value taken thence, for e, however, by 1°.

It may be considered, that the actual velocity of projection was a little *greater* than 14·765 feet per second, as there was some little adhesion between the blocks; and, in fact, if this problem be treated in the same way as the "Caisine at Polla," to which the nature of its fall and *overturn* was analogous, it would give a rather higher velocity, but the elasticity of the wall itself, measured the apparent velocity of the wave.

It hence would seem a legitimate conclusion, that here in the dense shaly argillaceous rocks, forming so much of the great mountain mass, between Padula and this valley, the earth wave actually did assume, a slightly increased velocity, over that which it has been ascertained to have had in the limestone; and thus we have an additional ground, upon which to account for the fearful destruction, at Saponara and Montemurro. The Casa Marotta stands at the opposite side of the street, a heavy building, well built, and but little damaged, while Don Antonio's, opposite, is demolished. Its long axis is 28° W. of north; the furniture still remains, as it is inhabited by the owner in some parts. The pictures along the middle walls *a a a* (Fig. 279)

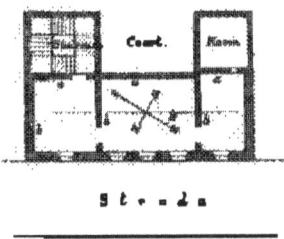

Fig. 279.

are uniformly thrown to the south, in the plane of the wall, and by friction of the backs, remained so, nothing having been disturbed in these large reception rooms, since the shock, as the dust and fragments from the fissures, in the walls and ceilings still unswept, when the rooms were unlocked for my examination, testified. One painting, 6 feet wide by 4 feet high, hung by two nails, and it has drawn or rather dragged and bent down, the projecting part of the nail, at the N.W. end, so that that corner of the picture, is below the level line 2½ inches. All the pictures on the walls *a b*, at both sides, are gone off out of plumb, towards the east, and those 1 foot 6 inches high by 2 feet 6 inches long, which hung from a single nail, are 1 inch out of plumb, in their length; two others, 4 feet long by 3 feet high, are 1½ inch out of plumb in the height, towards the east.

The pictures on the respective walls are not sufficiently

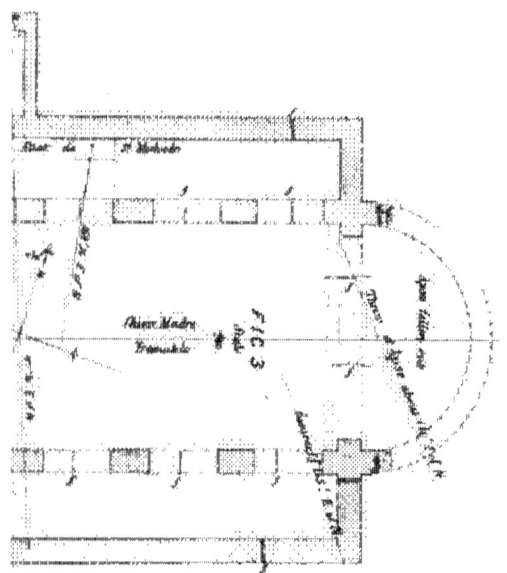

FIG. 3

similar, to compare their movements accurately. Generally, however, the displacements in the north and south plane, appeared nearly twice as much as in that east and west.

The walls of this house (three stories) are very thick in proportion to its size, 2 feet 9 inches, and nearly solid for the lower story; the apertures, few and small comparatively, and the mass of masonry large, above the tops of the upper windows, all of which, with its good class of work, have conspired to its safety, as contrasted with Don Antonio's house opposite, which is of brick in great part, and full of apertures in thin walls—a good example of the utterly diverse effects producible by the same shock.

The Chiesa Madre, a heavy Roman, arched structure, has its axial line 72° E. of north, or nearly east and west (Photog. No. 280, Coll. Roy. Soc.). The apse at the east end (Diagram No. 282 *bis*, Fig. 3), has fallen wholly out, towards the S.E. The great organ, that stood on a gallery over the west door, was projected on to the floor of the nave, in a direction S.E. All the other walls and the roof, are still standing, but heavily fissured. The heavy square piers, 6 feet by 3 feet 6 inches, of the nave, and the crowns of the arches between, are much shattered, but owe their still standing, to the shock having passed through them diagonally, and to their great dimensions. There is a formidable fissure, right across from side to side at the west end, due undoubtedly to the inertia of the organ, elevated at above mid-height, and many other fissures, the positions of some of the chief of which are marked; but little could be deduced from these here, the wave-path being obviously so very abnormal, and the walls of the church being externally propped and interfered with, by the movements of other buildings standing around and against it.

A sandstone statue of St. Leonardo, in the Capella Sta. Anna, on the north side of the church, stood elevated on a pedestal, in a niche on the north wall, in front of which was a stone and stucco slab or altar-table. (See Photog. No. 281, Coll. Roy. Soc. and Figs. 3 and 4, Diagram No. 282 *bis*.) It stood loose upon its base, 7·78 feet above the floor level, and was thrown in a direction, which finally was 102° 30' E. of north, but which, by marks upon the altar-slab and east walls, &c., seen in the Photog. No. 281, indicated that its first projection had been in a path about 144° E. of north, and that then, in pitching forward head foremost, over the edge of the altar-slab in front of the niche, it had altered the plane of its descent, to one more south, and, at the same time, thrown a complete somersault before it reached the floor, upon which it was found lying with the feet towards the south, and broken in two. The original height of the figure was $3\frac{1}{2}$ feet. It weighed entire, by careful estimation, about 160 rotuli = 314 lbs. The centre of gravity, being about $1\frac{1}{2}$ foot above the base, and the centre of oscillation over the front edge about 2 feet above it, it is not conceivable that its descent, to the position in which it was found, should have been made without the intermediate somersault. This so perplexes the effects of the original throw, that any calculation as to velocity, founded upon the horizontal distance, would probably prove fallacious. It might have reached its distance shown, viz. 7·45 feet from the front edge of the pedestal (having slided and turned over together, on the front edge of the altar-slab), by a force only just sufficient to upset it; and for this a

SALVTTELLO.

EROSION, Valley of the Arbellas.

FOG FROSTED STUBBLE.

velocity of under 13 feet per second would have sufficed, although, from its irregular figure, a precise calculation is not possible.

From the altar on the north side of the north aisle, a wooden figure of St. Michael had been thrown; it had been gathered up, but the Sacristan replaced it for me on the floor, in the position in which he said he found it. This proved to give a wave-path about 168° 30′ E. of north, one so far divergent towards the north, from those otherwise arrived at, that he was probably mistaken, or the figure had been thrown aside by something in its descent.

The Chiesa dell' Rosario, stands close to the preceding church, a vacant rectangular building, with a capella opening into it, on the north side. The belfry, seen from the outside in Photog. No. 283 (Coll. Roy. Soc.) has been fissured heavily, and part of its roof thrown down, but the bells stand. The "bambino" from the arms of the Madonna on the altar, was thrown behind the altar (they told me) in the direction marked (Fig. 5, Diagram No. 282 *bis*). This was possible, for I found the figure of the Madonna, if pushed from the N. W. or S. E. gently, assumed a gyrating rocking round its base. The axis of this church, is parallel with that of the preceding. Its great fractures, run both north and south, and east and west, and some of them are open 6 inches, at 40 feet in height; but in this case also, measurements were useless, owing to the surrounding buildings, some of which are seen in Photog. No. 283 (Coll. Roy. Soc.)

The heavy, red and white alabaster balustrade and capping, (Figs. 5 and 6, Diagram No. 282 *bis*,) that ran across and separated, the chancel from the nave, was prostrated over the steps on top of which it stood, and the fragments were still, *in situ* as they fell. All that half, to the south side which abutted against the south side wall, remained standing, the projecting force having been resolved principally against that wall; but the other half, having no such support, and the heavy-hinged doors of the same pattern and material, being open to the west at the time, in the way shown in Fig. 5, (as explained clearly to me by the parish priest), which gave freedom of fall to this half, but support by inertia (or back weight) to the preceding; the north half was wholly thrown, and the separate blocks of the capping, as well as the pilasters indicated the direction to have been 120° E. of north.

A general examination then made through the buildings of the town, as seen from the streets, and occasional admeasurements of several pairs of fissures, gave wave-path directions, from 120° to 150° E. of north, and uncertain indications as to emergence, but all proving it, from the north.

Upon a comparison of the whole, and attaching the most weight to the best observations, and in the most favourable conditions, I concluded here, a general wave-path between 150° and 160° E. of north, or more exactly one 152° 30' E. of north.

In the Punta della Chiesa, I found again one of those little stone crosses—"Il Croce della Chiesa" uninjured, and, of course, pointed out with superstitious wonder. This one was nearly 15 feet in height, but socketed together, and of hard limestone.

CHAPTER XXVII.

TRAMUTOLA—RETURN TO THE CERTOSA.

Leaving Tramutola, I purposed to have penetrated by Marsico Vecchio, and the towns to the N. E. on to Vietri, but I here found, that at this season the attempt, through that mountainous region was impracticable, or, at least, certain to be attended with great loss of time. I was therefore compelled to retrace my path, over the pass of Arena Bianca, by Lago Maorno, back into the Val di Diano, and thence by the military road, to Vietri di Potenza.

On commencing the ascent in return from Tramutola, looking back to the N. N. E., I see Marsico Vecchio, with miles of mountain, ending in Monte Voltorino, capped with snow behind them. The bedding of nearly all these mountains, appeared almost vertical to the summits, up to 2500 feet above the bottom of the valley of Tramutola. They all appear to have a general strike, to the N. N. E.; I can see at least 15 miles in that direction towards Calvello.

It had been reported to me, that heavy falls of rock had taken place at Marsico Vecchio, but my informants at Tramutola contradicted this. I should have before stated, that the noise at Tramutola, was described by Signor Morano and others, as lasting very long, beginning, they thought, at the same instant with the movement, but lasting a sensible period of time, after it was over. They described it in the usual terms as a "rolling," "murmuring," "*trampling*" (calcamentura) sound, &c. There was noise with the second shock, of an hour after the first. They had no accurate information as to the time of either, nor had any of the people in the valley of the Agri or its tributaries, any notice of unusual lights having been seen.

I had now traced the shock in a south and S.E. direction, to nearly the parallel of the head of the Gulf of Policastro, and it seemed more important to push the examination north and N. E. than to devote much more time, to the region I was in.

My return from Tramutola was made by an entirely different track over the great ridge; crossing two small ridges of hills, and the Torrent Cauoli, near its source, we struck into the valley of the Aggia, a branch of the Agri falling in on its right bank, and ascended by it, to the north side of the Piano of Maorno, leaving the lake upon the south of us, and diverging at Paterno, to the N. E. of Monte St. Elia, a mile or two north, for the purpose of examining cursorily Marsico Nuovo.

At about 2 miles from Tramutola, I lost the argillaceous beds, and came again upon white limestones, which are again succeeded within less than a mile, by the clay slates and clays—green, red, and yellow—with highly ferruginous beds, all twisted and disturbed in every direction. At the junctions, I passed many singular metamorphic rocks; at about the fifth mile the slates, &c., again disappear, and are succeeded by limestones, after which there were several short alternations, nearly to Paterno.

At Paterno I diverged northwards towards Marsico Nuovo,

already visible, distant 2 miles, perched on the conoidal summits of two low masses of limestone, (Fig. 286, Sketch Coll. Roy. Soc.), with the lofty Pietra Maura, covered with snow behind it, from which the Agri derives its source.

Paterno, a rather large and important town, had suffered severely, as the Photogs. Nos. 284 and 285 (Coll. Roy. Soc.) of the cathedral from the S. E., which shows the scalloping off, of the circular tower walls, as referred to in Part I., and of the archbishop's palace, may indicate. My object, however, was not to examine its buildings, but to discover the heavy falls of rock alleged to have taken place here; these I found were, to a great extent, fabulous. Some dislodgements of loose stones had occurred, from the limestone cliffs near the place, and of these my Photographer obtained the view (Photog. No. 287, Coll. Roy. Soc.), which is chiefly interesting, as giving an excellent idea of the petrological character of the soft limestone. I directed my attention also, to a sulphurous spring issuing not far from the town, and of which I had been told at Naples, that the volume of water had surprisingly increased after the shock, (Photog. No. 288, Coll. Roy. Soc.). As the result of my inquiries, this did not seem to be founded on fact; it had become turbid for some time, like the springs at Padula and elsewhere.

On returning, we topped the pass between the Serra Mandrano and Monte St. Elia, and gained a glorious sunset view, over the plain of Diano, as we descended.

I stopped on commencing the descent, at a moment when the sun's disc became visible, to take an observation for declination, but before the instruments were adjusted it had become again cloudy and barely visible. I record the observation, though not trustworthy, merely because the great change of declination given by it, occurs near the same region where in passing southward, I had found the local action of the ferruginous rocks so great, and as an indication to some future traveller, of the desirableness of ascertaining afresh, the declination upon these iron shot rocks.

The point of observation was at north lat. 40° 13', E. long. 15° 23', at 3ʰ 16', Greenwich time, by chronometer (19th February, 1858), sun bore 76° 3' W. of N.

Hour angle	= 61° 44' 12"·45
Sun's azimuth	= 62° 34' .. .. W.
Sun's bearing by compass	= 76° 30' .. .. W. of N.
	138° 37'
	180°
Western declination	41° 23' W.

13° to 15° W. being the usual declination everywhere else hereabouts. Although I cannot rely upon the observation itself, made through a thick haze, it yet derives I find, a strong confirmation as to its truth, from the only possible observation of a terrestrial azimuth. The town of Buonabitacola was the only one visible, and it bore from this spot, by compass, 84° 30' W. of north. Referring to its bearing from the true meridian, by Zannoni's map, I find it = 136° W. of N.

and 136° 0'
84° 30'
——
41° 30' difference = declination.

Barometer at this point marked 27·72 inches, thermo. 43° Fahr., which gives about 2146 feet above the sea for the elevation.

I arrived belated at the Certosa again, and had a welcome reception from the good-natured monks, wrote up my notes, and verified several dimensions as to facts at the monastery, &c.

CHAPTER XXVIII.

NORTHWARD FOR AULETTA AND VIETRI.

Early next morning I started northward for Auletta (20th February). In the hard gray morning light, the *peakedness* of the limestone mountains, of the high ranges, and the *end-on-edness* of the beds, are very striking. Passing Diano (in reverse direction) I remark, that the low spur that connects it with the hills behind, seems to be chiefly loose material, so that no push of the wave from the north could be transmitted through it, without immense loss and retardation.

Passing La Sala again, I got a good observation of the sun, at a point about 100 feet above the great plain.

$$\text{Lat. } 40°\ 20'\quad \text{Long. } 15°\ 32'$$

Hour angle	$= 33°\ 52'\ 3''\ 90$
Sun's azimuth	$= 33°\ 10'\ \ldots\ \ldots\ W.$
Bearing by compass	$= 52°\ 30'\ \ldots\ \ldots\ W.$
Western declination	$13°\ 20'$

The observation was made at $1^h\ 23'\ 47''$ by chronometer, Greenwich time.

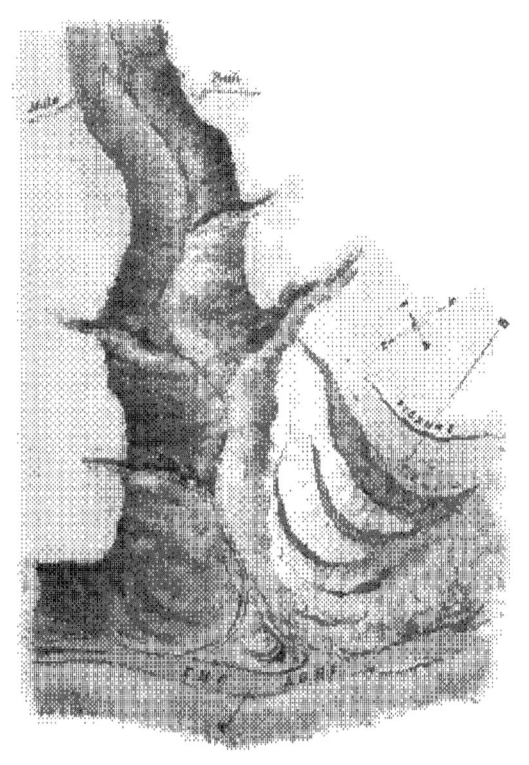

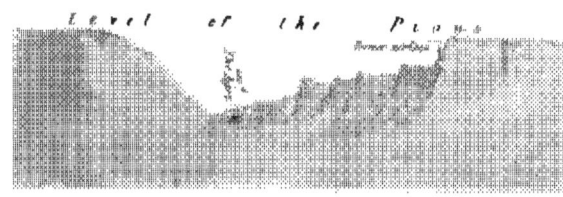

SECTION A TO B

From the same spot—

St. Arsenio bears 38° W. of north = 14° W. Declination.
St. Rufo   .. 72° W. of north = 15°   ..   ..
Diano   .. 115° W. of north = 15°   ..   ..

by reference to Zannoni's map, from which, however, it is impossible to take off bearings of *towers*, nearer than to about 1°. These observations are consistent, and show that the declination in the limestone, at least, is uniform.

If there be anywhere, in the inland regions shaken by this earthquake, in which a permanent elevation or depression of the land within a limited area would indicate itself, it should be in the great plain of Diano, where, from the extremely small fall of the numerous branches of the Calore, and of its irrigating channels, a very slight change of level would at once become apparent. I looked out narrowly for this on returning, but could not discover the least trace of changed level anywhere.

The enormous rate of erosion by the winter floods, and prodigious transport of material into this plain from all around, was very striking, now that for a time, my mind was free to observe, that and other geological circumstances. One of the most remarkable examples is that at the Certosa, where, by the torrent that comes down from east of Padula, boulders larger than a man's head, angular shingle, gravel, sand, and mud have been accumulated to a depth of nearly 10 feet, over a space of at least 200 acres since the monastery was built, or in about 150 years, for we cannot suppose any of it was then visible or likely to be deposited there, or they would not have chosen a site that now appears likely to be eventually overwhelmed.

From one of the summits between Atena and Campostrina I was enabled to get a view of Brienza with the telescope, and regretted much that time would not enable me to visit it. The place had obviously suffered terribly, apparently quite as much as Atena, and enormous avalanches were visible of white rubbish from fallen houses, that had shot down the sides of the abrupt rock on which it stands. The Castello on top, had great masses fractured and prostrated from its thick walls. The Photog. No. 289, (see p. 217,) gives an excellent notion of its appearance; I could not obtain the wave-path, &c.

I started from Auletta (21st February) for Vietri di Potenza, and to the far east north eastward. The road rises gradually for some miles, upon the north slope of a small valley running N. E., with Salvitello at its head, limestones at both sides, clays, and probably marl beds at the bottom. We surmount the ridge, separating the great valley of our old acquaintance the Tanagro from that of the Bianco, and get out upon the Piano Cerzeta, at the church of St. Giacomo, almost in ruins. At this highest point the barometer read, 28·50 inches, thermo. 47° Fahr., at 9·45 Naples mean time (21st February); the reduced level is, therefore, 1409·5 feet above the sea, and 647·6 feet above the Locanda of Auletta.

From this station I took several bearings for magnetic declination.

			W. Declination.
Buccino	bears 16° W. of north by compass		14°
Castelluccio	80° W. of north	..	13°
Auletta	due S.	..	15°
Caggiano	115° E. of north	..	East 12°

These results are all consistent except that from Caggiano, which I have every reason to think, is misplaced by about quarter of a mile, upon Zannoni's map.

Salvitello is now before me (Fig. 200), after a descent for two miles, perched upon a very blunt conoid of limestone. At less than half a mile distance, I scan it with the telescope, but except numerous fissures, do not observe much damage. One large mass of wall of rubble, has fallen, and the roof of a tower, and those of several houses have fallen in. These, and the directions of the fissures, indicate steep emergence of the wave: I can get no idea of its path, however. The people at the Taberna below the colline, tell me two houses only are prostrate, and that it is a generally well-built town. This Taberna Vigiliano is completely gutted by the shock, however, and the floors and roofs generally, indicate an angle of emergence, from about the S. E. of not less than 46° to 50°.

The long, straight, narrow valley of the Landro, stretches out before me to the S. S. E., coming down from above St. Angelo delle Fratti for more than seven miles in length, before the river falls into the Bianco, after turning about a mile and a half towards the westward. This valley has every look of a deep cleft filled with clays and loose material, and from its great length and depth, must have exercised a powerful influence in cutting off the effects of the shock, in its way eastward, if it indeed be, on the line of a deep dislocation.

We have crossed the Landro to its right bank, and still mounting, and passing along the south slope of Le Malde, about two miles from Victri, I see Caggiano, perched high up about three miles distant to the south. With the telescope

I see considerable signs of damage: an old Castello on the summit is in ruins, and in several other places walls are down, and even at this distance, in the morning light, I can see some fissures, and several roofs fallen in. We are still on limestone of the average "fucoid" look; the hills high and precipitous, the loose material upon their slopes thin; a very thinly-peopled country, few houses, and few evidences of earthquake. As we pass the Landro and the bottom of the valley, I see that the section of the latter is like that of all the small valleys that I pass hereabouts, and as in sketch Fig. 291.

Fig. 291.

Limestone in ill-distinguished beds forms the upper hills, generally with east and west strike, and dipping slightly north or south; above it in the valley bottoms, a large depth of thin horizontal beds of indurated green and grey marls, and above that a bed of clays and limestone pebbles, and boulders with many included ones of harder extraneous rock, and in masses often of great thickness. The marl beds, once extended all across, and have been cut into by the rivers to great depths; but nowhere is the limestone visible at the bottom, the banks of clay constantly shedding in, over the eroding marl-beds, and leaving a skeleton of boulders, in the beds of the streams.

A mile further on and Vietri de Potenza comes close in sight, a rather low-lying town, on the comparatively gentle, winding slope, of a hill side broken into hillocks. The low Colline upon which it stands, is almost insulated, the town being very near the fork of the rivers Turno and Landro, so that it is situated at the junction of three small valleys, all diverging from the town: the side of the Colline next the Turno to the N. E. is the steepest. (See Photog. No. 292, Coll. Roy. Soc.)

The summit of the town is, by estimation, from 350 to 400 feet above the river beds below. The town at top lies on bare limestone, the beds, so far as any can be traced, seem to run south and west, and dip to the south. At a very few feet vertically below the summit level down the slopes, clays begin to cover the limestone, and lie in very thick masses, increasing in thickness to the valley bottoms.

CHAPTER XXIX.

VIETRI DI POTENZA—EMERGENCE AND DIRECTION FIXED FOR THE PLACE.

It is Sunday, and I find Don Fortunato Gorrosi, the Judice, and several of the chief inhabitants lounging in the main street, and they conduct me over the place. There is a large and long fissure, 5 to 6 inches wide, and above 250 yards traceable in length, which cuts right across the military road, leading up to and close to the town; it is obviously due to a landslip of the deep clays upon their inclined limestone bed. Its general direction, though curved, is not far from north and south, and has obviously been determined, by the contour of the spot and of the rock beneath.

Almost close to the entrance to the town, at the east side of the street, stands a small and new, square monumental structure, intended for a water conduit, and to commemorate the completion of a new road: it is built of well-chiselled blocks of white limestone. See Photogs. Nos. 293 and 294, (Coll. Roy. Soc.,) and Fig. 295, Diagram No. 1. Its axial line, *i. e.*, the plane of its front and rear faces, runs 137° 30′ W. of north. It is greatly shaken and dislocated, but not thrown down. The lower part of the structure was built up solid, to the level of *e f* (Fig. 1.); above this it was hollow, and consisted of the parallelopipeds of limestone, laid

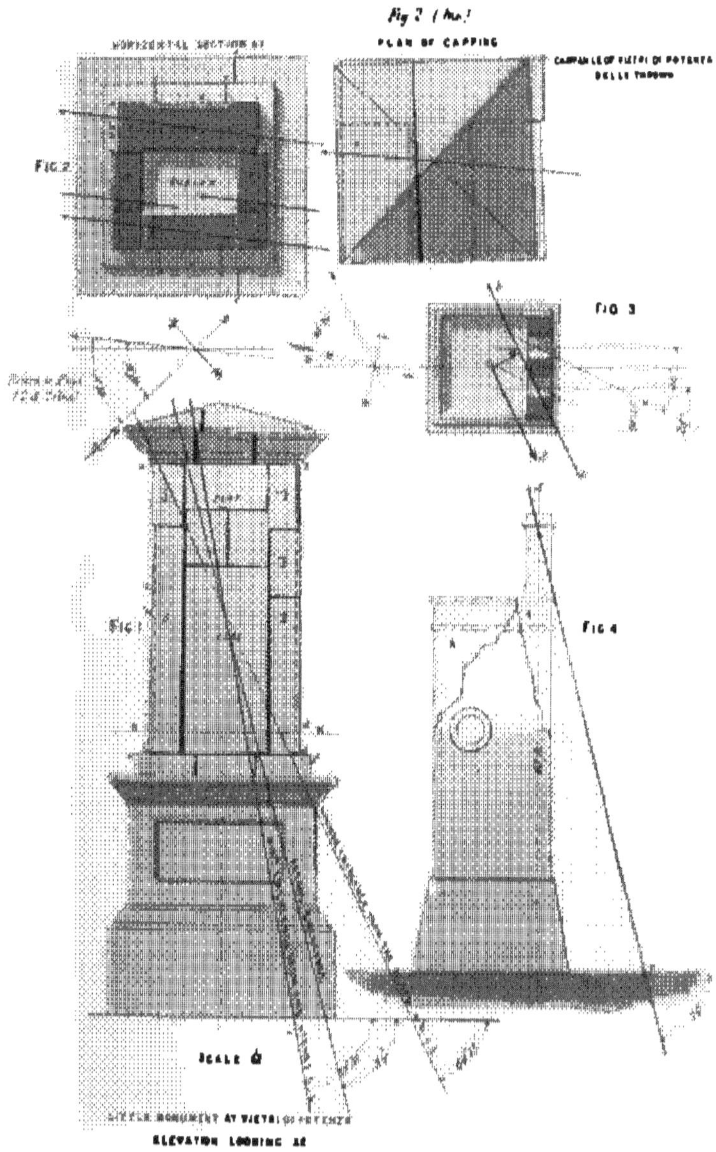

HORIZONTAL SECTION OF

Fig. 2 (No. 1)
PLAN OF CAPPING

CAMPANILE OF PIETRO DI POTENZA
DELLE TORRONE

FIG. 2

FIG. 3

FIG. 1

FIG. 4

SCALE

LITTLE MONUMENT AT PIETRA DI POTENZA
ELEVATION LOOKING AT

together with "lime putty" in the joints, which, from their recent formation, had, in fact, no adhesion but the friction of their mutual contacts. It was obvious at a glance, (as may be seen on studying the positions of the blocks in the Figs. and Photogs.,) that the whole of the upper part of the structure, above the line $e\,f$, had been subjected to rocking to and fro, in a line not far from parallel with the front face, or S. E. side; but that the large block, 6 feet × 3 feet × 1 foot, which formed this side ($a\,b\,c\,d$, Figs. 1 and 2) had *not* been so moved at all. It is unnecessary to go into details, as to *how* all the individual blocks assumed the positions shown, which are from careful sketches and measurements. Their movements are resolvable into rocking through small arcs as above.

The large front block ($a\,b\,c\,d$) acted upon *edgeways*, or nearly so, was *not* upset; but its large inertia *shoved* it, with its base, about 0·3 inch S. W. and opened the joints, $t\,t\,t\,t$, &c. The wave-path, therefore, was nearly in *its* plane, and its direction was from the S. W. to N. E.

The side blocks, $s\,s$, &c., were not upset either. The wave-path, however, passed through them, transverse to their broad dimensions. Assuming that the wave-path was nearly parallel to the front and rear of the structure, or nearly in direction, 42° 30′ E. of north, we can calculate the *limiting value* for e, *greater* than which, the angle of emergence here must have been, so as to leave this little structure standing; for the front block, taken alone, possesses the greatest stability edgeways, of any one in the structure, to a force as above. In determining its amount, we must take into account, part of the mass of the superimposed capping, on the summit of the monument. We may consider so much of it as affected the *front block*, as equivalent to 12 inches of material added to its height.

Applying the equation

$$V^2 = \tfrac{4}{3} g \sqrt{a^2 + b^2} \times \left(\frac{1 - \cos \theta}{\cos^2 \theta} \right)$$

we have $a = 3$ feet. $b = 6 + 1$ foot. $\theta = 23° 20'$ therefore,

$V^2 = 31\cdot71$ and $V = 5\cdot63$ feet per second,

which is the horizontal velocity that would have upset this block edgeways.

The actual velocity of the shock (*i. e.*, of the wave itself in the direction of its path) was found to be almost 13 feet per second, at Polla, and from the very short distance (under five geogr. miles) between, was, in all probability, the same here. Therefore, the direction of emergence of the wave here, must have been at such an angle with the horizon, that its horizontal component, was less than 5·63 feet per second, or otherwise this front block must have been upset; that is, e being the angle of emergence.

5·63 feet × sec e must be = less than 13 feet,

or, sec e = greater than 2·30 ;

therefore, e greater than 64° 15'.

This is therefore the *maximum* angle of emergence, derived from *the block of greatest stability*, in the structure; but it is not the greatest possible maximum; for with the same path as before, the wave affected either of the two side blocks, *s s*, in the line of their least horizontal dimensions, or direction of *least* stability. We may consider each of these side blocks $s\ s'—s''\ s'''\ s''''$, as one mass, the superimposed pieces, having the same effect upon the overthrow, as if united. The weight of the capping did not affect them, nor adhesion between it and base; because, as will be evident on considering Fig. 1 (Diagram No. 295), the instant the whole structure rocked, through a very small angle towards the S. W., the capping then rested momentarily only, upon the front block, and on those opposite it, (marked "flat" in Diagram), and the head of the block at s''' was left free.

Applying, again, the preceding equation, we have here

$$a = 0.58 \text{ foot.} \quad b = 6 \text{ feet.} \quad \theta = 10° 30',$$

therefore,

$$V^2 = 4.552 \text{ and } V = 2.356 \text{ feet per second,}$$

for the horizontal velocity, required to have overset either of these side blocks.

But they were *not* overthrown; therefore,

$2.356 \times \sec e$, must be less than 13;

or, $\sec e$ greater than 5·50;

and hence, e greater than 79° 30'.

This is therefore the angle of *greatest possible* maximum, for the emergence here, derived from this structure, assuming that there was not any adhesion or hold, of these side blocks by or upon the others, to prevent their fall. There was *some*, however, and therefore the true angle of emergence will be less than 79° 30', and will be further slightly reduced by the fact (now to be shown), that the wave-path here, was a little oblique to the faces of the monument.

The Chiesa Madre (Fig. 296, Sketch, Coll. Roy. Soc.) has its axial line 30° W. of north, and shows new fissures, fff, &c., obliquely across the vaulted ceiling of the nave, and oblique, but very nearly longitudinal to those of the side aisles, which give a direction of wave-path very nearly S. W. to N. E. There are some old fissures, which have been enlarged, but I neglected them. The candlesticks from the altar were thrown towards the north and east, but in directions no longer accurately ascertainable.

A picture hanging at *c* (Fig. 296) by a single nail from the east wall, 3 feet 4 inches high by 2 feet 2 inches wide, is swung off towards the north in plane of the wall 3½ inches in its own height out of plumb, and remains so, being high up. It appears, by some scales of whitewash detached from the wall just at the bottom of the heavy frame, and still on a ledge below it, to have swung *out* from the face of the wall, and, describing a short curve towards the west and north, to have struck sharply against the wall again, proving a path coinciding thus with that from the fissures.

The house of Signor Pescaroso, at the top of the town, shows two pair of very measurable fissures in the walls, which give a wave-path 50° E. of north, and 49° E. of north, respectively. The mean 49° 30′ E. of north, I conclude to be very near the true wave-path here; there are several other fissures, though none of great width, all of which indicate very great steepness in the emergent angle.

The Communal Campanile (Figs. 3 and 4, Diagram No. 296) had its two bells, of about 50 and 70 rotuli respectively, hung in slender brick arches, upon the summit of the square tower, at a height above the base, which Signor Gorrosi informs me was exactly 73 palms = 63 feet nearly: the tower since then had been taken down, to the level of the clock dial centre, below which there was not a symptom of fissure or injury. The upper part, had been shorn off however, and the portion left stood (as sketched for me on the spot) in the form shown in Fig. 4. All the fallen material, had been thrown towards the S. W., the portions at N. E. side, into the interior of the tower, carrying the floor down before it; that A (Fig. 4), a good distance off from the base of the tower, towards the S. W.; and the part B, which held the bells thrown with the latter, 25° oblique to the south face of the tower, or in a direction 10° E. of north to south; the tower itself having its faces or axial line 15° W. of north.

The bells had been found, at the very bottom of the rubbish; they had fallen mouth down, and struck the hard ground of the unpaved street, without any rubbish beneath to deaden the fall, and so left their marks when cleared around, at the exact points at which they had struck. These were given to me by the Judice, as measured, and were 16 feet from the vertical where they had hung, taken on the ground level, and in the plane of throw; nearly alike for both.

It was obvious, that they had been chucked out of the pintle sockets, by the sudden jerk, of the emergent shock, and had begun to fall just before the arches that they came from, began to follow them. (See Fig. 3, Diagram 295, for form of belfry.) The wave-path being in the direction a to b, oblique through the S. W. angle of the tower, and steeply emergent, this angle being the extreme fulcrum of *push*, and the resistance of the tower, being in the vertical line through the centre of gravity at c, and in the opposite direction c to d; a dynamic couple having a and c for its terminals, had produced a twist in the tower, in the act of falling; and part of this having been communicated to the bells at the instant preceding their fall, had thrown them more to the south, than the true wave-path. This somewhat reduced the distance, to which they would otherwise have been thrown from the tower, and the curvature of trajectory a little more; I estimated these both at about one foot additional, to the 16 feet of horizontal throw. Taking the latter at 17 feet, it was obvious that the bells had fallen almost precisely at the angle of emergence, or reverse to the wave direction, and thus we obtain for $e = 75°$, or only 4° 30' less, than the maximum angle of emergence given by the monument; and as this coincides very accurately, with the final conclusion arrived at from the calculation of the latter structure, I adopt 75°, with confidence, as the angle of emergence here.

This campanile was founded on the solid limestone, and the complete preservation of all its lower part, to about two-thirds its total height, is an additional confirmation of the great steepness of emergence of the wave here.

Surveyed from the existing top of the walls, the general direction of the valley of the Landro, looking west, is 65° N. of west.

Caggiano is visible from it, and bears 135° W. of north. According to Zannoni's map it bears 165° W. of north, and taking the declination at 15° its bearing should be 150° W. of north. It appears, therefore, to be misplaced upon that map about 5° of azimuth, and as the distance is not above two miles, this would place the town nearly half a mile too far west.

CHAPTER XXX.

FIRST APPROXIMATE CALCULATION OF THE DEPTH OF FOCUS OF THE EARTHQUAKE.

I HAD now the first decisive proof, that I had passed, beyond the point of the surface, vertically above the origin of the shock; and on comparing the emergence and wave-path ascertained for Polla, with those here obtained, I saw that that point, must be somewhere between the two towns (Polla and Vietri di Potenza), and not very far to the westward of the line joining them. With much curiosity, I made the calculation, for *the first approximation to the depth of the focus, ever attempted for any earthquake*. On the assumption that this point was in the vertical plane, passing through both Polla and Vietri, we have the emergences:

$$At\ Polla\ \ e_p = 55°\ 49'$$
$$At\ Vietri\ \ e_v = 75°\ 00'.$$

The angle made at the focus by their respective wave-paths therefore

$$\phi = 180° - (55°\ 43' + 75°\ 00') = 49°\ 11'.$$

The distance from Vietri to Polla, viewed as a right line, is 5·35 geographical miles. Then calling $r =$ the distance from the focus to Vietri,

$$\sin \phi : 5\cdot 35 :: \sin e_e : r,$$

and $\quad r = \dfrac{5\cdot 35 \times 0\cdot 827}{0\cdot 757} = 5\cdot 84$ geographical miles;

and for the vertical depth D of the focus we have

$$r : D :: 1 : \sin e_e = \cos 15°;$$

or $\quad\quad$ D = 5·64 geographical miles.

But this is below the true depth, as the focus is more to the westward, than in the right line joining the two towns as assumed, and were it worth while here, we might correct for this by a further trigonometrical operation.

Vietri is a tolerably well-built town, and does not present much antiquity in its edifices. Considering its proximity to the origin of the earthquake, it has escaped wonderfully, very few houses being actually fractured and thrown, though many fissured. It owes this in part, no doubt, to the steep emergence of the shock; but that alone would not account for it, nor for the difference in extent of injury, as compared with Auletta and Pertosa. Something in the deep formations, between it and the focus, or in the direction of the original impulse, has buffed the blow here. The frequent alternations, of clays and loose deposits, with the limestones, seem far too superficial, to account for the fact. The shock here, however, was severely felt; according to Signor Gorrosi it "fu ondulatorio e sussultorio e vorticosa e in tutti i sensi;" which is just what should be expected from so steep an emergence.

As to the character of the sound; he and the other "abitatori" agreed, "udite, grandi e subitano detonazioni nel lontano aere." They thought, the great shock and the awful subterranean and aerial thunder, came at the same instant; but some of them affirmed they had first felt "una leggerissima trepidazione precedente," and that it was accompanied by a low sound, "pissi pissi," *i.e.*, a sort of hum or buzz. With the exception of the suddenness, of the great sound, this was tantamount to the description given elsewhere. They spoke of but two great shocks, with the interval of about an hour between.

As regarded the time of the occurrence of the first; three public clocks were stopped by it—one of these being that of the Communal Campanile—and were stated all to have been arrested at a quarter past five, Italian time. They set all their clocks by sunset, and this Communal clock, was affirmed to be thus regulated, at frequent intervals, and to have been almost reliably correct. The first hour commenced (according to very common usage) at a quarter of an hour after the disappearance of the sun's disc. At some places, the immemorial usage, is to consider a quarter of an hour after sunset, the commencement of the first hour; at others half an hour after sunset; and at a few, sunset itself, commences the first hour.

Sunset took place at Vietri, on the 10th December, 1857, including refraction, that is, the sun's centre being apparently on the horizon at

$$4^h \; 32^m \; 46^s,$$

and adding the sun's apparent vertical semi-diameter $= 16' \; 17''$, to the zenith distance, $= 1^m \; 41^s$ in time, we have for the moment of disappearance of the sun's upper limb

$$4^h \; 34^m \; 27^s$$

mean time at Vietri di Potenza.

But five hours and a quarter, Italian time, is $5^h\ 30^m$ after sunset; hence

```
h.   m.   s.
 4   34   27
 5   30    0
───────────
10    4   27
```

mean time (Frankish or English reckoned) at Vietri.

A degree of longitude, at the latitude of Vietri, is = 45·56 geographical miles; and Vietri is 9 miles east of Naples.

Therefore the difference in time between them is $5^m\ 10\cdot 8^s$, deducting which we have

```
h.   m.   s.
10    4   27·0
      5   10·8
───────────
 9   59   16·2
```

as the moment of the occurrence of the great shock at Vietri di Potenza, by Neapolitan time.

I recurred to inquiries here, as to the light before alluded to, as reported to have been observed on the night of the shock, but the Vietrians had no information, beyond what they had heard affirmed by others.

CHAPTER XXXI.

PICERNO AND TITO OVER THE MARMO.

I LEFT for Picerno; the road for about three miles passes on a side cutting half way down the slope of the side of the narrow valley of the Turno. In the cutting to the left hand (north) I pass repeated alternations of limestones with variegated clay slates in their beds, approaching horizontal, but twisted in every conceivable direction. I can see with the telescope that the opposite side of the valley presents like characters.

Upon the surface, such a conformation must present prodigious obstruction to the propagation of a shock of earthquake passing eastward towards Picerno.

We continued to ascend for several miles (about five), passing over the shoulder of the Monte di Marmo, a huge lumpy and lofty mass, which interposes nearly in the right line between Vietri and Picerno. At $3^h\ 10^m$, Naples mean time, we reached the highest point: the barometer marks $27"\ 20'$, thermo. $38°$ Fahr., and the reduced level above the sea is 2605·5 feet. The summit of the mountain seems to be nearly 1000 feet above this.

We descend rapidly into the valley of the River Marmo, running nearly due north, and in a nearly straight and narrow valley, like that of the Landro, for five or six miles. The Marmo then turns westward, and falls into the Platano, which, passing between Reciliano and Balvano—both towns that have suffered severely—is joined by the Landro at Vietri, and both then become, Il Fiume Bianco, the head waters of the Tanagro and Salaris. The country all about here is very thinly inhabited, and the land appears very poor: we have scarcely passed a house between Vietri and Picerno. Crossing the Marmo, half a mile brings us to Picerno. The town is full 500 feet above the river at the bottom of the valley: it stands upon a rounded mass of diluvium, clays, and gravels of great depth, with argillaceous slates beneath. It is nearly insulated on three sides by erosive gullies of enormous depth, cut though the clays, which seem once to have filled all the valleys in this part of the country, to a depth of 400 feet or more above the levels of the existing water-courses. Off to the S. W., I can see with the telescope from the precincts of the town, some crevasses, produced by prodigious slips of these diluvial clays (of a purplish-red colour), upon the steep sides of the gullies, for those, though large enough, can scarcely be called valleys, whose sides are as steep as 40° to 50°, and nought but banks of clay and boulders, without a blade of vegetation. The town is about the same size and style as Vietri: it has suffered most upon the north and west sides, which consisted of the poorest and worst buildings.

Part of the west wall of the church is down, as also part of the north one, which has fallen upon the roof of a side aisle and crushed it: it gives a wave-path 45° E. of north from fractures. The Campanile of chiselled limestone, with brick at the base, five lofty stories in height, and of the usual square form, and without *visible* tye-bars of iron, stands entire; it leans a little out of plumb towards the N. E. The two bells which had hung from timber in its top story, were thrown out and on to the ground; and it was affirmed to me by several persons that one bell had chanced to fall right over the other like an extinguisher, both falling mouth down, and the upper one getting split. The spot upon which they were alleged to have alighted was pointed out to me, and the plane of fall indicated a wave-path of 63° 30' E. of north. Many of the houses indicated a wave-path from fissures, approaching west to east.

The day was so extremely cold that very few inhabitants, and none of the better order, were visible. The place did not present any very striking features, and having a very heavy march to complete before nightfall in order to reach Potenza by Tito, I therefore did not attempt to look for evidence here as to emergence, and left with a cursory examination.

A steep and continuous ascent of more than three miles to the south, leads up a long mountain ridge, the Serra Alta, the highest point of which is very little lower than the shoulder of the Marmo. From this I see Barragiano, at about six miles away to the north clearly, and with the telescope can see that it has suffered a good deal. A church to the south side of the town (which latter is perched, as usual, upon a lofty colline, broad and lumpy) shows distinctly, even at this distance, that the wave-path there was about from S. W. to N. E. Far away, beyond it, and over a tumultuous ocean of mountains and valleys, I see the town of Muro, perched upon a lofty mass of mural crags, and far behind it again, the huge forms of the highest ridges of the southern Apennines rise peaked up, and shaggy with dark pine forests, their summits diademed with snow. Muro bears 29° W. of north, and Picerno 13° W. of north, Barragiano being between them. Commencing the descent which, in order to reach Tito, we have to make again nearly to the bottom of the valley below it, I see a large building below me at about a quarter of a mile distance, the huge north and south fissures in which, show the wave-path hereabouts, almost exactly west to east.

Tito was a highly interesting and ancient town of about 5000 inhabitants, before the earthquake, and would have well repaid a longer examination than I was enabled to bestow upon it. It was very roughly handled, and had nearly 260 people killed. It stands upon a lofty eminence, like almost every other, and is 400 or 450 feet above the Fiumara di Tito, that rolls its little torrent close beneath it, in the bottom of the gorge, to the west and south. It stands upon rock, with more or less diluvial covering, and occupies the S.W. slope of the hill; thus presenting a free outlying surface to a wave-path here approaching S. W. to N. E.

Numbers of its houses are down, and the fractures of the walls all give evidence of a steep emergence about 30° (Photog. No. 299, Coll. Roy. Soc.). A most quaint-looking little old church, St. Antonio, on the very top of the hills above the town, which may be seen in the distance in Photog. No. 299, gave from fractured wedges at the quoins, about the same emergence, and a wave-path 74° 30′ E. of north. The wave-path from the several houses examined, gave a mean value of 87° 30′ E. of north; but this is probably incorrect, as I had not time to make measurements, and had to trust to eye alone, and many of the houses were highly ordinal, preventing very correct guessing. The Chiesa Madre, seen from the interior of the nave, Photog. No. 297 (Coll. Roy. Soc.), and externally, looking in the same direction, Photog. No. 298 (Coll. Roy. Soc.), has lost the whole of its roof, which has fallen into the body of the church, much of the rubbish being thrown towards the west side.

The west end wall, gave evidence by its fissures, and by the descent of the mass above the doorway, of the steep emergence, which gave the angle $= 33°$, and this was sustained by the wedge-shaped pieces thrown from the quoins externally. The wave-path deduced from its fissures was $59° 30'$ E. of north. I find I omitted to record the direction of the axial line.

Here, surrounded by a number of miserable huts, run up for temporary shelter from the ruins of the houses, was one of the little stone crosses, a Roman Doric column, on stepped base, with ball and cross on top (Photog. No. 300, Coll. Roy. Soc.), which, contrary to the usual fact, *had* been overthrown, and apparently broken right through the shaft, at about one-third of its length above the base.

The structure had not been socketed as in most cases, but united by iron dowals, which appeared to have split the stone by rusting, so that it easily separated, and the parting of the shaft, appeared to be at an old fracture. The stone was also bad and shattery. It did not appear to warrant any conclusion as to unusual velocity of the wave here. Yet Tito has suffered vastly more than Picerno, though not six miles from it, and both at nearly equal distances from a point, which must be somewhere about vertically over the origin. I cannot see anything upon the surface sufficient to render account of the difference.

The hill upon which Tito stands, is well connected with the range to the N. E., the Serra del Cerro. One circumstance, however, may probably be sufficient fully to account for the severity with which it was shaken. Directly to the east and S. E. of the town, with a slight depression between, rises the immense mass of limestone, of the lofty Monte Petrucco, a continuous ridge, running for four or five miles about S. W. and N. E., and distant about two miles from crest to town. This ridge runs almost transverse to the wave-path. The shock reaching Tito, therefore, had an earthquake echo from this mountain, and must have received a shock in reverse, nearly as severe as the original one. This shock was necessarily a divergent one, with reference to an horizontal plane; reflection and refraction, both sending the return waves back at different angles, from the great axial line of the chain; and this, no doubt, is sufficient also to account for the great discrepancy in the wave-paths, given by the different buildings, the extremes being 69° 30' and 87° 30' E. of north.

The more I become acquainted with earthquake effects, in this mountainous country, the more important I perceive the effects to be, of position with reference to adjacent great masses, in modifying the effects of the primary shock.

From the summits above Tito, looking off to the westward, Il Torre di Satriano may be seen, at about two miles, with the telescope, perched on the top of a low colline, midway between Monte Corona on the north and the Serra di St. Vito on the south. This is surrounded on all sides by the heaps and ruins of the ancient town of Satriano, of which I could get no account but that it was the "Citta (Civita) diruta." Like numbers of others, it is most probably the witness, of some extremely ancient earthquake, and the examination of its ruins with a careful and skilful eye, would afford decisive information as to the direction, and probably the depth, from which those shocks were delivered that centuries ago overthrew them. The information would not be without its fruit, as respects the question of secular change of energy and focal centre, in volcanic regions.

CHAPTER XXXII.

POTENZA.

I DEPARTED when it was already late in the afternoon, 6·40 P.M., having before me, some twelve miles of hilly and difficult road, before I could reach Potenza, where alone I could hope for shelter for the night. A fatiguing ascent of four miles, brought us upon the highest point of the S. E. flank, of the Serra del Cerro, and from this the remainder of our descent was made in the dark; a dreary ride, with a dense wet mist driving before a harsh N.E. wind into our faces, and nothing visible beyond a few yards. The mountains passed over, were wild, lumpy, and quite uninhabited. They appeared to be limestone in the highest points, no part of the road being higher, than the shoulder of Mormo passed in the morning, and lower down, all sorts of strange-looking, argillaceous slates and sandy clays.

It was past ten at night when we got to Potenza, and then an hour and a half was spent in rain and darkness, groping about through streets encumbered with ruins and props, before we could get lodged. It is a large place, the capital of the province (Basilicata), an archiepiscopal city, and standing at the eastern verge of the high Apennine ridges, with a vast fertile rolling country, stretching westward before it, to the Adriatic, has a great traffic, and current of country travellers. For their temporary accommodation, the Locanda being nearly wholly destroyed, the small theatre had been applied as a lodging, and of this, I expected at first to become an inmate. Nothing could be conceived more grotesque, than the scene of the interior of the house, from the parterre, all the tiers of boxes, being converted into sleeping cribs for the time being; but the cold was intense, from absence of any means of warmth, and the whole of the house lying open and fallen, from the curtain outwards to the back of the stage; so that I gladly availed myself of a prompt visit from the police, on our arrival, to get an escort to guide us to the Locanda della Corona di Ferro, where, although to a great extent in ruins, they had begun to restore, and gave me a tolerable "camera." It froze hard all night, and melting snow lay six inches deep in the streets in the morning, and all the surrounding ridges were white-topped.

Potenza lies high, and has a bleak and cold climate, in winter at least. At 8·30 A.M., Naples mean time (22nd February), the barometer at the Locanda first-floor window, reads 27" 21", thermo., 31° Fahr., and the reduced level is 2581·9 feet. The mean level of the summit of the ridge upon which the town stands is about 2550 feet above the sea. This ridge, however, does not rise more than 400 feet above the streams, the Aritello and Vasento, that run at its opposite bases, and unwater the wide-spread sweeping basins that surround it. We have passed the great Apennine crest, between Tito and here, and the watershed, is now all towards the Adriatic, the Vasento that rises here (at Vignola), reaching the sea a great river.

The ridge is four or five times as long east and west, as north and south. The long axis runs about 70° E. of north, and the general configuration may be seen from Diagram No. 301, in plan, Fig. 1, and in north and south section Fig. 2, and east and west section Fig. 3 (Sketches, Coll. Roy. Soc.). The top, of the ridge occupied by the town, is nearly level, but beyond its verge, circumscribed in many places, by parts of the ancient towered walls. The flanks slope down rapidly, to the bosoms of the great basins below. Looking northward from the town, the basin spreads away for miles, with low, rounded, swelling, knolls and hills, some rising tolerably high, but all, like the ridge of Potenza itself, covered over deeply, with clay and diluvium. The highest summits visible are the ridges of the Serra della Fontana, to the N. W. ten miles away.

From the south side, a rolling mass of mountain and valley spreads away, abutting up much closer upon Potenza, to the west and south, and amongst which the Bosco de Cerrito and Monte Acuto rise high. To the S. E. we look up the straight little valley of the Vasento to Vignola, only about three miles away. No limestone is visible, except in the highest peaks: all is rounded clay, and beneath the town and everywhere around it, appears to be a vast variety of argillaceous rocks, passing continually into sandstones, and again alternated with the clays and slate beds. These are twisted in all directions, and do not, upon the whole, seem to have any determinate horizontal position. Beneath Potenza, there are obscure indications that the rock is argillaceous, and that the beds have their strike, something about the lengthway of the ridge, and dip towards the north and N. W. generally.

The aspect on the north side, is seen in Photog. No. 302 (Coll. Roy. Soc.), looking towards the S. E., and that of the east end in Photog. No. 303 (Coll. Roy. Soc.). In the latter a number of the fallen walls, &c., are visible, and, to an eye that has become educated to such observation, affords evidence of the general wave-path, from a little south of S. W.; as about being described.

The Photogs. No. 304 and No. 305 (Coll. Roy. Soc.) of the market-place, convey the extent to which the place has suffered. The damage done was very diffused over every part of the town, though greatest upon the free lying flanks, to the east, west, and N. W., and many buildings are prostrated or fractured; but the intensity of the shock was obviously reduced here, a good deal below that, nearer the origin, and at the other side of the Apennine ridge.

A greater amount of popular notoriety was given to the supposed destruction at Potenza than it deserved, owing to the tragical circumstances connected with the unfortunate political prisoners in the prison, whom the local authorities (responsible first of all for their safe keeping) did not feel themselves authorized to remove from the tottering walls, until some of them had been buried beneath them. Out of a population of above 12,000, however, the deaths only amounted to about twenty-two, a sufficient proof of diminished action, when compared with Montemurro, for example.

I proceeded to the Intendenzia (Photog. No. 306, Coll. Roy. Soc.), and delivering my credentials from Naples, obtained letters to the Sotti Intendenti of the Communes, far to the north and N. W., and proceeded thence, to examine the city, accompanied by an intelligent officer of gendarmerie, Don Carlo Gonzales, Cancelliere di Polizia, in Potenza, who was appointed by the Intendente to attend me.

The Intendenzia is fissured much; it is at the east side of the market-place, and the east or front wall has bulged outwards, and is strutted and propped for its entire length. All the cross walls are fissured. The shock displaced much of the furniture therein—fissures not fitted for measurements.

The Casa Communale is at the north end of the same market-place, Photog. No. 307 (Coll. Roy. Soc.), and

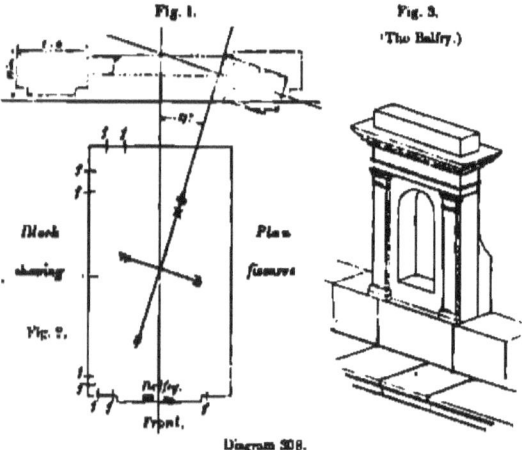

Diagram 308.

Diagram 308: its axial line, is 17° W. of north. (See Figs. 1 and 2.) It has several thread-like fissures, which indicate a wave-path about 47° 30′ E. of north, *from* the S. W.

Upon the front wall above the centre, stood a small arched campanile of brick and plaster, (Fig. 3). Its piers, only 1 foot 0 inches × 11 inches, have both been in great part thrown down, and the arched part fell in upon the roof, in a direction nearly N.E. The east pier has been twisted precisely 17° (Fig. 1), so that its narrow faces are just north and south by compass now, this is a mere accident, however. The evidences were not sufficient for calculation, but it was obvious to *tact*, that the shock must have had, a low horizontal velocity, or the whole of this little structure, must have been broken off at the level of the entablature, of the front of the Casa, and projected to the ground.

The Church of St. Angelo della Trinita, has in great part been thrown down; the campanile tower, fissured both north and south, and east and west. (See Photog. No. 309, Coll. Roy. Soc.) The fissures give a wave-path about 77° E. of north, from the S.W.; indications bad.

The Collegio di Jesuiti, has the axial line of its principal mass 18° E. of north. There are fissures though not measureable, on the north and south and east and west walls, (Fig. 310). The east wall of the great hall, has gone out towards the east, about 7 inches at top.

In the entrance corridor, a large picture, which hung from two nails, its size $6\frac{1}{2}$ feet × 5 feet, upon a wall ranging east and west, has drawn the nail to the west end, and is down six inches, resting upon a ledge at that end, indicating emergence from the west at a pretty sharp angle.

The ceiling of the great dormitory on the first floor, a room about 70 feet × 26 feet, is flat, and covered with thick white paper, on canvas below the boarding beneath. It is said to have been all flat and smooth, previous to the shock of December; it is now wrinkled all over, more or less in lines the directions of which are shown in Fig. 310. The average direction in length, of the wrinkles, about the mid-length of the room, is 50° W. of north. The west wall has gone out much, towards the west; the fissures produced are 2 inches wide at top, and a large piece of the south end of this wall, has fallen out to the west.

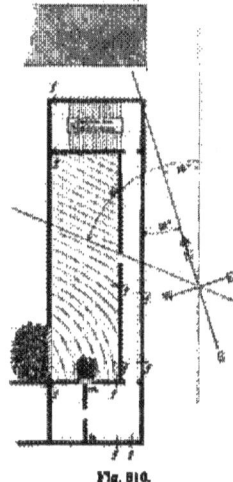

Fig. 310.

A doorway at m had been bricked up for a long time, with one brick thick: the whole is thrown about 22° E. of north. A partition south of it, $m\,n$, prevented its fall in that direction: the brickwork was thrown in one flake, nearly, twisting eastwards as it fell.

The staircase at the north end, is of limestone on groined arches, and constitutes that end of the building, a rigid tower; as respects the remainder, the groining is full of complicated fissures. Comparing, the twisting of the ceiling, the directions of the main fissures, and their relative sizes in the main walls, the directions of throw of the fallen walls, and the indications afforded by the fissures, in the groining of the staircase, I conclude, that the direction of shock was one from west to east, and not far from 80° E. of north.

The Gardien, Il Padre Salvatore Paligonice, told me, that he was in bed at the time of the shock; the lengthway of his bed was east and west, the head being to the east; and he distinctly felt the first shake, to be from the foot of his bed, towards the head of it, so that he felt a tendency, himself, to slip off from his pillow, in the direction towards his own feet. He was wide awake, with a light in the room, and cast his eyes on the instant, towards the foot of his bed, close against which a table stood with some things upon it, at about the same level as the coverlet. He felt the table push against the foot of the bed, and the moment after he saw some of the small things on the table, (books, crucifix, &c.) leap from it, on to the foot of his bed, and roll off to one side.

Within a second or two afterwards, he felt another shock, less violent, that shook him transversely, and tended to roll him out of bed, and, at the same moment, as nearly as he could say, he felt himself shaken in all directions " vorticoso."

He rose and dressed himself, hearing the noise and cries, and falling and splitting of walls, and was standing up, on one of the floors of the college, when he felt the second shock about an hour after the first, and this appeared to him to be very much, up and down: he added, however, that some students, who had hurt themselves by falling in the dark, at the first alarm, and were then lying down, thought this second shock, was about in the same direction, as he himself felt the first, and that they did not perceive the up-and-down movement, much, if at all. It appeared to me very probable, that those *standing up*, would feel the *vertical* movement most, and those *lying down* the *horizontal* one.

The evidence of Padre Paligonice is conclusive, however, as to the direction of wave-path, being very nearly from east to west, complicated directly afterwards, by reflected and refracted waves, from other directions, even so far divergent as north and south.

An ancient cylindrical tower, near the west side of the town, of the Hospital of St. Carlo, part of an old Capuchin monastery, has been split by three large fissures, running nearly to its base. It is about 20 feet diameter internally, the walls 8 feet thick, and has no floor nor roof, and is about 45 feet in height.

Two of these fissures which slope off a few degrees towards the N. E. at their lower ends, are in the same diameter, and in direction 42° W. of north. The other one is exactly at right angles to the preceding, and hence in direction 132° W. of north. (See Fig. 311.)

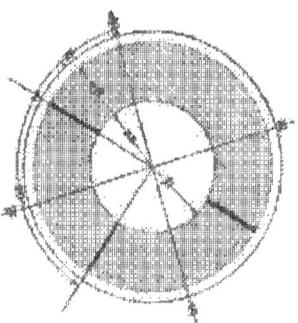

Fig. 311.

The N. W. fissure was the widest, 2¼ inches at top (nearly); the S. E. one, about 1 inch wide at top, and the S. W. one about 1¼ inch.

They appeared to have been formed at the same moment, or in immediate succession, by a force that had acted upon the tower, in a direction about from west to east; had split it through the weakest vertical lines, viz., through the heads of old apertures, &c., and that the S. W. half of the tower, had instantly separated again, by that fissure, and moved over towards the west. The direction of wave-path resulting from the whole was about 100° E. of north.

In the Magazino del Summano, a large storehouse of ponderous masonry (for grain, &c.), a wall running 30° W. of north has been fairly thrown to the S. W. in a direction 81° E. of north.

This wall near *a*, (Photog. No. 309, Coll. Roy. Soc., but not visible in it,) gave me a tolerable measure of velocity: it was not materially bound or constrained by other walls, or by timbers. Its whole height was thrown, moving upon the angle at ground level, its length was about 43 feet unobstructed, and its thickness at fracture was 2·0 feet. The masonry was of the calcareo-argillaceous stuff of which they form their rubble here, and applying the equation, of horizontal velocity for fracture,

$$V_f = 21\cdot46 \times \frac{L\beta}{a^2},$$

solving, we have $V = 4\cdot61$ feet per second.

We must add to this the horizontal velocity for overthrow from the equation.

$$V_t^2 = \tfrac{1}{3} g \sqrt{a^2 + \beta^2} \times \left(\frac{1 - \cos\theta}{\cos^2\theta}\right).$$

We have therefore

$$V_t = 6\cdot665 \text{ feet per second.}$$

The total horizontal velocity of both fracture and overthrow, is therefore

$$V_f + V_t = 4{\cdot}61 + 6{\cdot}665 = 11{\cdot}275 \text{ feet per second} = V',$$

and not greater, as the two surfaces of the fracture lay close together, at the angle of rotation. The angle of emergence here, however, as will immediately be shown, is $e = 23° 7'$, and hence the total velocity of the wave

$$V = V', \sec e = 12{\cdot}255 \text{ feet per second};$$

a sensible though apparently not very large reduction in velocity from that ascertained for points much nearer the focus.

In passing along the streets I noticed that several of the lamp irons had been shaken down from the walls. They consisted of wrought-iron arms, extending horizontally about 6 feet from the faces of the walls, with three spur braces or stays, also of iron, two above and one beneath: all being spiked into the mortar joints, and carrying a lantern for an oil light. The chuck that would be required to dislodge these, must have been pretty sharp: they would scarcely warrant calculation, however.

The house of Don Dominico Antonio Durso, stands upon the old town walls to the north side, (under *b*, Photog. No. 302, Coll. Roy. Soc.,) between the two old semi-cylindric towers. It is on a free-lying brow, of the slope to the north, and is considerably fissured, and the north walls have gone out. It gives a wave-path 119° 15' E. of north. The towers rather indicate a wave-path, from the south due north.

CHAPTER XXXIII.

CONCLUSION OF THE EXAMINATION OF THE CITY OF POTENZA.

Proceeding to the Chiesa Madre, I found the lofty square campanile free from all injury, and without even a fissure, or dislodged tile. It is about 24 feet square at base, and nearly 100 feet in height, (Fig. 312,) which stands perfectly independent, but close to the cathedral, and is a new building erected about four years, of excellent and well-bonded rubble masonry, with three tiers of iron tye-bars at each floor, crossing in both directions.

Close to it is the cathedral, riven and fissured from base to summit, and to such an extent as to be unsafe to enter, and requiring in great part to be rebuilt.

It is quite a modern building, the ancient one having been thrown down some years since, by earthquake also. Roman Doric in style, the walls of pretty good rubble masonry and brick; brick arches to the nave and transepts, a semi-cylindrical brick arched roof, and a dome also of brick, and rather higher than a hemisphere,

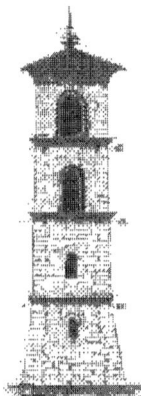

Fig. 312.

constructed above the crossed arches of the nave, chancel, and transepts.

From the regularity of the structure, and its great size, I at once saw that the fissures presented data of the highest value, and devoted some hours to their exact drawing and admeasurements. When I had completed my work, one of the "Canonici" offered to bring me to Signor Guiseppe D'Errico, the architect of "the Chapter," from whom, he said, I could obtain much information. I found Signor D'Errico to be a gentleman of learning, great intelligence, and observation; he had already had accurate drawings made, to scale, of every fissure in the cathedral, with reference to the possibilities of reparation, and he obligingly offered me tracings of them. The Diagram No. 313 gives his figuring of the fissures in the vertical section along the axial line looking north, and also in horizontal section or plan. The fissures drawn in the latter, so far as the roof is concerned, are drawn as if looking up at them from the interior, those of the walls, &c., as if looking down on them. The vertical section and dome plan, are from the hand of Signor D'Errico, and bear his signature, drawn "dal vero;" and as he had no theoretic views whatever, as to any relation that might subsist between the directions, &c., of fissures, and that of the shock producing them, this drawing, which agreed with my own sketches and measurements, may be adduced as a valuable confirmation from a thoroughly competent and yet wholly unbiassed observer, of the correctness of the views advanced on this subject in Part I., as well as affording data of the most reliable kind. It will be needless to describe in detail those fissures and fractures which will be most perfectly understood by a careful

examination of the drawing. Besides the great mass of fissures which run transverse to the axial line of the church, which is precisely east and west, and having a prevailing slope at the top towards the west, there are others parallel to the axial line, one, in particular, extending right along the soffit of the nave and chancel, and which has sent the whole length nearly, of the south side wall out of plumb, in its whole height 1½ inch to the south. There are also transverse roof fissures at various oblique angles through the arches, and a huge mass of the dome at the west side has parted off from the remainder, and the spherical triangle has gone westward, leaving fissures of 7 to 8 inches wide open to the sky. There are innumerable *small* fissures in the dome, and many small and short fissures in the walls and side arches, &c., produced by local structural causes, which are at angles having all possible directions. Some of these, particularly those at the crown of the first arch next the north transept to the westward in the nave, present evidence of having ground their surfaces together, by the oscillation of the elevated mass of the dome rocking the sub-structure.

The west end wall is fractured and split in its own thickness, and the east end of the chancel merely hangs together, a mass of dislocated fragments. The precisely cardinal position of this cathedral, and the nearly subnormal path of the wave, all favoured the exact determination by fissures of its path. The result of my measurements produced a wave-path, (the mean of nine sets of fissures,) having a direction $92°\ 30'$ W. of north, and an emergence of $23°\ 7'$ from the west towards the east. The widest departure from the mean in these nine sets gave

88° 30′ W. of north; and the mean from the fissures of the body of the edifice, precisely corresponds with the direction of throw that is given by the spherical triangle, broken from the dome at the west side. The greatest and west fissures in the arch of the nave and chancel, evidence a separate shock, which must have been within 10° or 15° at most of north and south in path. This fissure, however, has been widened, and many others in the same general direction, in the soffits of the great arches beneath the dome, by its rocking high above; the oscillation at first, in the plane of the primary wave-path having, as usual, become gyratory.

The fallen masses, from the roof and roodloft, at the extreme east end of the chancel, were thrown westward and southward. From the altar at the north end of the north transept, a little alabaster image was thrown from a shrine, and found on the table beneath, having been thrown 1·5 foot to the south and west. The figure was 15 inches high, the base round 3½ inches diameter; the centre of gravity was about 8½ inches above the base, and it weighed 7 rotuli by trial. The irregular form of the figure rendered any calculation of velocity from its throw useless. The episcopal throne and canopy, which stood against the north wall of the chancel, was thrown forward south, from the wall. An image of St. Michael, that stood in a niche in the west wall of the north transept, was found leaning back against the rere of the niche (*i. e.* thrown westward). In the sacristy are a number of old oil paintings high up the walls, hung from single nails. All those, upon the two north and south walls, are thrown more or less out of plumb towards the south, and all upon the two east and west walls, similarly out of plumb towards the west; but the east and west movement has been by far the greater. Upon the whole, I conclude that the wave-path and direction, of the great primary shock, are given very accurately by the cathedral; that, standing, as the town does, upon an elongated ridge, which received the impulse of the primary wave obliquely, the ridge itself vibrated, in many different directions, by transverse and reflex waves; and that from the lofty ridges to the south and S. E. of the city, a reflected wave, or oblique echo, was delivered back, and produced a powerful secondary shock, nearly orthogonal to the primary. I am hence disposed to reject all wave-paths, given by other buildings than the cathedral, as respects the primary wave, and view them as evidences chiefly of the secondary waves.

The clergy of the cathedral informed me, that they had learned from others of their cloth, at Brindisi and at Tricarico, that at both these places, the direction of shock had been exactly west to east.

At Vignola, also, they said it had been felt from west to east exactly, but of course such statements cannot be relied upon within 5° or even 10° either way. Signor D'Errico after I had explained my views to him, considered the direction from, as evidenced by the injuries done, to the churches of Sta. Maria Maggiore, and D'Annuziata (Photogs. No. 314 and No. 315, Coll. Roy. Soc.), as about 70° or 80° W. of north, and from the S. E.

I was unable to get any reliable information, as to the instant of time of the first shock. They all spoke here of three shocks. The first great one, which they thought, continued vibrating more or less, for about twenty or thirty seconds, and was succeeded very soon, (after a moment of quiet,) by another minor shock, differing in direction from the first, and more undulatory as they thought, and lasting nearly the same time. There was then the shock, of about an hour after, but that they felt with much less violence than the two preceding, and it did but little damage, except to what was ruinous, from those that went before.

The noise, was described by the Intendente, and by several others, as a rolling, deep-toned, rombo, like the sustained but irregular fire of artillery, at a distance; and it appeared to them, to be heard at the same instant, with the arrival of the shock, and to continue as long, if not longer, than the vibratory movements which were felt after the great pulse.

They had seen no strange lights, but had heard that others *had*, back to the westward. All sorts of exaggerated stories were current, however, as to some extremely oppressive state of the atmosphere, during the shock and after it, for which there seemed upon examination to be no good foundation.

There were several heavy landslips, in the upper part of the valley of Vignola, and fissures, open only a few inches, but some hundreds of feet in length, at the east side or slope of the valley, in the diluvial covering.

CHAPTER XXXIV.

SIGNOR D'ERRICO'S DOCUMENT—CALCULATION OF THE MOMENT OF SHOCK AT HIS STATION.

Signor D'Errico, was not at Potenza on the night of the earthquake, but at a country-house a considerable distance to the east of it, and from him I received a written statement of his observations, which are of much interest, more especially as respects time. I subjoin a translation of his communication (with the exception of some speculations as to the cause of earthquakes) which he obligingly wrote out for me, while I was occupied elsewhere in the city, and handed to me before my departure.

Translation.

"I, Guiseppe D'Errico, architect, do truly certify, the following narrative of facts to have been observed by me, during the terrible earthquake that occurred in this province of Basilicata, on the night of the 16th December, 1857:—

"On that night, I was a visitor at a large country-house, known to the surrounding inhabitants as 'Il Casone'—the Big house—and had made all my preparations with instruments, &c., for commencing early the next morning, a survey and geometrical plan, of the place and its environs. The house alluded to, is situated in the eastern part of the boundaries of the province of Basilicata, and is part of the estates called Piano Cardone di Montefermo, and is built upon level ground. The surrounding country is composed of semi-planes, hillocks, and elevations more or less high. It is open in the direction of N. W., which is that in which the boundary of the adjoining province of Bari runs.

"On the one side of this line (viz., to the east) the prospect opens upon a gently rolling country, the horizon of which is lost in the blue waters of the distant Adriatic, and on the other side (viz., to the west and south) terminates with the abrupt and lofty peaks of the Apennines, near which are seen the cities, Monte Peloso, Oppido, and Genzano. The place is therefore quite open to distant observation.

"I was seated at the corner of a large fire-place, one of the sort generally built in the country of Puglia, surrounded by many persons, and thus I had every opportunity of carefully observing all that was passing, from the two happy circumstances, of being perfectly awake, and close to the open fields.

"The first shock took place at five minutes past five o'clock, Italian time, and all of us who were in the Casone immediately left the house.

"Once in the open air, I found myself without chronometer or any other instrument of precision, so I counted the duration of the first and second shocks, by the tread of my feet at intervals of a second, as nearly as possible. I remarked that the sky all round was serene, but the stars emitted a dim and reddish light. There was not a breath of wind in the atmosphere, but a sense of stifling heat, as it were from a very hot steam-boiler, surrounded us, and, as it were, seemed to take away the power to breathe, and this continued to be severely felt by us, during the whole time of the first and second shocks.

"The duration of the first shock, in my opinion, was not less than from 30 to 32 seconds. It went on, waning slower and slower, but without ever leaving off entirely, and at about four minutes after the first (*i.e.* the commencement) came the subsequent one, which lasted from 27 to 28 seconds.

"The second was the most violent, so much so that none of us who were congregated at the spot could readily stand upon our feet, but were compelled to throw ourselves down upon the ground.

"I had scarcely recovered from my first surprise, when I bethought me, of the many things which were hanging round about the house, such as lamps, saddle-bags (bisacce), fowling-pieces, and other things, hanging like pendulums; and returning to the house, I noted accurately the directions of their oscillations, which lasted some time after the shock. Having afterwards set the compass of my theodolite on the spot, I ascertained more accurately still, that the direction of oscillation was from S. W. to N. E., or between that and west to east. The oppressive heat which I have already described, decreased gradually after the second shock. At the same time, and from the same direction (as the shock, namely), we distinctly heard a deep and rolling thunderous noise, like the report of artillery at a distance (un rombo ed un fremito cupo simile al rimbomba di artiglierie lontane), which advanced from the S. W. direction, and proceeded to be lost and dissipated towards the N. E.

"My profession as an architect has given me opportunity

of remarking the effects of this terrible phenomenon on many buildings. The upper floors, of houses built on level ground, suffer most. Churches and public buildings of large dimensions were shaken with great violence, and suffered, comparatively speaking, more: where, however, the buildings were strongly constructed, and well cemented with mortar, their resistance was greater, and in a great measure they remained intact and unshaken. Iron chain bars, the good qualities of which we have ere now appreciated, have saved a great number of buildings."

The station referred to in the preceding, at which Signor D'Errico was situated on the night of the earthquake, is almost midway and in a right line, between the towns of Genzano and Gravina: it is precisely in the latitude of Naples (39° 45′ N.), and is 89 to 90 geographical miles, due east of that city, or long. 16° 13′ 15″ east of Greenwich.

The time of sunset at this station on the 16th December, 1857, was

	h.	m.	s.	
	4	33	22	mean local time.
Naples, west of station, in time	0	7	50	
	4	25	32	sunset at the station

by Naples mean time.

We must assume, however, that Signor D'Errico's watch, was going by Potenza, (his own town's) time.

The time of sunset at Potenza (N. lat. 40° 40′) on the 16th December, 1857, was

		h.	m.	s.	
		4	33	58	local mean time.
Naples, west of Potenza, in time . . .		0	6	19	
		4	27	39	Naples mean time of sunset at Potenza.
Signor D'Errico's time		5	5	0	
Add the customary 30 minutes . . .			30	0	
		10	2	39	time of the shock at his station, Naples mean time.

The customary time here *must* be the half and not the quarter hour, for the latter would bring the time *before* the occurrence of the shock as observed at any point whatever.

According to Signor D'Errico, the wave-path at Monte Peloso, was between 45° E. of north, and 90° E. of north. The latter coincides more closely with the direction derivable from Potenza and many other places, which would be about 103° E. of north. It seems probable, therefore, that the wave-path here, was disturbed by the large mass of comparatively low hills, to the N.E. and east. According to Signor D'Errico and the clerics of Potenza, the shock was felt at Accrenza, Genzano, Oppido, Lupino, and Minervino, in the same or nearly the same direction. The shock was severe, at Matera, Gravina, and Altamura: at the last place the direction was west to east. At Ruvo, Terlizzi, Bitonto, Bitetto, and Bineto, it was scarcely felt at all.

All these places are situated out upon the rolling plains

of the "Murgie," at a distance from the main axial chains, but with lumpy hills, in masses, here and there, and beneath them all, the stratification is generally much more uniform, level, and unshattered, than further east and north, amongst the Apennine limestone.

Monte Peloso, is the most eastern point of which I have facts from direct personal observation, (Signor D'Errico's,) save those of the Canonico Campanelli, as to the Adriatic coasts. Whether the "stifling heat" spoken of by Signor D'Errico, be a reality, or a sensation dependent upon powerful and sudden nervous excitement, may admit as yet of some question. It is remarkable, however unsupported by positive evidence it may be, that several of the local historians, of *other* earthquakes in these regions mention the same thing as having been concomitant to the shock.

CHAPTER XXXV.

DEPARTURE FROM POTENZA EN ROUTE FOR AVIGLIANO.

On leaving Potenza, the ruins of a place known as Reviseo Diruta, are seen northward upon the summit of a low hill, the Pietra Colpa, and are said to be the result of an ancient earthquake. Within half a mile, I pass a great monastery on the east (Di Santa Maria), in the lofty boundary walls of which, are very large fissures, 5 to 6 inches wide at top. The building is nearly cardinal, and has a low hill to the north, upon the slope of which it lies, as also another to the eastward.

The fissures run nearly north and south, a little west of north, and, so far as I can observe them, without going into the monastery, are confirmatory of all I have determined at Potenza.

The hills all around to the east, and in the immediate neighbourhood, are rounded in sweeping outline, and not lofty, but large; they have generally a deep covering of clay boulders and detritus. The rock beneath, is the argillaceous slaty stuff, with limestone here and there. The beds, wherever I can see them exposed, are at very various strikes, and much dislocated, but all steeply inclined.

I am obviously, here upon the western edge of the vast tertiary deposits, that form the low hills and great plains of the Murgica, stretching far away to the Adriatic. To the westward, the lofty ridge that I am mounting and have to cross to reach Avigliano, consists, towards its upper part, of the upper limestones, and there are limestone peaks behind me, at 8 to 10 miles to the south and S.E.

Near the summit of the ridge of Monte Foj di Potenza, I pass some gigantic calcareous breccia rock, very similar lithologically, to the breccia wherever I have met it hitherto; but here, the nodules were almost absolutely spherical, and from 20 inches up to even 5 feet diameter, a size to which some that I measured attained. Nothing distant is visible. I have been enveloped the whole way, in dense fog and hoar frost, and, what is remarkable, not with a calm atmosphere, but with a driving north wind. The crystals of hoar frost driven before it, accrete upon the windward side, of every stubble stalk, and branch of brushwood, and stand off in horizontal lines of white ice, in a very singular manner. (Sketch No. 316.) It is intensely cold, yet the water in pools, &c., thawed upon the ground by the sun of the morning, is not yet frozen. The thermometer marks 27° Fahr. at 4·0 p.m. There is a continual light sort of clinking sound, borne upon the sighing wind, from the breaking off of these icicles from the branches of the savage-looking pine forests, that now and then show like dark spectres, through the rack and hoar fog.

The barometer reads 26·34 inches at the highest point, and the reduced level shows that I am 3414·4 feet above the sea and 827·5 feet above the city of Potenza.

Not far from the commencement of the ascent, I passed, upon the west side of my route, the debouchure of a tributary of the torrent of the Aritello, which comes down from the higher steeps, and joins the Vasento below Potenza.

The mass of detritus swept down and delivered out upon the hollow plain was truly surprising. Much of it consisted of slaty angular blocks of large size of the soft argillaceous rocks, with smaller fragments of the upper limestone, and round lumps of the calcareous breccia, all mixed with or imbedded in, torrents of red mud.

The huge talus, projected several hundred yards into the valley basin, and its central slope was probably not more than 20° to 24°. The torrent of muddy red water, rushing from the narrow gorge at top, soon separated into innumerable rills and cascades, and brawled sinuously over the heap, spreading it in all directions, and rendering more than a square mile desolate and infertile. (See Sketch No. 317.)

Even at the highest point, which I find is called Il Topo di Meta, there are no craggy summits, all is rounded. A mile further, and I see Avigliano, perched upon the east slope of a rather steep hill; and half a mile south of it, near the town of Ruoti, pass a gorge with twisted limestone beds, and bands of red ochre between, all cut through, by a ravine running east and west. At the next gorge, both flanks, are composed of an immense deposit of loose detritus, with boulders of great size, and angular, both of limestone and argillaceous rocks, embedded in a red ochrey clay. I begin to mount the steep ascent to the town, and come in upon, a part of the military road; and in the side cutting on the left hand, I see the first evidence of approaching the volcanic district of Monte Vulture, in beds of dense yellow tufa, with pebbles occasionally, embedded in curved and twisted beds. It is like that of Vesuvius, but of a deeper yellow, and might at a casual glance be taken for a coarse yellow sandstone.

CHAPTER XXXVI.

AVIGLIANO TO ATELLA.

I ARRIVE at Avigliano after sunset. It has taken more than six hours to get over about twelve miles of country, and the men positively refuse to venture on to-night, over the ridge and snow, to Rionero, which I had purposed to reach. So I occupy the remaining twilight in examining this place. It is a large town, but more filthy even than Potenza, and much more hilly and uneven in its streets and the ground upon which it stands. The line of perpetual snow at this time of year appears to pass through this town. The upper part is all frozen, and snow lies thinly upon it, while, at the lower part, the streets are wet and slushy.

It seems to stand on limestone. At $9^h\ 0''$ P.M., Naples mean time, the barometer reads at the Locanda, which is rather below the mean level of the town, 26·5 inches, thermo. 38° Fahr., and the reduced level gives 3308·2 feet above the sea.

The Castello, at the upper part of the town, a very ancient, barrack-like old building, now used as a Gendarmerie, is ordinal, and shows fissures both on the south and west walls. All appear to be enlargements of old fissures of the shock of 1851. The direction of path generally given by them is S.W. and N.E., but obscurely.

At the Chiesa Madre it is almost dark, and I can examine it but incompletely. The axial line is very nearly east and west. There are fissures crossing both side walls, and there are two minor ones in the west-end wall. They generally indicate a wave-path from S.W. to north-eastward, and at an emergence that does not appear by the eye only to exceed 20° to 25°. The amount of damage generally done in the town, seems to be small. There are a few houses propped, and several are fissured, but none were prostrated.

The son of the Padrone at the Locanda, a rather intelligent youth, gives me an account of the earthquake, as he experienced it, and of what occurred in the town. His account agrees generally with that at Potenza. He says, however, that there was no shock noticed at Avigliano, after the two first, which were very close together. I could not ascertain clearly from him whether there were even two, or only one prolonged movement, with two more distinguishable pulses. The movement, he said, was back and forward only, he thought. His account of the noise was very much the same as that of Signor D'Errico. No clocks were stopped, that he or the Capo d'Urbano on duty at the guardhouse opposite the Locanda, knew of. The time of the first shock, they only thought to be, about a quarter past five, Italian time, the usual estimate everywhere.

It was too late to call upon any of the communal officers or ecclesiastics, for better information ; and it hardly seemed of much importance, until I should get further north. I arranged to leave, with a gendarme and lanthorns, at four o'clock in the morning, so as to insure reaching Monte Vulture before the ensuing night. We started punctually to time, and commenced in darkness and intense hoar frost, with a driving mist from the north, the dreary ascent of about four miles, to the ridge of Monte Caruso. About four inches of snow, at the level of Avigliano summit, and about seven inches, on the crests of Caruso.

At 6·30 A.M. (23rd Feb.), Naples mean time, barometer reads 26·27 inches, upon the highest point of the road; thermo. 29° Fahr., and shows that we are 3581·2 feet above the sea, and only 275 feet above Avigliano, from which we had descended much, on first leaving it. I hung a thermometer here, so as to be freely exposed to the wind and hoar fog, and after about half an hour, found it was at 17° Fahr. The cold was intense. The rounded tops of Monte Caruso, rise against the dawning sky-line to my right, apparently 800 feet above me. As daylight approaches, we commence to descend, between low rolling hills, along the course of the little stream, the Agromonte, and through the valley of the same name, opening out upon the nearly level plain of Atella. Tufa beds and ancient lavas, are visible to the right, at the opposite side of the stream, which has cut away its steep banks. It is obvious that the superficial covering of volcanic formations here, extends far beyond the boundaries assigned by Collegno's geological map, which marks their limit at Atella, five miles further north. To the east, at about half a mile, I pass the great Castello di Lago di Pesole, the lake itself being about a mile further east, but not visible—the property of Prince Doria Pamphili; its massive curtain walls present no sign of fissure or dislocation. The tufa and volcanic rocks have now become the universal formation. A little further, near a place called Iscalonga, are many inhabited caves, excavated in the dry tufa, of extreme antiquity: some of the Troglodytes came out to see us pass, and looked savage and queer enough, in their rough brown blanket-cloaks with peaked hoods, and sheepskins. At length we arrive at Atella.

CHAPTER XXXVII.

ATELLA TO RIONERO.

ATELLA, a town founded in the early days of Greek settlement, and presenting still every indication of its remote origin, and of the successive races that it has owned for masters, was terribly handled by the earthquake of 1851 that destroyed Melfi, and its remaining crazy and ancient buildings have suffered considerably by the late one. On entering the town from the south, a large building on the west of the street, that looks like an old palazzo, three stories in height, shows some heavy fissures from top to bottom, open three inches at top. The wave-path seems to have been about S.W. to N.E. from these; and the slope of the fissures indicates a small emergence from the S.W., not more than 12° to 16°. The Palazzo Sarracino, and also a large nunnery, the two best-built and most modern buildings in the place, do not show a sign of injury; the cupola of the latter, is seen above the road in Photog. No. 318. The Chiesa Madre (Photog. No. 319, and Fig. 320,) a Lombard building of venerable antiquity, has its axial line 110° E. of north. It is severely fissured (new fractures) in the north side wall, in the arches of the chancel, both along the axial line and transversely,

ATELLA
AND PART OF THE VULTURE RANGE

and at and in the campanile. The general indication is from the S. W. to N. E., but the fissures will not admit of exact measurement. The old clock in the octagonal roof of the campanile, which has been much shattered, still shows by its index, Fig. 320, that it was stopped on

Fig. 320.

the night of the 16th Dec. last, at twenty-two minutes past five, Italian time. The Canonico tells me, it has not been touched since.

	h.	m.	s.
The sun's upper limb set at Atella on the 16th Dec., 1857, at	4	30	38
Clock shows Italian time	5	22	0
Add the customary quarter hour after sunset	0	15	0
Frankish mean time at Atella	10	7	38
Naples is west of Atella, in time	0	5	44
Clock therefore stopped at Frankish mean time of Naples, at	10	1	54

The two ancient bells, had been chucked out of their old timber fastenings, and thrown against the N. E. side of the octagonal part of the belfry, which they had carried away and fallen with it, but in a way so disturbed by obstacles, as not to afford any indication, beyond the general confirmation, as to wave-path.

A large building, to the north side of the piazza in front of the Chiesa Madre, has its front wall which ranges exactly with the axial line of the church, bulged and thrown outwards towards the south. It is also fissured transversely, and is propped from the piazza, as are many of the larger buildings along the main street, which runs nearly north and south.

Two other smaller churches, both at the east side of the main street, have their axial lines quite parallel with that of the Chiesa Madre (110° E. of north). One of these, (Chiesa di San Beneditto,) is heavily fissured, transversely and longitudinally, and the west end wall has gone out. The brick groined arching of the roof, shows irregular fissures; the building is small, its indications not *absolutely* clear, but its main fissures indicate pretty distinctly, a wave-path 45° 30′ E. of north from the S. W., and, an angle of emergence of from 15° to 18° from same direction, (see Diagram No. 320, Fig. 2, Coll. Roy. Soc.).

Very near it is the Chiesetta of St. Johanes, a strange dark little vaulted "cella," tremendously fissured at the S. W. quoin, in the west wall over the door, and longitudinally along the crown of the vault. Both piers at the western quoins are of well-built limestone ashlar, in large blocks about 3 feet wide on the face and 18 feet in total height. The S. W. one, is thrown five inches out of plumb to the S. W. (see Diagram No. 320, Fig. 3, Coll. Roy. Soc.). The arched roof is elliptical, of rubble ashlar limestone. The longitudinal fracture has let down the crown and forced out of plumb both the side walls.

Everything has been removed from the interior of St. Johanes ; but in San Benedetto mass was still said, and in it are a number of silver relic shrines, large-sized human busts, apparently of extremely early Byzantine workmanship, that would reward the examination of the archæologist. The priests knew nought of their history, but that Atella had possessed them time immemorial. The wave-path given by St. Johanes was about 10° more east, than the preceding, or 55° 30′ E. of north. The building was too low to afford any satisfactory evidence as to emergence.

As I leave Atella, I pass beneath, the old Roman or early Norman, gateway of the town, and looking back upon the place towards the south (Photog. No. 318), see the tower of the Chiesa Madre to the left, and to the right, a fine old cylindrical tower, now forming the keep of a small fortress or fortified barrack. It is of squared and coursed ashlar, well put together, apparently Roman work, and has not had a stone displaced by the shock.

Atella stands upon a gentle swell above the plain, and leaving it, we descend into a great hollow Piano or basin of deep rich soil, upon still deeper yellow tufa, with Monte Vulture due north, visible from base to summit, and the rich plain to the N.E. studded with towns. Rionero, Ripa Candida, Ginestra, and Barielli, are all within view.

Between Atella and Rionero, looking east towards Ripa Candida, I can see that the latter appears to stand upon calcareous breccia, covered more or less by volcanic deposits; and in the deep cuttings of the smaller streams in the same direction, there are evidences of calcareous rocks beneath the superficial volcanic beds; and the inclination of the beds seems to be towards Vulture, and not from it, so that they have not been tilted from it, as a centre of elevation; and it is probable that these underlying calcareous beds may alternate with other volcanic ones, and abut up very much closer to the actual cone of Vulture; which thus seems to have simply broken through the stratified rocks, and, as my barometrical measurements show, at a very low comparative level.

LOOKING at CHURCH — APOLLO

Houses on the ground three miles from BELLA

CHAPTER XXXVIII.

RIONERO AND THE COUNTRY TO THE FAR-OFF SOUTH
AND EAST TO THE ADRIATIC.

I ARRIVE at Rionero at 9·45, and having hired fresh pack mules and horses, to ascend to the Monastery of St. Michele, or Monticchio, on the N. W. shoulder of Vulture, proceed to examine the place, accompanied by the Judice, on whom I called.

The Locanda, though fissured, is habitable. It is about at the mean level of the place: at twelve o'clock noon, Naples mean time, barometer stands at 27·94 inches, thermo. 40° Fahr., and the reduced level gives a height above the sea of 1957 feet. This is not very far from the general level of the great plain or basin, to the east and S. E. of Monte Vulture, and shows that it is very far below the level, of the mountain and table-lands to the south and S. E. of Avigliano, consisting of the tertiary clays and the upper limestones.

Rionero is a prosperous-looking town, nearly as large as Potenza, inhabited by a people of Albanian descent, picturesque in dress, and very commonly handsome in person. The ground upon which it actually stands, is very uneven, and consists of all sorts of alternations, of tufa and solid hard lava rock.

Nearly one third of it was destroyed in 1851; but many new and substantial buildings have arisen since. A good, substantial-looking house, of two solid stories, opposite the Locanda, which is nearly cardinal, is fissured in four places. It is insulated, and gives good indications, and shows a wave-path 45° 30′ E. of north, and an emergence from the S. W. of about 16° or 16° 30′. The streets are desperately steep and tortuous, (Photog. No. 321,) as seen in the view of the town looking towards the highest summit of Vulture in the distance. The Aqua Francesca, a stream which flows through the town and supplies its fountains, is in the foreground. It falls into the Ofanto, to the S. E. of Vulture. The building high up upon the right, is a great monastery not far from Barielle.

It soon became obvious, as I examined the town, that every one of its separate knolls or crags of lava, had shaken in secondary directions of its own, dependent upon the path of the main wave and its own free-lying faces; and hence, I might have found here (without attention to this condition) evidence of wave-paths in every point of the compass. It afforded an excellent instance of the caution as to conditions, that an earthquake observer requires, ever to bear with him. The extremes that I found, were south to north, and 18° E. of north.

At the top of the town the Palazzo Catani, a large and lofty four-story building, well built, and with iron tye-bars inserted at each story (probably put in after the shock of 1851), has escaped without a visible shake or flaw.

Returning to the house I first observed, and remarking the position of its ground, I returned again to the east and N. E. of the town, and comparing the few indications of

MONTE VULTURE, FROM NEAR RIONERO.

wave-path that I could find there, in houses standing on level ground, and without any steep scarps near them, I found them to agree pretty well with the first. There were in many quarters, obscure indications of a subordinate shock, from about 25° W. of north to south, which direction, points almost exactly, towards Monte Vulture. This rendered it highly probable that a reflected wave from that mountain mass, had been transmitted through Rionero, and added to the complication of its phenomena, the path of this reflected wave being nearly orthogonal to that of the primary shock.

At the Locanda of Rionero, I fell into company with the Canonico Il Padre Felice Campanelli, of Spinazzola, a priest of a good deal of knowledge and intelligence, and received from him some valuable information as to the effects of the shock far away to the east, and upon the Adriatic coast, with all which country he was familiar, and had travelled over it since December.[*]

At Spinazzola, his own town, (Photog. No. 323, Coll. Roy. Soc.,) which lies upon an undulating plain of the Murgie, with rolling hills to the east and south of it, a good deal of mischief was done. He was there, and felt the shock severely. The direction of the great movement was, he

---

[*] Since these pages were written, I am informed, that this gentleman fell into the remorseless grip of the late tyrannical government, and was one of the last of its incarcerated victims, his ostensible crime being his having expostulated as to the savage treatment of an overdriven line of fainting and roped-together prisoners. But he was a marked man even when we met; a brother had fled from "being suspected." Don Felice hoped he was in England, but had heard nothing of him for some years, and dared not write even to any third party to make inquiries.

thinks, a little to the south of from west to east. It was a strong horizontal shake, succeeded by a continued tremor for several seconds; then another heavy horizontal shake, and then a second tremor. Altogether, he thought the movement must have lasted from three to five minutes, but added, that he only judged so, and that people judged badly when frightened.

There was a rolling noise, heard by many around him, but he did not hear it himself, which he ascribed to his whole attention having been otherwise directed; others said the noise began when the shock did, and ended with it. The Campanile of Spinazzola, he said, had been fissured, but the mischief done, was chiefly confined to old and very ill-built structures.

Part of a church had fallen at Spinazzola; but it was before the shock in a tottering and dangerous state, and might have come down at any moment.

I caused my photographer to obtain the two Photogs. Nos. 322 and 323 (Coll. Roy. Soc.), the former being a view of this Campanile, looking eastward. It was fissured right through the north and south walls, nearly vertically; but the fissure appears to have been too narrow to show distinctly in the photograph; the fact, however, supports the narrative of Padre Campanelli.

Upon the east coast, the shock had been felt as far down as Ostuni, but did no damage whatever. It was perceived at Brindisi by some persons, but was not perceptible at all further south, as at Lecce and Otranto.

Passing northward along the coast, it was distinctly felt, but without damage, at Monopoli, Polignano, Bari (where it was severe), Molfetto, and Barletta, and was perceptible at Manfredonia, and even in upon the mountain table-land of the peninsula of Gargano.

Passing again south, he said, that at Cassano and Gioia, towns which are upon the last lines of prolongation of the Apennine chains, but upon Murgie, (the tertiary rocks,) and low hills, the severity of the shock had been thought much greater than at Matera, and at many of the other towns in the central part of the great rolling lands, to the N. W. of the Gulf of Tarentum.

At Gravina and Altamura, where the shock was felt from west to east, there was some damage done, but not great.

At Tarentum, at the head of the gulf, the shock was not noticed. At Canosa, he had heard from other priests, that the direction of the shock, was rather to the north, or from S. W. to N. E., which would be about 49° or 50° E. of north, and was also there from south to north.

CHAPTER XXXIX.

A RIDE ROUND VULTURE AND UP TO MONTICCHIO.

I LEFT in the afternoon for Monticchio monastery, situated close above the lakes of the same name, that fill two of the ancient craters upon the west side of the Vulture.

Leaving Rionero, we ride across the rich and nearly level plain of about $2\frac{1}{2}$ miles wide, all sown with even now sprouting grain, and have to make many detours, to pass the deep and wall-sided chasms, or "nullahs," that are cut into the mass of tufa underlying it, by the rain torrents descending from the flanks of the cone. (Fig. 324.) Many of these torrent courses are 50 to 100 feet in depth, and some not 30 feet across, though generally they are more; the sides are perfectly plumb, or shed in and sloped here and there, tortuous and winding in plan. The bottom is generally quite flat, and not above 10 or 15 feet wide between the high side banks of tufa, strewed with large lapilli, fragments of lava, numbers of limestone pebbles, and a fine black sand, of titanate of iron, which is deposited in whole banks in some places.

These chasms are almost invisible at a short distance, and perfectly impossible to be crossed when deep. On

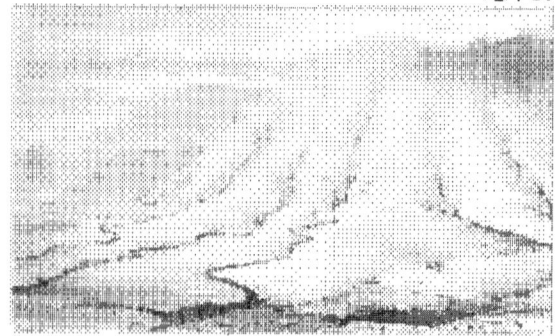

S.W. Shoulder of MONTE VULTURE.

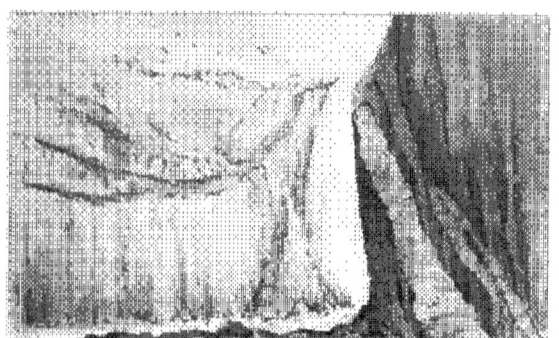

TORRENT, MONTE VULTURE.

North End, MONTICCHIO.

following any one of them up to the head, it is found that several minor rain torrents from the sides of the cone have coalesced, and that after having run upon the surface with a gradually lowering bed for some distance, they suddenly plunge down (Fig. 324) over a vertical wall of tufa, forming a cascade of from 2 or 3, to 20 or 30 feet in height (Fig. 325), but which only runs during rains. Here the cutting back of the tufa proceeds at a visible rate, and what is very remarkable, although the total depth of the ravine slowly decreases, as it is eaten out, upwards towards the cone, the abrupt perpendicularity of its head, over which the waters shoot or trickle, never changes, or becomes levelled to a talus.

Here is the point at which any one of these ravines can first be crossed; some hundreds of which intersect the flanks and plains around the great cone,—if cone, the vast irregular mass of Vulture, may be called—and form the feeders to the upper forks of the Ofanto, which drains the whole region.

The cone itself, upon its S. E. side especially, presents in its outlines and surface the most striking characteristics of enormous erosion by rain (Sketch, Fig. 324). Not a vestige of lava or hard rock is visible here—all is a rounded, furrowed, and worn mass of consolidated tufa.

As we leave the slopes that blend the plain with the mountain, and ascending some two miles more, reach its S. W. shoulder, isolated blocks of lava crop out here and there, and in some places are exposed in mass in the ravines. Thence the way lies wholly through the forest, El Bosco della Pietra, or De Bucito, for about two miles more.

Nothing could exceed the impressive beauty of this forest scenery, with its hoary moss-grown oak and beech trees, its silence broken only by the rustling fallen leaves, the bark of the distant shepherd's dog, and the far-above cry of the descending charcoal burner to his laden mules. I discern the two craters, now deep circular lakes, through the interlaced branches, and having topped one of the shoulders of the mountain now, far below me; the further dark and clear, the nearer turbid and yellow green.

I descend amongst aged trunks and overarching limbs, and pass over masses of rounded lava blocks—tufa—cemented lapilli. I am at the margin of the first lake. All is quietude; the soft breeze of a quiet winter's afternoon, fans across the embosomed water, from the early wheat-fields and the furrowed acres of the opposite steep slopes, and brings the gentle ripple lapping, amongst the roots of the old hazles at my feet.

Off before me, and to my left crowning the slope, are the grey ruins of some ancient church or castle, a few piled stones only. Far above me, and to the right, nestled against the lava crags, behind and above it, standing out white and clear, I see the strong buttressed mass of the monastery of St. Michael.

Not a sound but the rustle of the dead leaves, beneath the pawing of my little stallion mule, breaks the solemn silence; how hard it is to realize that this noble and lovely scene, full of every leafy beauty, that life and time can bestow, upon fair Nature's aspect, was once the innermost bowl of a volcano; that every stone around me, now glorious in colour with moss and lichen, sedum and geranium, was once a glowing mass, vomited from out that fiery and undiscovered abyss, that these placid waters now bury in their secret chambers. Yet the same effort of imagination must be made, before the geologist can realize, that every acre of surface whose landscape now delights him, with wood and flower, bud and insect, once produced nothing but algæ, and nourished the slimy things of the great deep innumerable. In either extreme, vitality asserts its power, and in a few short years obliterates the rude formative traces, whether they be by fire or by water.

CHAPTER XL.

IN THE MONASTERY OF MONTICCHIO.

A SHORT and sharp ascent, leads up to the monastery from the margin of the lake beneath (Photog. No. 327). As I approach it, the path is, I find, blocked by a huge fallen fragment of lava, dislodged by the shock from the cliff above. It has fallen in a direction 67° E. of north, towards the S.W. A fine young walnut tree of two boles, each of 14 ins. diameter, lies crushed and mangled beneath the fallen mass. (Sketch No. 326, Coll. Roy. Soc.)

The block is 13 feet long, 11 feet wide, and 8 feet thick, mean dimensions: it has fallen from a height, at A, of 43 feet, pitched upon its lower end at K, 14 feet horizontally from the point of displacement, and then falling over forward upon the steep slope, has overwhelmed the tree and been arrested by its timbers. If we assume the angle of emergence at Monticchio, to be about the mean of those given by Melfi, Barielle, and Atella = 15°, we obtain the following as the velocity of the wave of shock here.

Bearing in mind that the fissures in the building (as immediately after given) prove that the return stroke from the mountain which projected the rock was made with a

local emergence of 40°, we have the horizontal velocity—

$$V^2 = \frac{g}{2} \times \frac{a^2}{b - a \tan e}$$

$a = 14$, $b = 43$, $e = 40°$,

and $V = 11{\cdot}36$ feet per second;

but V, the velocity in the actual wave-path (i. e. the primary path) $= V \sec e$, and e here $= 15°$; therefore

$V = 11{\cdot}36 \times 1{\cdot}035 = 11{\cdot}757$ feet per second,

which is probably very near the truth, though derived from data somewhat unprecise.

The monastery has its long axis north and south, 10° W. of north: its broadside faces the lake or crater, and its rear is, in great part, built up against the lava cliff behind, in a cavern of which, the church which contains the miraculous image of St. Michael, said to have been found embedded in the solid lava, has been excavated. The church has its axial line west and east 118° W. of north. In the masonry portion of it outside the cavern, one large fissure is visible across the side wall and arch of the nave, on the north side of the church next the altar. There is also another smaller one at the east quoin at the north side. At the south side of the church, at its actual abutment with the lava rock, there is another fissure. The direction of wave-path given by these, is about 33° E. of north, and they are much sloped towards the S. W. at top, nearly 40° with the vertical. I hesitate to conclude anything positive, from these fissures, as the contact direct with the mountain side must have powerfully affected their directions.

The body of the monastery itself, is diffusely but not severely fissured. The best and most reliable fissures (as least affected by the rock behind) that I can find are in the north end gable, as seen from the terrace outside. (Sketch No. 328.) These three, with corresponding pairs in internal walls, give, I find, much about the same direction of wave-path with those of the church, viz., 33° E. of north, and the slope is nearly 40° for the two inner and 11° for the outer. I remark that the two former are nearly perpendicular to the face or slope, of the steep talus of bank beneath the monastery, and owe their extreme obliquity, as do those of the church, most probably to the reflected shove outwards from the rock behind; whose direction would, when coupled with the structure of the building, be in something like a line parallel to the slope of the bank. It is impossible to conceive them indicative, of a true angle of emergence of 40° here, in conflict with all other evidence.

The ancient fissures left by the shock of 1851 along the soffits of the corridors, which were 10° W. of north, and at right angles to that azimuth, prove that the wave-path then, could not have been very different from that of December last. The fissures in a few of the rooms on the second floor, to the front or west side, in which they are still visible, indicate the same. These cannot be confounded with the recent fissures, as those of 1851 have since been coloured over, in "tempera;" the recent ones are clean.

The monks, and especially the vicario, who has command (the priure having gone upon some mission), and who afforded me hospitality, agree in stating, their sensations to have been, that the shock came nearly horizontally, and almost from south to north, or a little from the west. They seem to have paid but little heed to it however, as they can give no clear information of how long it lasted, what time it occurred, or whether there was a noise with it or not. They say they did not discover that the building had been fissured until after daylight next morning.

I found here that the centre of the western lake surface, bore exactly due west, from the front and centre of the length, of the monastery; and comparing this with the bearing given by Zannoni's great map, the magnetic declination here proves to have been 14° westerly, which is within 30′ of the declination now given at the Observatory at Naples.

At $9^h 26^m$ Naples mean time (24th February), the barometer read 27·65 inches on the first-floor level of the monastery, thermo. 36° Fahr., and the height above the sea proves to be 2107·5 feet. It is therefore not above 200 or 300 feet above Rionero, although the high shoulder of Vulture, which I passed over, intervenes, nor above half the height of the mountain itself, the highest point of which, is given by Palmieri and Scacchi ('Memoir on Melfi Earthquake of 1851') at 4356 feet, and who give 1880 feet as the elevation of Rionero, and by Don Arabia (Del Tremuoto di Basilicata, &c.) at 4128 feet. Abich makes the level of Monticchio lake as much as 2332 feet. There was a sudden local disturbance of weather, on the night of February 23rd, and a considerable fall of snow took place, which may have rendered the comparison of my barometric height, with that of Naples Marine Observatory for the same time less to be trusted, and my height is possibly below the truth.

I left for Barielle, and found considerable difficulty in

CHAPTER XLI.

ON TO BARIELLE—EXAMINATION OF THE PLACE.

BARIELLE, a place of nearly 6000 inhabitants, who are said to be descendants of Albanian colonists, and of much antiquity, (Photog. No. 329, Coll. Roy. Soc.,) lies upon a high offshoot of Vulture to the eastward; upon deep beds of yellow and grey hard tufa, with large masses of included hard and elastic lava visible in many places. Four of the large torrents from the flanks of the mountain, pass through and around the town, dividing, to a considerable depth, the blocks upon which it is built, and uniting to the east of it, in the little Vallo della Fica, fall into the Olivento, which joins the great stream of the Ofanto, about twelve miles to the N.E. The Pizzuto of Vulture, bears west of north, from the highest point of the town, and compared with Zannoni's map, confirms previous determinations of magnetic declination. The Syndico, Don Vincencio Piancentini, and two or three of the chief inhabitants, accompanied me over the town, which has suffered severely. It is diffusely and in many places severely fissured, and several buildings wholly prostrated. Two persons were killed by the fall of these.

A large building opposite the Casa Communale,

L shaped in plan, whose front walls run 70° W. of north, shows large fissures, in both the east and west and north and south walls. Two pairs are measurable, and both give a wave-path 33° E. of north from the S. W. The emergence seems very small, (but rather ambiguous from structure,) about 8° from the S. W.

The church of St. Nicole, has its axial line exactly north and south. The south end gable wall, has been split off by a large east and west fissure, upon 1¼ inch open at top, down to the springing of the semi-cylindrical vault of the roof.

There is also a long narrow fissure, open about half an inch and extending north and south along the soffit, as far as the chancel. These two, which are the only main contemporaneous fissures, are unfortunately, by structure, not strictly comparable. They afford to "tact," however, an *estimate* of direction, which cannot be far from 25° to 35° E. of north, and from the S. W.

A large painting which stood upon the top edge of the cornice, beneath the vault-springing, at the west side of the nave, and leaned forward, or towards the east, being kept in position by a cord and nail behind the top of the frame, has been thrown back, and now leans against the vault behind it, having thus been thrown at top westward.

The Palazzo of Prince Torella (Photog. No. 330, Coll. Roy. Soc.), is nearly cardinal, and stands on the edge of a deep ravine of tufa to the north of it. It was ruined in the earthquake of 1851, and the fissures then made, which are still visible, show a wave-path *for that shock* from south to north. There are large fissures from the recent shock, both in north and south, and in east and west walls; and the mean of several sets gives a wave-path 45° 30' E. of north, from the S.W. The emergence still is apparently very small, not above 3° or 4° here, or, therefore possibly, horizontal. The whole north side, has been thrown outwards, and the fall indicates the wave-path also towards the N.E.

The smallness of the angle of emergence, I can now see from the highest points of the town, has arisen from its isolated blocks having oscillated separately, and confounded the emergence due to the wave with their own line of oscillation, which was approximately horizontal.

I remark from this point, also, that the mass of the south flank and shoulder of Vulture, lies right in the line of wave-path from the town, which, isolated as its blocks are, may be viewed, as placed upon a free lying surface, in the direction of the wave transit. The Piano della Croce, and other hills to the north and east, must also have sent back reflected waves, and a direct earthquake echo.

The Chiesa Madre was completely demolished in 1851, except one Capella and the Campanile. These show by the *old* crevasses, that the wave-path was *then* south to north. They afford no indications as to the recent one.

A very heavy wall (Photog. No. 331, p. 7) adjoining a vault beneath some large building, close to the west of the Chiesa Madre, is far out of plumb, twisted and thrown to the south and west, but still standing. It has been a little supported by a bank of earth to the southward of it, which at the end still remaining nearly plumb, reached to about one-third its height from the base; but the other end, that in front of the photograph, was unsupported.

The precise direction of wave-path cannot be calculated,

but may be judged by "tact" to have been very near 45° E. of north, or between that and 55° E. of north, the plane of the wall being 110° E. of north. It gives a tolerable measure of velocity. The wall was 20 feet in height, 4 feet in thickness at the base, and the velocity was obviously not quite, but very nearly sufficient, to overturn its unsupported extremity; the angle θ is here = 6° 30'; $a = 20$; $b = 4$.

The horizontal velocity necessary for overthrow is therefore first to be calculated without reference to the dislocation of the masonry, which was of inferior quality, and not above one-fourth the strength of the best limestone rubble work, and then the fracturing velocity for the latter, and both added, and resolved from the horizontal direction, and perpendicular to the plane of the wall, into the direction of the wave-path.

The horizontal velocity of overthrow is

$$V^2 = \tfrac{4}{3} g \sqrt{a^2 + b^2} \times \left(\frac{1 - \cos \theta}{\cos^2 \theta} \right);$$

$$V^2 = 42.93 \times 20.3 \times 0.0112 = 12.64;$$

$$V = v_i = 3.555 \text{ feet per second.}$$

The horizontal velocity for fracture is

$$n = \tfrac{4}{3} g \times \frac{L \beta}{a^2}$$

L here = $\tfrac{59}{4}$, one-fourth the coefficient for the best rubble masonry, and,

$$V = v_f = 42.93 \times 0.153 = 6.568 \text{ feet per second.}$$

$v_i + v_f = 3.555 + 6.568 = 10.123$ feet per second,

therefore, would have been a velocity, which if applied

horizontally, and square to the face of the wall, would have fractured and overthrown it.

The wave-path, however, was oblique in azimuth to the wall, i being $= 25°$, upon the data preceding; and we may take the emergence here at about $15° = e$, from other determinations, whence we obtain, for the total velocity, in the path of the wave, that would have prostrated the wall,

$$V = \frac{v_i + v_j}{\cos i} \sec e = \frac{10 \cdot 123}{0 \cdot 906} \times 1 \cdot 035 = 11 \cdot 564$$

feet per second; on the supposition that the wall had received no support from the bank of earth to the south; which, however, did prop it sensibly at one end, as the vertical fracturing due to torsion, seen in the photograph, proves.

A velocity in the path of the wave, *greater* than 11·564 feet per second, therefore, would have been required for its overthrow; and it was *not* overthrown, but was upon the *verge* of it, being out of plumb nearly three feet. The actual velocity of shock to which it was exposed, therefore, was very little below, 11·564 feet per second; but we already have found from the thrown rock at Monticchio, that the velocity there $= 11 \cdot 757$ feet per second, which harmonizes closely.

The Syndico, had a large silver pocket-watch, which on the night of the earthquake, hung by its ring upon a nail, driven horizontally, in a north and south direction, upon the south side, of a wall of his chamber running east and west. The nail projected about 3 inches from the face of the wall, and the watch was hanging so from it, that the back of the case, was in contact with the wall. He happened to have his eyes upon the watch very nearly at the moment of the great pulse, of the first shock, and he saw the watch run forward upon the nail, from the face of the wall, nearly as far as the latter would permit, namely until the ring should come in contact with the head of the nail. At the same time, the watch oscillated, in a plane parallel with the face of the wall (east and west) from 30° to 40°, i. e., or half these at each side the vertical. The moment it got stopped by the head of the nail, the watch began to gyrate, i. e., to oscillate as a conical pendulum. The Syndico, a gentleman of shrewd observation and with all that clearness of mind that characterizes the people of Southern Italy, repeated the movements for me with the watch, by hand. We obtain from his observation a very tolerable estimate of the horizontal amplitude of the wave at Barielle, which was obviously about 1·25 inch, or 1·30 inch, in a north and south direction, and a little less in the direction of east and west, or about 1·76 inch in the path of normal vibration.

He noted the time of the first shock by this watch, which, in Frankish time, was 10ʰ 8ᵐ, Barielle time. The watch was adjusted by sunset, but he could not guarantee that it was right within a minute or two. In Naples time it is as follows :—

	h.	m.	s.
Watch noted at Barielle .	10	8	0
Naples, west of Barielle, in time .	0	5	45
Time of the shock, Naples mean time	10	2	15

The clear impression of the Syndico, and of two or three of the inhabitants then present with us, is, that the direction of the shock was from the S. W., and from a point rather more south than S. W. He was in the town in 1851, and is of opinion that the shock *then*, was from south to north.

A general ramble over the buildings of the town, however, convinced me that here, as at Rionero, and elsewhere, there had been several secondary waves, crossing the primary wave-path, and producing complicated minor phenomena, and wave-paths in direction, south to north.

They had no measures of the time of the occurrence by public clocks, stopped or observed. Their reports as to the noise, were not very distinct; the sound was low and prolonged, but obviously had not attracted much attention nor had the second shock of about an hour after the great one.

CHAPTER XLII.

RAPOLLA AND ITS NEIGHBOURHOOD TO MELFI.

I pushed on for Rapolla. It is a place of about 3500 inhabitants; nearly two miles further removed to the N. E. from Vulture. It lies upon a spur of tufa, of enormous depth of deposit, which points towards the N. E., and whose general direction is the same. It is insulated by ravines of great depth and steepness, to the north and south sides of the spur. The upper part of the town, Photog. No. 332 (Coll. Roy. Soc.), suffered terribly in 1851, and is still almost wholly in ruins. The fine old Norman cathedral, was then quite destroyed; the present is a modern and very plain structure.

This town has suffered very little from the recent earthquake: it is hard to find even a few fissures, that will give measurable results. Three sets, of two, each, narrow and thread-like, I did find, in new and substantial buildings in different parts of the town, which gave wave-paths of

45° 30′ E. of north from the S. W.
24° W. of north from the S. E.
S. to north from the south.

Emergence from the first, 12° from the S. W., from the two others $e = 0$. The first, was from a building at the S. W., side of the town, and upon the most broad and level part of the spur; the two others on the north and south sides respectively. The two latter are obviously local secondary oscillations of the spur itself.

The main cause of this place having suffered so little, appears plainly enough to be the sifting that it received in 1851, which demolished all the old and less firm buildings, so that it now consists only of the stout ones that remained, and which are but few, and of the numerous new and substantial buildings since constructed. I could obtain here no information worth recording from the chief inhabitants, and in the afternoon I pushed on to the city of Melfi, and at once waited upon the Intendente, whom I found at his palazzo, and who obligingly brought me in his carriage over the town and its immediate neighbourhood.

Melfi stands upon a rolling country of swelling hills, all of deep tufa, with great beds of lapilli interposed, often of great size, and masses of lava here and there; it is of exuberant agricultural richness, as the Photog. (No. 333 Coll. Roy. Soc.), close to the town, with Vulture in the distance, may indicate. The great rounded mass upon which the city stands, is more than a mile and a half across both ways; it is surrounded nearly, by the Torrente di Melfi, and the Aqna Negra, whose beds, in the bottom of deep ravines of erosion, are probably 300 to 350 feet below the mean level of the place. The elevation above the sea is given by Palmieri and Scacchi at 1600 feet; by Don Arabia at 1688; and I made the level of the Castello yard 1700 feet, by an imperfect observation, however. It is therefore about 200 feet lower than Rionero, and about

400 beneath the water surface of the ancient craters at Monticchio.

From the neighbourhood of the Castello, which overtops the highest part of the city, and is at the edge of the most precipitous scarp around the walls, the summit of Vulture bears 156° W. of north,* and, comparing this with Zannoni's map, the magnetic declination is about 15° W.

Melfi suffered terribly in 1851, when 800 persons were killed; 170 houses were prostrated; with churches, the cathedral and many other buildings nearly destroyed; the shock then, as numbers of old fissures show still, having had a wave-path nearly from south to north, and having a steep emergence. The people of the place say, if their account be reliable, that the movement of 1851 was first nearly vertical and then became oscillatory, lasting, in all, nearly a minute. It has, however, escaped very well on the present occasion, and upon an examination afforded such evidence, that I had got nearly to the verge in this radius, of such energy as had left any permanent marks of its effects, that I resolved to halt here, and return upon a new track.

There are a good many fissures to be found throughout the town, which give wave-paths from 30° to 40° E. of north.

The Intendenzia has got some rather heavy fissures in the front and interior walls, which give 45° 30' E. of north.

The Church of Morteelli, a modern building, has its axial line east and west, and shows a recent fissure through the soffit of the nave. The east-end gable has parted off from the vault, widening here an ancient fissure of 1851. The wave-path shown is about 45° E. of north, but does not admit of precise determination. There are many old fissures, and difficulty in deciding which are new.

Fissures at the east and S. E. flank of the town, gave some very discordant results, showing wave-paths 16° W. of north, and others south to north; but, from the situation, these are, no doubt, all local oscillations or reflected waves.

The Agricultural College, which is situated on tolerably level ground to the west of the city, has its long axis 72° E. of north. There are fissures in the south walls (external), and at both sides of the S. E. quoin, in front; and the whole south front wall has given out a little. Other fissures in north and south walls, on the west side of the building. All are recent, and the average wave-path that they give, is 30° E. of north to 32° E. of north.

I could get no measures of emergence of a trustworthy character except from this building, and from the Church of Mortcelli, both of which gave pretty clear indications; the former 15° emergence from the S. W., the latter 16° 20′ from the same.

Very many of the smaller buildings were fissured nearly vertically, and in some instances I could detect no structural cause determinant of that direction, and therefore conclude that there was some great local oscillation of the ground beneath Melfi, in one nearly horizontal path.

The Intendente told me, that at Ascoli, a town about fourteen miles north of Melfi, the shock had been felt almost precisely from south to north. He had a pendulum clock in his entrance hall, vibrating in a plane nearly east and west, which was not stopped.

The precise time of the first shock of 16th December was determined here, with greater accuracy, than anywhere else except at Naples, so far as I have been able to collect. The Sotto Intendente carries a pocket chronometer, which, he states, goes with remarkable precision, and which he compares occasionally by telegraph with Naples time. He looked at this chronometer at the instant of the great shock, and found the time to be $10^h\ 3^m$ Naples mean solar time. Melfi is in longitude 1° 26′ 40″ E. of Naples, and the difference in time $= 5^m\ 46·6^s$.

The Intendente did not hear any noise himself, but states that very many persons in the city did. The people at the Agricultural College, and more particularly the teacher of natural philosophy there, described it as a low, prolonged, rumbling sound—"Sotterra ò in aria rimbombi quali produce il cannone lontano."

The Sotto Intendente said, that several persons in the city, spoke of having heard such sounds repeated several times during the night. They had observed nothing of unusual meteorological phenomena; the weather was calm and serene at the time of the shock. Their own *sensations* were, that the great shock had reached them from the S. W.; that it was nearly horizontal, and was succeeded by small up-and-down oscillations, that lasted for several seconds, the total duration, being very variously and obviously very vaguely estimated, at from twenty seconds to a minute or more.

CHAPTER XLIII.

FIRST MOVEMENTS IN RETURNING—SNOWING UP ON MONTE CROCE.

I commenced my return, through Rapolla Barielle Rionero and Atella, a long and fatiguing ride of about thirty miles, to Muro, intending now to traverse the extreme N. W. region of the shock, through the valleys south of the great ridge of Monte Calvello and Monte Accellico.

On re-passing Atella, and looking back upon it from the south, I see that on this side it stands on a pretty steep escarpment, with large beds of lava, showing a rapid slope from Vulture, exposed and cut through, along with the beds of tufa. Denudation here, at the torrent Fiumara d'Atella, running west, has cut through at least 300 feet of volcanic deposits. Yesterday I noticed, near Rapolla, lava beds reposing on tufa, and cut quite through, which had by the eye a slope of at least 30°, dipping north and N. E. from Vulture. The whole of the volcanic phenomena of the Vulture district, are developed upon a scale of grandeur, to which Vesuvius is insignificant.

Crossing the Artuso and the Vonchia, two nearly parallel torrential streams, descending from Monte Pierno to the south and west, and running northward to fall into the Fiumara d'Atella, I came upon, green yellow and brown metamorphic rocks of great beauty, and very hard. They are not only seen here and there *in situ*, in extremely disturbed beds, but the whole country, and the beds of the rivers, are strewn with the rich-coloured boulders, whose angles only, have been rubbed off.

Somewhere about here, must be the very edge of the volcanic tract to the north, and these rocks are apparently the result of the reaction of the ancient volcanic rocks upon the argillaceous beds, which, owing to their original contact with the cretaceous limestone, had acquired such a dose of lime, as enabled them to bake into the magnificent natural terra cotta that is around me.

Creeping along beneath the great forest of Maurella, that rises continuously for two or three miles upon the N.W., and whose growth attests the richness of the mixed volcanic and calcareous soil, we commence the long and steep ascent of Monte Croce, having necessarily to pass somewhere, the great Apennine ridge, in order to return into the valleys whose watershed is towards the Mediterranean.

The monks at Monticchio, upon the coming on of the fall of snow there, had hinted that I should find difficulty in crossing the pass of Monte Croce; and the Padrone at Barielle had expressed great doubt of the possibility of accomplishing it.

I was extremely anxious to return that way, as leading me over new ground, and finding, after the best inquiries I could make, that the other passes across the chain, south of Potenza, were still higher and known to be worse in deep snows, I finally resolved to attempt the passage of Monte Croce. The whole of Vulture now lay covered, and even the plain beneath, had about six inches of snow, as we left before daylight, and we found nowhere less than three or four inches on the ground.

As we commenced to ascend now the exposed northern steeps of Monte Croce, the depth of snow rapidly increased, and before we had reached the Taberna of Caputo, upon the sloping back of the great spur, between Monte Fieno and the little vallone of Pierno, at 11 A.M., we were brought to a standstill, in snow of two, to two and a half feet deep. A train of muleteers with produce, which we had seen before us, were here also brought up. All trace of road or path was lost. The air, though lightsome and still, was filled with a fine powdery crystalline ice, whose minute falling particles rapidly filled outside pockets and boots, with some pounds of heavy ice. The snow, where it lay in pits and hollows, showed its density and depth, by the starchy blue aspect it bore; and we were still five or six miles from the summit of the ridge. The opinion of the leading muleteer, of the train we had come up with, who had been snowed up at Caputo, for three weeks the preceding year in April, was, that a heavy fall of snow might be expected that night, and that unless we could make good the passage before sunset, it would become impracticable.

He and his companions, experienced carriers of wine and oil upon the road, also thought that it would be possible, to clear a track in good time, if sufficient labouring help could be collected. Matters looked urgent; money was to be weighed against time. I promised him and his "banda," a liberal donation and five piastres each, and one piastre to every labourer they could collect, provided they had the passage cleared so that we could get over, before sundown.

We all returned about two and a half miles down to the

Taberna de Caputo, nothing but a rude and ponderous mule shed, with a single small sleeping-room, in which a man and his wife lodge, and have charge of a supply of flour and wine, maintained here by Government, to prevent starvation in those who may be snowed up, upon these solitary steeps.

The men started off downward, plunging through the snow towards the Vallone of Pierno, to some hamlets said to be there, and in about an hour, groups of wild-looking fellows, with their large hoes, began to pass upwards. At last we had collected, in all about fifty hands, in addition to the muleteers, who got tools from Caputo, and stretching them along the line pointed out by the leader, I found they soon began to make a sensible impression, partly treading down, partly excavating the snow.

As we gained height, the scene was impressively grand: The saddle-backed slope of unbroken snow, up which we toiled, and the rapid *pente* to the right, were lost in air filled to obscurity, with floating and falling ice particles. To the left, the steep slopes clothed by the noble pine forest of Pierno, lay below us; the black spiral forms and laden boughs of the huge pines, now and then visible for a few moments, and then fog and ice particles, again shutting out all around. After two or three hours we hailed another party of eight or ten of the Guardiani della Strada that we found were at work above us; and about the same time the fall of ice particles ceased. I had now good hopes of a passage, and returned alone to the Caputo, to order up a supply of wine for the men. After three hours and a half more, occupied there in writing up notes, the leader muleteer came down, with the joyful news that the passage was, he thought, practicable. In less than half an hour more, the proof of this was given in the arrival on his mule, wet and exhausted, of Il Padre, Vincencio Barra di Melfi, who had been endeavouring to force his way from an early hour of the morning, going towards Melfi. He was engaged, as a sort of rural dean, in an ecclesiastical inspection of the injury done to church edifices in this province; and I obtained from him much information of a valuable character, during the hour that still elapsed before we could start, as to the effects of the shock, in the districts of Bari, the Capitanata's, and the north and east of the Tierra di Lavoro, and Molise.

The scene of snow and desolation at the top of the ridge, where I paid off my wild band of excavators, was worthy the pencil of a Carravaggio. I took on, for two or two and a half miles down the slope towards Bella, ten or twelve men, and fortunately, for we had there to cut through a short abrupt drift, that was forming across the road to a depth of more than 18 feet. I found we had in all, wrought a path of about a mile and a half long, upon an average two and a half feet deep, above the trodden snow beneath; in many places three to four feet deep, and for about 300 yards, a continuous drift that measured 8 feet 6 inches above the hard snow below.

Had it not been for the fact, that owing to some peculiar set of the wind at this season, or time, due probably to the eddies of the smaller valleys or great gorges, the snow is swept off the highest part of the pass, as fast as it falls, and drifted away down the slopes to the westward, (as the muleteers assured me before we began was always found to be the case,) the attempt to get through six miles of deep snow would have been hopeless.

I rejoiced to find myself once more upon the solid earth, with the forest boughs above me, and my face towards Naples, and that at this side it was thawing fast.

A rough observation at the Taberna showed that it was about 3000 feet above the sea. Upon the highest point I found the barometer read 26·13 inches, thermo. 36° Fahr. at 4·40 Naples mean time, and the reduced height above the sea was 3654·5 feet.

The summits of Monte Croce were quite invisible, but the men I had brought down with me, said they rose more than a thousand palms, above the highest point that we had passed.

CHAPTER XLIV.

MURO AND BELLA—THE APENNINE KNOT AND GREAT LINE OF DISLOCATION.

The first rock that I saw from under the snow at the west side, proved to be nearly, vertical beds, in the variegated clay slate—Apennine marls, I suppose—and within two miles down from the top, we came upon cretaceous-looking limestone, having passed some intermediate beds of red metamorphic rocks.

The view now opens upon Bella, a town perched upon, and stretching along the top, of a thin-edged ridge, of soft rock and diluvium to the westward. The general direction of the ridge, is 110° W. of north, and it abuts and is connected with, much higher ridges at its east end.

The torrent of Carpineta, runs at its east and south bases, which falls into the Platano, and ultimately into the Salaris far away.

The town has suffered, but not severely. The church, whose axial line is 140° E. of north, has had its campanile thrown from the north end, on to the roof of the church. The church itself, is fissured both longitudinally and transversely. The direction of throw of the Campanile, indicated a wave-path of 25° to 25° 30' E. of north. Several other buildings were fissured, but the near approach of darkness compelled me to make but a most cursory examination, so as to reach the Taberna della Aqua Bianca to sleep.

Descending on foot, the steep hills towards Muro, I fell into conversation with an extremely intelligent young man, whose name, I regret to find, I neglected to take, and who gave a good account of the earthquake, as observed about Bella, to which place he belonged. He alluded to the strange atmospheric light (before I had asked any question about it), which, he said, was noticed by nearly every one, like a pale diffused moonlight, for half an hour or more, *before and after*, the great shock. The first shock, he said, was a double one, with an intervening tremor. The noise was distinctly heard, and seemed to come, not only from the same direction as the shock, which, he said, most persons hereabouts agreed was from the S.W., but also " out from under Monte Croce." On looking at the relative position of Monte Croce, from that of the house down towards the bottom of the valley, where he says he was on that night, I find the wave-path prolonged goes through the northern shoulder of Monte Pierno, and it may be concluded that the sound from beneath Monte Croce was, in fact, a subterraneous echo. It was long and reverberating, he said.

This lad was the first who noticed to me, the vast landslips that have occurred beyond Muro.

The rock hereabouts is cretaceous-looking limestone, in some places a coarse, irregular, limestone breccia; but the surface is covered with very deep clays, in and upon which, great limestone boulders are lying, all in directions that lean and slope towards the valley bottoms, and are indicative of the enormous amount of slippage of loose material, and of the denudation which has taken place.

Muro is before me (Photog. No. 334), at the opposite side of the deep narrow valley, clinging to the precipitous N. E. end, of a huge mass of solid limestone mountain, that comes up in the midst of a great amphitheatre of far larger and higher mountains, amongst which Monte Croce towers above all.

All the bedding discernible about Muro, seems nearly vertical, and the rocky sides of its mountain base, are murally steep. It is not more than a mile distant in a right line, and yet I find, it will take two hours and a half at a trot, to reach the town from this. I therefore remain at the Taberna dell' Aqua, or della Muro, and pass the evening with the padrone, and his family of three sons and four daughters, all grown up, chatting over the earthquake around the "Camine."

On the road side approaching Muro from the north, is a remarkable example of the movements by slippage, of the

Fig. 326.

vast masses of unctuous clays, of this region, into which the thin marl beds dissolve when saturated in water.

The Photog. No. 335 (Coll. Roy. Soc.) and Sketch

No. 336, the former taken, looking down the slope, and hence showing the inclination badly, the latter looking diagonally up towards the S. E., represent the ruined walls of the Taberna della Duc di Gravina, which was destroyed by these "illuviones" in 1836. After a long period of drenching rain, the sloping side of the valley upon which it was founded, began to give way and move bodily downwards, towards the stream at the bottom. The large edifice has been thus launched, above 100 perches west of its original site, and as the mass of clay was shoved on, a mighty plastic mass, (a mud glacier,) over an uneven rocky bed, its surface rose and fell irregularly, but with extreme slowness, and the long walls of the building, were riven nearly vertically, presenting still, in some places, evidence upon their surfaces of the shearing and grinding action. The intermediate great fragments of wall, hence are thrown out of plumb, in the planes of the walls, some up, some down the slope; others are out of plumb across the wall faces, and, what appeared most strange, the whole general line of base, originally quite horizontal, was now out of level, and had assumed the general slope of the slipping mass that carried it, the upper being nearly the height of the walls, 10 feet, higher than the other end, the slope of the land surface generally being about 18° or 20°. The whole mass had also obviously sunk and buried itself, about 3 feet below its original foundation level, and the plastic masses around it, have swelled and risen upon it about the upper end, from inequality of resistance.

The sub-soil upon which it stands, is rendered visible by a streamlet close by, and shows itself to be a deep, slippery, blue marly clay, of great depth, and easily dissolved into

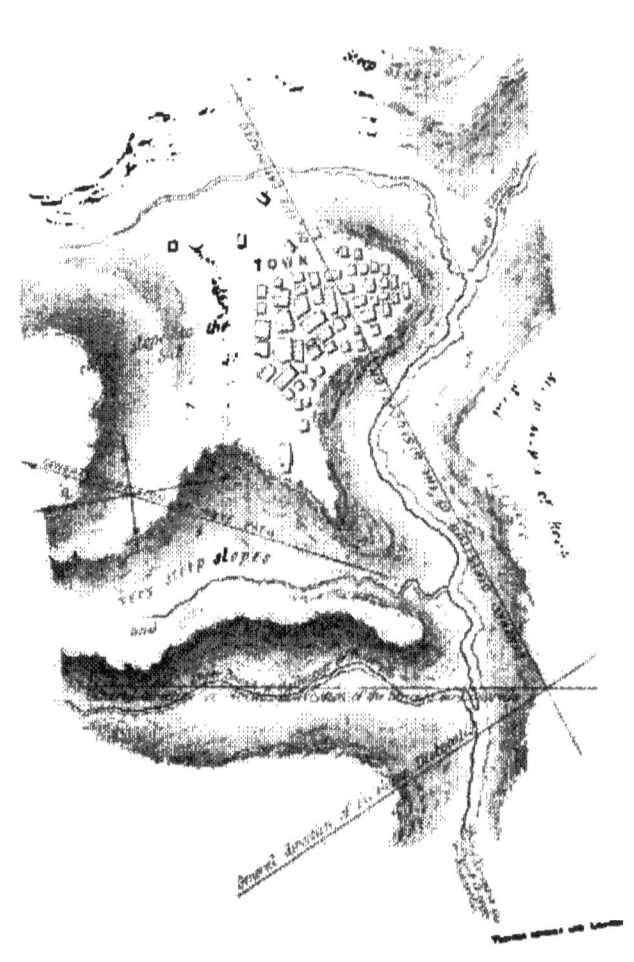

ELLIA
VIEW NEAR THE N END OF THE FIORD

mud when wet. Here and there, huge limestone boulders, and others, of metamorphic rock, are scattered through its mass, and have been moved *pari passu* downwards with it, towards the bottom of the valley; and as far as the eye can stretch westward, along the lower slopes of Monte Carozze, Guardiola, and Croce del Topo, and towards the valley in which Castel Grandine lies, the whole country seems composed, of like masses of clays, bearing like enormous detached masses of rock, all, from their slopes and positions, in process of slowly and insensibly going downwards, into the beds of the torrents and rivers, in the valley bottoms.

At daylight, I descended the steep slopes to the S. W. of the Taberna, to examine Muro, and the grand chasm through which the Giacojio rolls, upon the opposite side of which Muro is poised, upon the shelves of the spur, looking S. E. between that stream and the Malda, that falls in just below it. At the Taberna, at six A.M., Naples mean time, barometer reads 27·65 inches, thermo. 34° Fahr., and the reduced level gives 2178 feet above the sea. The older part of Muro, stands terraced, about 300 feet above the bed of the torrent, and is about on a level with Bella. The newer portion, stands about 150 feet higher, and is apparently about 200 feet below the Taberna, so that the level of the torrent bed, beneath Muro, may be about 1500 feet above the sea.

The town stands upon solid masses of limestone, on beds almost perfectly vertical, that rise like a wall; upon the south and east sides of the grand chasm of dislocation, that here is rent for above two miles in length, in a general S. E. and N. W. direction, through the limestone rock. (See Diagram No. 337, Figs. 1, 2, and 3.) For above a mile in length, its sides are not above 100 to 200 feet across, jagged and saw-like, the salient and re-entrant angles, and even the opposite beds, (whose strike is very generally transverse to the great chasm,) corresponding, and everywhere presenting evidence of actual fracture; the mural precipices to the west side frequently 500 to 700 feet in height, above the torrent bed.

This great line of dislocation, is joined by others at several points, at angles more or less acute; so that both Bella and Muro, stand upon spurs having chasms of dislocation at two sides, the former between those of the Carpineto and the Fumarella, the latter between those of the Giacojio and the Malde.

On examining Figs. 1 and 3 it will be seen, that the bifurcation of these chasms, in relation to the general wave-path at each place, is such, as to interpose the breadthway of the dislocations, filled in with loose material, dropped down between their rigid jaws, between the towns and the advancing shock; and to this condition must be attributed, the almost entire immunity from injury, that they have experienced. Situated, both on solid limestone, with free lying surfaces opposed to the direction of wave transit, and at no enormous distance, from towns which were totally destroyed, these must have likewise perished, had it not been, that these deep trenches, broken up by nature, and loosely filled in with a compressible cushion, of boulders gravel clay and such-like loose materials, had stood like great buffers, to receive the shock of the wave, and destroy at once, to a great degree, its velocity and its further propagation, by compression of the filling material between the jaws of these profound chasms. A new and unexpected

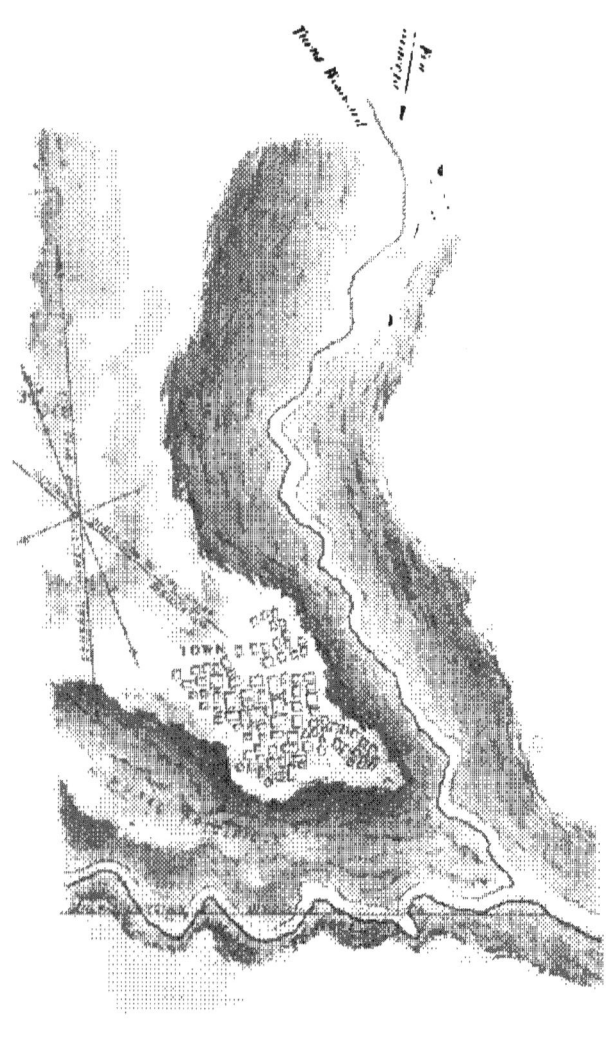

cause, for the sudden changes often found, and frequently so apparently capricious and inexplicable, stood revealed, in two separate but adjacent instances, and upon a scale so vast as to compel conviction. From below Muro, nearly twenty miles in length of the general line of the valley, may be traced by the eye, and its whole direction down to the junction of the Giacojio or Fiumara de Muro, with the Platino, generally coincides with that of this great dislocation, namely, N. W. and S. E.; so that it may fairly be inferred that the vast fracture extends for miles beyond the portion visible, and is now covered to the southward by the loose deposits of the valley bottom. Its influence upon the shock would be, however, scarcely altered by such covering, and must be great in proportion to its length, depth, and width.

Examining Muro with the telescope, from the eastern steeps opposite, at only about three furlongs' distance, I can see that it has suffered scarcely any injury. A few fissures are visible, and I find from some of the buildings near the base, that the direction of wave-path is 16° 30' E. of north. These correspond narrowly with those at the Taberna and other buildings upon the slope below it, which give 16° E. of north. I find from the Padrone that Bella and Muro are not the only towns that have escaped so well; that, in fact, all the towns that lie to the N. W. of the valley of the Giacojo and within a short distance, have had the like immunity. Thus Pescopagano, St. Andrea, Castelgrandine, Rapone, Ravo, and St. Fele, have all come off with little more than fissures, while at an equal distance to the S. E. of the same line, the towns that I have already passed over and examined, are mostly in ruins.

At about three miles to the S. E. from Bella, were the great "Voragines," of which I had heard so much, Photogs. No. 338 and (No. 339, Coll. Roy. Soc.), which, as I expected, turned out to be landslips, produced, no doubt, by the shock as secondary effects. They lay upon the gently sloping flank of a wild mountainous region, between the Carpineto and the Costa Carlotta, called the Carlotta d'Isca di Muro. It seems all to consist of these deep slippery clays, with soft limestones coming up through here and there. The general direction of the trench-like fissures, now getting rapidly obliterated by rains, &c., was N. W. and S. E., or parallel to the strike of the slope of table land, and they had opened very variously, at different points. The largest were open, at top, 10 or 15 feet, and from 5 to 8 feet deep, the turf, &c., torn across, and the land had descended at the lower side. The movement of land, once commenced, by the *jog* of the earthquake, had obviously gone on for a considerable time, and might possibly be even then slowly proceeding. The greatest of the fissures, the people about said, had been traced two miles. The land that had visibly slipped, and the surface of which was wrinkled and furrowed more or less, appeared to be about 400 or 500 English acres in extent. In some places, pressure from behind, had forced portions of land completely over, so that the original surface had been buried and the subsoil had turned up and become the surface. The changes of level within short distances produced by this forcing up and fissuring were considerable, so that when a trench ran right across the length of a ruined shepherd's hut, one end of the building had got out of level to the right, and the other, the opposite way, to the left. All these fissured lands, lay to the east of the great valley gorge of the Giacojio and the Platano, &c.; and except the minor torrents, such as the Marmo and others delivering into the Platano, were not cut off by any great and continuous valley courses from the neighbourhood of the focal region of the earthquake, between which and this place many of the prolonged lower ridges assume a direction about north and N. E., or end on to the wave-path.

Moreover, the great mass of Monte Marmo lies nearly (a little east) in the line of the wave-path from the southward. All these circumstances conspired to make the shock considerably more severe about the Isca di Bella, than at Bella town, and at Muro, which, although so near, lie at the west side of the great chasm.

A very small amount of shaking, however, upon this unctuous and treacherous soil, might set in movement the most enormous slippages; so that there is little necessary connection between the extent of the landslip, and that of the shock originating it; in fact, the common phenomena of slippage in heavy railway embankments, which are generally brought to the final point of moving by the vibration of a passing train, is a case in point; indicating how little the violence of the shock can be judged of by the extent of such landslips. There was nothing, except the large scale of the occurrence remarkable, beyond what I had already carefully examined at Campostrina, at Auletta, in the valley of Viggiano, where the dislodgment was quite as striking, and elsewhere.

Judging from the character of the wild region, that for many square miles seems to consist of these clay formations around, it is probable that a careful examination would detect numbers of other examples of such slippages; upon all which, the case of the Locanda di Gravina of yesterday, was an instructive commentary.

All that is seen in the engravings Nos. 18, 20, 27, 29, 30, 34, 36, 37, 39, 41, 42, 45, and 49, of the ' Istoria di Fenomeni del Tremoto nelle Calabrie, nell' anno 1783, dalla Reale Accademia delle Scienze di Napoli, fol. 1784, Naples,' allowing for the barbarous drawings, and gross exaggeration of parts, and still more barbarous engraving, is perfectly and easily accounted for by the phenomena disclosed, by these various fissures and landslips, whether superficially dry or ponding water, whether running, or stagnant and lodged beneath the surface.

Subscription of CATALDO.

SLIPPING ROCKS, Valley of the Maida.

CHAPTER XLV.

MURO TO LAVIANO OVER THE BOSCO CERRETA.

I LEFT Muro to the south, taking the road to Laviano by a wild country on the north slopes of the little valley of the Maklo, and over the ridge of the Bosco Cerreta. Immense blocks of limestone lay half buried upon the deep clays in every direction, all pointing down the slopes. About three miles from the Taberna, the Rio de Santa Muffeo comes down from the recesses of Monte Carozzo, through the little gorge of Cataldo on the north, and presents a very remarkable debouchure upon the valley. Far away, and high above, in the gorge, I see lofty and frowning crags of limestone at both sides; but below, the advanced slopes and masses, are all rounded grey and yellow clays, and soft sandstones, in pretty level beds, presenting, by their outlines and enormous detritus, all the characters that the glacialist would attribute to ice; but the extreme softness of the rocks forbids this, and it is obviously due to ancient marine tidal action, and later, to pluvial scouring away, and constant slippage (Sketch No. 340), which together can simulate everything that ice can effect.

All about here, appears to be the geological boundary, of the yellow and grey soft sandstones, and of the soft, cretaceous limestones. At between five and six miles from Muro, still going N. W., I remark traces of the great dislocation, still retaining (on the large scale) the same general N. W. and S. E. direction. I pass on the west great beds of yellow grey sandstone, soft, mouldering, and crumbly, and inclined downwards to the valley bottom at the east side of the stream; and on them limestone has rested more or less conformably, with their beds of clay or marls interposed.

The limestone has slid in immense masses, upon the subjacent rockways, greased by these clays when wetted, and becoming dislocated, now lies in enormous slabs and masses, some of them blocks of 60 and 80 feet long, and 10 or 15 feet thick, half buried in the clays and slimy detritus, and gravel, all over the slope, for about a mile and a half up and down the valley, by nearly a mile wide of the slope, whose average angle may be about 12° or 14°, with a much steeper talus where it approaches the river at the bottom. (Sketch No. 341.)

Zannoni's map, and still more the others, are all astray in this region, which is left quite a terra incognita.

We now begin the ascent of Monte Cerreto, the last ridge separating this valley from that of Lavinno. At the highest point of our path the barometer reads 27·15 inches, thermo. 30° Fahr. at 11·40 Naples mean time, and the reduced level is 2645·2 feet above the sea. A keen north wind blows over the ridge, and is bitingly cold. Last night it froze hard at Muro, down even to the level of the torrent.

We have the yellow-grey sandstone, all the way over the ridge, and a long way down, into the new valley to the eastward, where the white limestone again appears. We pass through a beautiful little gorge, flanked by precipices of this last rock, with the charming little nameless stream below us, and I remark that this gorge *also* has a N. E. and S. W. general direction. We continue to descend rapidly for a long way, towards Laviano, and within a mile of the town, to the east of it, I find specimens of the white, cretaceous-looking limestone, with chloritic slate and ferruginous bands enclosed in it. All is again limestone now around me, and it bears, lithologically, an uncommonly " green sand" like character.

Nothing that I had hitherto seen in the Southern Apennines equalled the savage grandeur, and, in many places, the great natural beauty of the scenery I have passed through between Monte Croce and Laviano, a region capable of well rewarding the prolonged visit, of either geologist or artist.

CHAPTER XLVI.

LAVIANO TO VALVA BY THE RIO TEMPATE.

Laviano stands nearly at the head of the great valley, which now gradually opens downwards towards the west to Eboli and the sea, and upon the head waters of the Rio Tempate, which, winding round the base of Monte Spagarino, whose large mass rises to the west and N. W., falls into the upper forks of the Solaris, below Calabrita.

The town, a small and poor place, is placed upon the summit of an eminence of solid limestone, which rather crosses, in its greater length, the main general line of the valley, which is here very sinuous, though not abrupt in character.

The mass of limestone upon which it is built is no more consistent than so much soft, sandy chalk. Close to the mass to the west and north is the junction of this cretaceous limestone with the beds of yellow-grey sandstone, which appear to overlie it, and whose strike here is N. W., and dip 35° from the vertical to the north and N. E.

The eminence on which the town stands is steep, almost abrupt, steepest and highest above the valley bottom at the north and N. W. sides, but nearly insulated to a considerable depth upon the south and east, by a deep ravine and small stream at the bottom.

At the bed of the Rio Tempate, immediately below the town, barom. reads 29·00 inches, thermo. 43° Fahr., at 11·15, Naples mean time (26th February), and the reduced level is 1010·5 feet above the sea. At the mean level of the town on the top, at 10 A.M., barom. reads 28·26 inches, thermo. 41° Fahr., and the reduced level is 1627 feet above the sea. Laviano is, therefore, rather more than 600 feet above the bottom of the valley under it, and about 1000 feet below the ridge of the Bosco della Cerreta. The monastery of Cappucini, perched upon a rock that seems hard Apennine limestone to the telescope, stands 150 to 200 feet above the town. It is said to have suffered no injury.

The people of Laviano, as well as those of Calabrito, about six miles to the west, felt the shock with alarming distinctness; but no injury was done to the buildings generally, beyond some "piccolo lesione" in the walls, of which there are a good many visible. The churches, of which there are two or three, have suffered no injury.

I could find few of the fissured dwelling-houses, sufficiently distinctly fractured, or enough isolated, to obtain any results. From one of the largest, however, the palazzo of Signor Antonio Durso (filio) Don Carmine, now let in miserable tenements, I got pretty good indications. Both external and internal walls are fissured: the building is three lofty stories above ground. In the upper floor, which, as is common, opens upon a roofed but open-fronted terrace overlooking the street, the west-end wall has gone out. It and the "spauling off" of the plaster from the wall and ceilings under the beams of the ceiling of the floor above indicate a movement from the south and east.

The fissures of the west quoin, which are open in the

north and south walls, 0·53 inch. in 10 feet, and 0·30 in the same length, in the east and west walls, indicate a wavepath of 32° to 34° W. of north, and from the S. E. The general slope of the large fissures here and in other parts of the edifice, (which is built of soft, badly put together, rubble limestone chiefly,) gives an angle of emergence from 21° to 26° 30'.

The present owner of the house, was just going to bed at the time of the shock, and he brings me to his bedroom, and placing himself in the same position he then occupied, points out to me the exact direction in which he states he felt the second or undulatory movement, swaying him forward and back. The head of his bed stood against a north and south wall to the east, and he was standing with his back to the bed, or looking north, undressing himself at the north side of his bed, when he felt first the strong "sussultatorio" shock that seemed to lift him with the floor and throw him forward, at the same moment, and directly after he felt, several times repeated, an "oscillatorio" movement, that swayed him forward and back, to the N. N. W. and S. S. E., and the direction of which I found, as pointed out by him, was 20° W. of north. Allowing for the impossibility of *exactly* observing and pointing out afterwards the direction of movement, this corroborates the determination from fissures. The priests at the church, however, declared their opinion to be that the movement had been exactly from south to north. They seemed, however, amongst the many here having no clear notions as to points of the compass. Both they and the persons at the Palazzo Carmine, as well as some of the people in the town, all agreed that the first movement was "sussultatorio" (they were not conscious of a second great shock), and that it was immediately followed by the oscillatory movement, which seemed nearly horizontal, and lasted some seconds, and died gradually away. It was the first movement that did the mischief, however. It made the beams of the floors, bend and creak, and displaced various articles of furniture, &c. They all heard the "rombo," which continued during the whole of the movement, or rather "seemed to lend it along," and most of them thought it *lasted after the movement was no longer clearly sensible.** It was a low, rolling rumble, like distant thunder. Several of the people here said, they felt giddy from the effect of the motion. They had heard of the unusual light on the night of the shock, and said the people of Calabrita and Capasole had seen it, at a great distance in the sky, to the south and S. E., but they had none of them seen it at Laviano. Had the shock been at all powerful here, Laviano must have been nearly destroyed, as secondary reflected waves of a formidable character must have reached it from the large mountain masses with which it is surrounded: Monte Marzano to the south, Spagarino to the N. W. and west, and the Serra Lunga, and Difesa di Castelnuovo to the north. The great valley depression, of the rivers Laudro, Platano, and Bianco, and the upper stream of the Tanagro, lie between this whole valley, and the region within which the centre of effort, (or point vertically above it,) must be situated, and no doubt to a great extent cut off the progress of the wave, towards this place. The extreme chalky softness of the rock upon which it is built, and the junction

* This viewed as a fact is curiously illustrative of Mr. Farnshaw's investigations as to the velocity of impulses, in relation to the power of the originating pulse.

close below, with the overlying beds, has also tended to its safety.

From the summit of Laviano, I can see distinctly Calabrita, about six miles distant, situated upon a low, stumpy, jutting shoulder of the Serra Longa, facing the north, its own small valley, running generally east and west, but extremely sinuous, and terminating the view with the lofty snow-clad summits of Monte Calvello.

Calabrita does not, to the telescope, present a symptom of injury. The priests of Laviano say, the shock there, was felt from N. W. to S. E., or 45° W. of north. It bears 68° W. of north, from Laviano, and, comparing this with Zannoni's map, gives the magnetic declination here, 15° W.

CHAPTER XLVII.

VALVA TO OLIVETO.

By miserably bad roads, and constantly descending, I approach Valva, the same cretaceous-looking limestone following all the way. None of the houses that I pass, present obvious traces of the earthquake: a few have fissures, but small. Within half a mile of Valva to the east, however, I pass a large house, in progress of repair, which had been much damaged, though nowhere overthrown. It stands almost exactly ordinal, is not far from square, two stories high, and two of its faces are 43° E. of north. The fissures are long and decisive, though fine and narrow, in walls but little perforated by apertures, and indicate a wave-path 25° 30' W. of north. The fissures were not far removed from vertical. I therefore am disposed to believe that at this spot, some powerful *secondary nodal wave-point* existed, to which the severe fissuring of this house was due, as, if produced by the direct wave, they must have shown a subnormal path, with appreciable emergence. I could not find any one to answer inquiries on the spot. The reflected wave from Monte Spagnrino, Marzano, and many other isolated masses, studding over, this region of sinuous valleys, must have given rise to great perplexity of movement here, which, had the shock generally been more powerful, would have left complicated traces of its action most difficult to decipher.

Valva stands nearly in the mid breadth of the valley, which, however sinuous, has so far had a general direction nearly east and west, but here is intersected by the larger and longer valley of the Salaris, which, before its junction with the Tanagro, runs nearly north and south, with many minor valleys, bringing its tributaries into the main river. The town of Valva, (a small place,) shows many old fissures of former earthquakes, but none of a measurable character from the recent one. The people whom I converse with, very generally state, that the direction in which they felt the great shock, was from the S. E. to the N. W., or a little more eastward of that, say 46° W. of north.

From the brow at the west side of the town, a very extended prospect is obtained; and I got several bearings for magnetic declination, which present very accordant results.

	By Compass.	Zannoni's Map.	Declination.
Calabrita bears .	26° W. of north	41° W. of north	15° W.
Coglietto ,,	62° W. of north	76° W. of north	14° W.
Sonarchia ,,	76° W. of north	92° W. of north	16° W.
Crest of Monte Polvoracchio ,,	80° W. of north	96° W. of north	16° W.
Oliveto ,,	134° W. of north	149° W. of north	15° W.
Contarsi ,,	149° W. of north	165° W. of north	16° W.

Mean magnetic declination, 15° 20′ West.

The summits above Oliveto, probably those of Monte Negro, are hidden in clouds.

The ancient fissures at Valva, showed a wave-path that had produced them, not far from east and west, direction indeterminate.

A mile below Valva, at Il Ponte Vecchio, on the level of the bed of the Salaris, the barometer reads 29·77 inches, thermo. 45° Fahr., at 1·30 Naples mean time; and the reduced level gives 309 feet above the sea. The course of the stream, from the Rio Tempate its head water, at Laviano, to Il Ponte Vecchio, is about eleven geographical miles, and the fall in this distance is 701 feet, or nearly 64 feet per mile.

I arrive at Oliveto. On entering the town, which, as usual, stands on an eminence, with an old ruined stronghold above it, I pass a large old monastery of "Zoccollante," and in the east end, of the semi-octagonal apse of the church, observe an ancient fissure, still open fully four inches at top, and forty feet in height: it indicates a west and east wave-path, in the shock that produced it. There are, however, no signs of "lesioni" by the recent shock. All the towns along this valley, seem to have been preserved from the violence of the shock, as felt further south, by having been *cut off*, from the more violently shaken country *by the deeply cleft and long continuous valley* of the river, bearing the successive names from Muro downwards, of the Giacojo, the Platano, the Bianco, and the Tanagro, a united length of valley, not less than 26 geographical miles, before their confluence with the Salaris.

The Padrone, with whom I dined here, gave the same account of the earthquake, as those at Laviano and Valva, and stated, that the usual impression at Oliveto was, that the direction of the great shock was from the S. E. to N. W.

He says, that at Senarchio and Calabrita the people felt it in the same direction. A Carthusian monk, who is present, however, says that he had heard at Calabrita that it was felt there, rather more to the south of S. E. to N. W. (or, say 44° W. of north). They heard the "rombo" at all these places; a very long, low, rumbling, continuous sort of grating thunder.

They had no information as to the exact time, and estimated the duration of the movement, commonly, at about half a minute. The second great shock, of an hour after the first, which was so disastrous, within the regions to the south and nearer the focus, seems to have been scarcely noticed here: many people, indeed, denied having felt it at all. The unusual light, was not here seen, and even the popular news, of its having been seen elsewhere, to the south and east and west, seems unknown.

Between Oliveto and Contursi, along the bed of the Salaris, upon the east bank, there are several copious springs of strong sulphureous water, issuant from the soft limestone rock. They suggest the probability, that the two nearly circular lakes further east—the Lago di Palo and Lago Pantone—may be extinct volcanic vents; and that a more exact geological examination, might considerably extend the number of such lakes in these regions, beyond those of Amsanctus and Monticchio.

CHAPTER XLVIII.

RETURN TO EBOLI—THE CIRCLE COMPLETED.

I LEAVE for Eboli, and after about nine miles of gentle descent, though with occasional ascents—the river in such points cutting through a deep bed—the grand range of mural precipices of Monte Alburno come once more to my view on the left, distinct and glorious with the rosy glow of the declining sun slanting upon the piled-up beds, and contrasting vividly their colour, with that of the purple sea that closes the horizon. Servitello and Puglietta are perched high amongst the crags also to my left. I had not seen the sun for days, and I was just enabled to catch an observation of his disc at setting, over the horizon from a point of the road a mile from Eboli (February 26), latitude north 40° 35', longitude east 15° 4'.

	°	'	"
Hour angle at time of observation, 5ʰ 50ᵐ Naples mean time	82	44	25.35
Sun's azimuth	78	4	West.
Sun bears by compass	88	30	W. of north.
	166	34	
	160	0	
Magnetic declination	13	20	West,

which sufficiently well confirms the results obtained to-day by intersections.

At the point where this observation was made barometer reads 29·64 inches, thermo. 48° Fahr., at 5ʰ 55ᵐ Naples mean time; and the reduced level is 407·9 feet above the sea. I am here distant nearly two miles from the bed of the

Salaris, at the lowest point of the valley, directly beneath, the fall down to which is between 200 and 300 feet by eye. The fall in the river bed has hence rapidly decreased, between Oliveto and this, as the volume of its united waters have increased, which now roll past a great river.

I arrive at Eboli once more, after a long and weary day's ride, and having thus completed an entire circle round the earthquake focus.

The night was clear and fine, and I arranged to have myself called up at midnight, after some sleep, to take an observation of the pole star, for correcting magnetic declination, as a check upon the more than doubtful solar observation made at Duchessa, on the outward journey.

The result, owing to enough wind acting on the legs of the theodolite, to disturb the image of the star, was less precise than I had hoped for. It gave 15° west as the magnetic declination.

Within the last few weeks I had "roughed it" a good deal, and had known most of the small miseries of camp life in the wet and cold of winter. Yet such is the undefinable charm, this sort of nomad adventure with an object clear in view, possesses, that this evening, while conscious that I had completed my circle of observation, and was about to return to the lights and fires of Naples, and of our so-called "civilized life," was almost the only one of sadness I had felt throughout my journeying, except when now and then in presence of suffering and wretchedness that I could neither relieve nor mitigate; and I am afraid I received the congratulations of my host of the Da Vozzi upon my anticipated return to "society" in a less courtly manner than they deserved.

CHAPTER XLIX.

LA CAVA BACK TO NAPLES—THE RECORDS OF THE MARINE OBSERVATORY.

I PUSHED on rapidly next morning over my former road (as there seemed no sufficient object for entangling myself in the labyrinth of hills to the N. E., where it was certain the earthquake had produced little decisive effects), for La Cava, and thence back to Naples by rail.

At Naples I compared my barometer with that at the Osservatorio Reale di Marina, and obtained the records of the barometric daily observations, as well as those of temperature, kept there, for the period corresponding to my journey in the interior; as also those for a considerable period preceding the earthquake. I learned from the zealous and intelligent director, Il Capitano di Marina Patrelli, that the clock belonging to the self-acting anemometer of the Observatory had been stopped by the shock of the 16th December. The pendulum vibrates quarter seconds, and in a plane 110° W. of north.

The connection of the pendulum with the clock movement was such as insured its stopping by a small motion transverse to the plane of vibration, but the bob touched nothing in the case. They had, unfortunately, not observed carefully the time of stoppage, before setting the clock again going.

I collected at Naples, in the very few book-shops to be

found there, a number of interesting and, in England, rare books and pamphlets, on the subject of earthquakes in the south of Italy; and having received by telegram through Rome, the authority of the Royal Society, to obtain photographs of the more important points visited by me in the earthquake country, I arranged for the production of the chief part of those which are intercalated with this Report, and the others which are referred to throughout by (Coll. Roy. Soc.), *i.e.*, as to be found in the Library of the Royal Society. These were produced by a resident French photographer at Naples, Monsieur Grellier, to whom I gave in MS. an itinerary, and descriptive catalogue with sketches, to direct him to locality, object, &c. The work was artistically, well performed by him, but somewhat unfaithfully, several objects and views agreed for, having been left undone, in places of more than usual difficulty of access; and, after great delay beyond the specified time for delivery, the whole of the views were sent to England, with the catalogue stipulated for it is true, but without any corresponding marks upon the photographs, by which identification by me, became wholly a tax upon memory, and involved great loss of time in completion.

When waiting again upon the Minister of the Interior, to thank the (late) Neapolitan Government for the assistance I had received in my expedition, I submitted, through the proper functionary, two letters, one upon the establishment of bench marks, as to level of the land at Naples (Appendix No. 4), and the other on the work of restoration, of the ruined towns in the earthquake region. I have stated, in a former paragraph, the views of this despotism, as to the reception of these documents.

CHAPTER L.

BACK TO NAPLES—VESUVIUS—JOURNEY OF OBSERVATION TO ROME THROUGH THE PONTINE MARSHES.

While waiting for my passport, I ascended Vesuvius, and examined with some care the courses of several of the ancient and the very recent lava currents, with a view to the theory of their movements.

At Resina and Vesuvius, I found that the town of Ottajano, had suffered considerable fissuring, (more, I was informed, than Nola); and that the shocks had been felt in two different directions, crossing each other—the one the same as at Naples and all about here, viz., nearly south to north; and the other in the direction pointing to Vesuvius, or, as they said, the shock "came from Vesuvius." This would be a wave-path nearly 40° E. of north, and would appear to be a secondary wave propagated from Vesuvius by the oscillation of the mountain as a mass, from the effect of the primary shock acting on it south to north, and ending in gyratory oscillation of the cone, transmitted to its base around. It might, however also, be a reflected wave, from the direct wave, of low intensity, reaching Vesuvius and the plain to the east and S. E. of it, immediately from the focus, in a direct line.

Finding that the earthquake was stated to have been felt along the coast, northward and westward, as far as Terracina, and probably farther, it appeared desirable to endeavour to observe the progress of its becoming insensible in those directions, and of the effects, of the Pontine Marsh district, upon its progress beyond. I therefore prepared to return to England by Civita Vecchia, in place of by steamer direct from Naples; observing the extinct volcanic country south of Rome also by the way.

The railway carried me to Capua, where the shock was sharply felt, but no mischief done; nor could I observe or hear, of any fissures having been produced, nor articles of furniture noticed to have been disturbed. No noise was heard, nor any other unusual phenomena, beyond the *one movement*, which lasted several seconds, and was described as a succession of short horizontal undulations, in a direction about north and south. Some of the officers at the railway station said, it was reported that some injury had been done to the lofty aqueduct of Madalone, a structure of limestone ashlar, carrying water to Caserta Palace, over three tiers of semicircular arches, and nearly 200 feet in height. Its great elevation, and its direction in length being nearly transverse to the wave-path here, I thought it worth while to go out to examine it; but it did not present a single symptom of earthquake effect. The guard of troops on the spot had been changed since December, and those on duty could give no information.

At Madalone the account given me by the country people was much the same as at Capua; and at the Locanda there, they said that the earthquake had been felt at Aversa and Acerra just the same as at Madalone and at Caserta, but that at Nola and Avellino, they understood, it had been more severe, but no serious injury, if any, done. At Pie di Monte, close under the great mountain knot of

Monte Matese, to the southward of the chain, they said they understood the shock had been felt very sharply, much more so than with them, which is what might be expected. It had been felt in Molise, to beyond Campobasso.

Whatever wave impulse may have been transmitted, from Naples and the south side of the bay, northwards and diverging east and west, into the great plain of the Terra di Lavoro, was in condition to become very rapidly extinguished. The great plain itself consists, of a vast heterogeneous deposit of level and loose volcanic materials, chiefly tufa, yellow and brown, and becoming dark grey and very ancient, at the north and west sides, with great beds of lapilli, and covering over in many places, travertino, and lava streams or outbursts, several of which may be seen cut through, in roads or opened for quarries. These deposits, surrounded to the N. E. and south by steep limestone hills, branches of which penetrate into the plain in various directions, lap against their bases, and wind in and out amongst their hollows, like an earthy sea, always abutting close upon the roots of the hills, but never rising upon their slopes, but like an irregular stone trough filled in level with dry sand. And the earth wave appears here to have been transmitted from the limestone range to the south of Naples Bay, through the deep bottom of the trough, and shaken the limestone edges of it to the north and east, very perceptibly more, than the loose dry filling within it, or anything that rested thereon.

Thus I found, in going northward at Sesse, which stands upon part of the great limestone spur, that comes down in a S. W. direction nearly to the coast at Mondragone, and terminates with Monte Massico, that all these towns and hamlets had been (so far as I could judge by the description given here), a good deal more violently shaken, than those twenty miles to the south upon the tufa; but from Naples northward, there are unfortunately no actual traces of the shock, and I am thenceforth obliged therefore to resort merely to cross-examination, and testimony far from satisfactory.

At Sesse, they said, the shock had been sharp enough to awaken all the people, there and at Corbara, a little village opposite.

Sesse stands on the S. E. flank (perched on rock) of a very deep and abrupt cliff, that comes down for some miles in a N. N. E. direction, and through which the Rivo Travata comes down, to join the Garigliano.

Leaving Sesse, we come in upon another great basin plain, of volcanic filling, with the large stream of the Garigliano flowing through it, and lose sight of the limestone, until passing under Trajetto, and Castro Onorato, which appear by the telescope to be on limestone brows. In crossing this plain I lost all trace of the earthquake; no one appeared to have felt it, (these perched towns I could not reach); and so it was, until arriving at Mola da Gaeta, on the coast, and close under the rather lofty hills of Monte Castellone and Suvoreta, the southern terminations of the next great knot of mountains, that spreads out towards the S. W., and here covers a large tract between this place (Mola), Pontecorvo on the north and east, and Fondi on the north and west, or about ten geographical miles by eight.

At Mola the shock was distinctly felt by great numbers, but not by every one; many persons, although awake and dressed, as well as many others asleep, were unconscious of it, by sensation. Mola, though close to rock, stands upon detrital material, which is cut into by small streams going down to the seashore to a depth of 30 or 40 feet; the shore being of rounded limestone pebbles, and singularly destitute of either animal or vegetable marine life. At the royal palace, or rather fortification at the opposite side (west) of the gulf, they had felt the shock, but it had produced as little alarm as here.

Itry lies about four miles northward, in the heart of the mountain mass, on the west side of the small stream, Aqua di Conca, that comes down south, to within a mile or so of Mola, passing beneath the spot where tradition says, Cicero died by the sword of the Centurion. Such of the people of this ignorant and wretched place, as I met with, seemed to know nothing of the earthquake. The road then rises rapidly over a low ridge, and a dreary descent of about nine miles further to the N. N. W., brought me to Fondi, which is at the base of the limestone, but at the head of another great basin plain, of deep marshy alluvium, not volcanic apparently, and resting on limestone beneath.

At Fondi I fell into conversation with the old Padre of the parish, who told me that there, most people had felt the shock, but not every one; he himself did: he was up and reading. He felt it as a sort of tremulous, forward and backward, gentle oscillation, most powerful at or near the end, but could not tell how long it lasted, or in what azimuth it moved; he was not conscious of any noise, nor had he heard of any such having been heard by others.

This old gentleman confidently attributed the small effects of the earthquake at Fondi, and its universal immunity from such calamities, to "the abundance of springs about it," that come from cavernous fissures, &c., in the limestone above and to the east of the town—a superstition, upon whatever based, that I found was popularly and widely diffused further south, has thus descended from early Roman days, as classical men will remember.

At Portella, on the frontier line, the Custom-house officer said they did not feel the shock; they were, however, asleep and in bed. It lies on the nearly naked limestone, of the steep east slope of Monte del Guardia, and but little above the level of the great plain and swamp lake, of Fondi. This side of the plain, is bounded by the third great mountain spur that comes down to the coast, at Terracina, terminating with Monte Rotundo and Paliarolo, close to the N. E. of the town, which stands upon the deep alluvium at the sea level, and at that of the great Pontine swamp, stretching hence far to the north, and with the continuation of this mountain spur, widened into a mountain knot, running parallel and bounding it, on the east side.

At Terracina, the clerics at the grand old cathedral told me, the shock had been quite unnoticed in the town, which stands upon the plain, on deep alluvium, though close at the foot of the spur of limestone mountains, one ridge of which comes down in an almost unbroken range, in a direction from N. N. E. to S. S. W. for several miles, and ends with an abrupt mass overhanging the town and sea; but by those who dwelt "in the mountain" they said the shock had been distinctly felt, though not universally. At Sperlonga, at the opposite side of the roadstead, upon the shore, and on the limestone of the last mountain mass passed by me, viz., that to the east side of the plain of Fondi, they told me the shock had been very sharply felt—enough so to produce alarm.

On looking back at Sperlonga with the telescope, distant about eight miles, it appears to lie, on the free-lying surface of considerable hills of limestone, rising to the north and east of the town; but there is nothing revealed above the surface of the sea, nor anything apparent, except difference of distance, to account for the difference in motion, there, and at Terracina, and the latter does not appear to stand, five miles north of Sperlonga at most.

I scanned Sperlonga from the ruins of Theodoric's Palace, on the limestone heights, above Terracina: there, if anywhere, fissures or displacements might have been found. I looked for any evidence of earthquake effects, however, in vain.

At Treponti, in the middle of the Pontine Marsh plain, along the Appian Way, and about twenty miles north and west of Terracina, the people said they had been unconscious of the shock, but that it had been felt pretty distinctly, at Piperno, at Sezze, and at Sermoneta, places standing rather high, upon limestone, in the mountain range to the eastward of the marshes, all which squares with the information at Terracina.

At Cisterna, also, close to the Appian Way, and upon the deep alluvium of the marshes, and about thirty miles from Terracina, all trace of the earthquake was finally lost: the people had neither felt it themselves, nor heard anything about it from the neighbourhood, and only knew of its occurrence, from Votturini, from Naples, &c.; and this continued to be the case, through Velletri and Albano, to Rome.

I reached the "mother of empires" late in the evening, which was intensely cold and windy, and after a very fatiguing day's walking and hammering, amongst the extinct volcanic crater lakes and deposits in the interesting country to the south of the city.

CHAPTER LI.

ROME.

The next day, I was prostrated by fever and pleurisy, by cold caught in examining the extinct volcanic tract between Velletri and Rome, where I was delayed thus a fortnight, and was able to make but few inquiries, before leaving by the first Marseilles steamer after my recovery, as to the distance and extent to which the shock had been felt, in the Roman states far away to the eastward, and towards the Adriatic shore.

At the Collegio Romano I found, on visiting the Padre Secchi, the able and active astronomer, that he had reason to believe that the shock had been *instrumentally* sensible, even as far as Rome.

He has at work at the college, a self-registering barometer, the principle of construction of which is based, upon the large iron tube of the instrument being balanced, its lower end dipping into a fixed cistern of mercury. The rise and fall of the whole tube, as its balance is disturbed by change of pressure, acts upon the registration apparatus, marking upon a band of ruled paper, moved by the clock. *Almost at the instant* of the occurrence of the shock, allowance being made for the difference of times at the two cities

(Naples and Rome), a remarkable and unprecedented disturbance, occurred in the curve of registration, on the night of the 16th December, indicating a sudden jar or tremor, communicated to the whole system; nothing similar to it, was presented by the register-cards, when examined for many months previous.

The singular and unaccountable circumstance, however, is the want of sufficient time for the wave transit, between the origin south of Naples, and Rome, if we assume the disturbance here, to have been due to the first great shock, as felt at and around the origin.

No doubt rested on Padre Secchi's mind, as to the correctness of the local time of the barometer clock, and we are compelled to assume, that this perturbation of the instrument arose, from some unknown local cause *not* seismic, which is, under the circumstances, highly improbable, or that it was due to the first great Naples shock, an error occurring in the observation as to the time at Rome, or that it arose from the deep propagation, of a previous or premonitory shock, delivered a few seconds before the first great one, perceived at the Naples origin, and around it. I am disposed to adopt the second of these probabilities.

In observing several of the remains of edifices of ancient Rome, with my eye fresh from the constant detection, and educated by the remarking of earthquake effects, it was interesting to me, to be able to distinguish in many places, the rents and fractures that had been made, by the tremendous earthquakes that desolated the city and Campagna, between the fourth and ninth centuries of our era.

This is peculiarly striking, in some of the great rents in the Coliseum, and in *the fractures* of the marble shafts of the columns of the Forum; *the forms of which* latter prove, that they were overthrown, not by Gothic hands, but by earthquake impulse.

In connection with Padre Secchi's observation, it may be well to notice here, the several minor shocks, which have been noticed and recorded as occurring, very nearly previous or subsequent to, the great shock of 16th December. Many others must, no doubt, have taken place, and had there been means to observe them would have been recorded.

Date.	Time (Frankish).	Occurrence of Shock.
1857. December 7	7·30 A.M.	At Potenza, a report from beneath like the explosion of a mine, and a slight shock.
,, 16	..	The great shock.
,, 19	6 and 10 A.M.	At Salerno, a harmless shock.
,, 21	..	Up to this date occasionally felt, with injury at Lago Negro.
,, 23	..	At Balvano, a slight shock.
,, 23	6 P.M.	At Saponara, two heavy reports, with interval of 30 seconds.
,, 26	3 and 6 A.M.	At Montemurro, strong shocks, which levelled remains of buildings.
,, 26	8 A.M.	At Viggiano, a powerful shock.
,, 26	9 P.M.	At La Sala, several shocks, each 10 to 12 seconds, followed by tremors less intense.
,, 26	6 and 7·30 P.M.	At La Sala, same as day previous.
,, 26	6·45 P.M.	At Potenza, a strong shock, and several minor ones afterwards.
1858. Jan. and Feb.		The occurrence of many minor shocks was reported, from Salerno, Potenza, the central region generally, and Naples, but none precise, or absolutely reliable.
March 6	During night	At Lago Negro, three prolonged but harmless shocks.
,, 7	3 P.M. and at 8 P.M.	At Lago Negro, two shocks, much more severe than on the preceding day, lasting 9 or 10 seconds each.
,, 7	2·50 P.M.	At Salerno.
,, 8	3 P.M.	At Lago Negro, and at Montemurro.

Date.	Time (Frankish).	Occurrence of Shock.
1858. March 8	At 12 to 1 midnight	At Salerno. All the shocks between the 7th and 8th were felt at Potenza, at Tramutola—which they greatly further injured—at Montemurro, at Vibonati, and at Sapri.
,, 13	,,	At Rodi, province of Capitanata.
,, 17	,,	At Potenza, and elsewhere in the province of Capitanata, the earth was said to have trembled almost incessantly.
,, 20	10 A.M. and 2 P.M.	At Potenza, the first slight—three or four at the latter hour more severe.
,, 23	2 P.M.	At La Sala (Val di Diano), four shocks, all harmless.
April 8	5·15 & 7·30 A.M.	At Palmi, sharp subsultatory shocks.
,, 10	8, 9, and 10 A.M.	At Reggio, three shocks.

My record does not extend beyond the last given date, but letters from private friends resident in the Neapolitan kingdom inform me, that such occasional shocks continued sporadically to be reported, even up to the month of May, in 1859. Those given, sufficiently indicate, that which is the general fact, in all earthquake regions, that, when once the state of seismical repose is powerfully broken, it is only resumed through a long-continued succession of these abortive and decreasing transitory commotions. The general tendency of the preceding table is also to indicate, that after the great shock of December, 1857, some subordinate centre or centres of activity, further south than the focus of the first, came on to a sort of expiring activity. To this sort of fact, apparently, Humboldt points in 'Cosmos,' when he says, that in South America, the tendency of earthquake activity, is continually to enlarge its circle of action round a given focus.

CHAPTER LII.

NEAPOLITAN STATISTICS—SURFACE—POPULATION—
KILLED—WOUNDED—LOSS OF PROPERTY.

The following tables of the superficial areas and population, of the Neapolitan kingdom, are the latest supplied by the (late) Naples government, and are returns for 1850:—

Province.	Area.	Population.
Abruzzo Citeriore	940	312,399
,, Ultra 1	935	229,728
,, Ultra 2	1,905	329,131
Bari	1,783	497,132
Basilicata	3,134	501,222
Calabria Citra	1,980	435,811
,, Ultra 1	1,859	319,692
,, Ultra 2	1,560	381,147
Capitanata	2,205	318,415
Terra di Lavoro	1,885	752,012
Naples	288	822,142
Otranto	2,171	400,000
Principato Citra	1,710	558,809
,, Ultra	1,064	383,434
Molise, or Sannio	1,344	360,549
Totals	24,583 geographical square miles.	8,610,873 total population.

The populations of the chief cities are thus stated:—

Naples city, in 1851	.	.	416,475
Bari city, 1850	.	.	27,297
Potenza „	.	.	12,362
Salerno „	.	.	16,892
Cosenza „	.	.	13,847
Foggia „	.	.	24,058
Caserta „	.	.	25,780

The following tables contain all the exact information that I was able to obtain, as to the damage and loss of life, or personal injury; they are defective of a large portion of the shaken country:—

Synoptic Table of the greater Disasters of the Earthquake in the District of Sala.

Commune.	Houses fallen.	Houses falling.
Polla	1,300	335
Atena	932	812
Auletta	186	310
Caggiano	43	50
St. Arsenio	121	526
St. Pietro	187	374
Padula	171	50
Montesano	140	100
La Sala	38	26
Diano	19	52
Pertosa	176	133
Totals	3,313	2,786

The damage done to buildings embraced in this return was estimated* at 1866 ducats in the government return, a sum obviously not one-twentieth of the actual loss.

Except in the case of Signor Ajosso, the Intendente of Salerno, I found obstacles thrown in the way of giving me returns of the number of persons killed and wounded; and

* No doubt according to order.

THE KILLED AND WOUNDED.

the following tables, which were the whole I could obtain, do not embrace the whole area of disturbance, but reach over the larger and most important parts of it:—

Return of the Killed and Wounded, of the Communes of the Province of Basilicata.

Commune.	Population.	Dead.	Wounded.
Potenza	12,511	22	11
Vignola	5,259	6	..
Picerno	4,769	20	9
Tito	4,030	257	..
Vietri di Potenza	3,425	1	..
Balvano	4,229	..	1
Brienza	5,350	151	30
Pietrafesa	2,867	4	..
St. Angelo le Fratte	1,644	63	22
Sasso	2,760	4	1
Calvello	5,820	90	40
Anzi	4,053	1	..
Abriola	3,414	1	9
Marsico Nuovo	7,528	89	..
Paierno	2,500	122	..
Viggiano	6,834	800	200
Marsico Vetere	3,403	90	..
Saponara	4,010	2,000	70
Tramutola	4,538	177	52
Montemurro	7,002	5,000	500
Gallichio	1,296	16	98
Missanello	1,064	14	50
Armento	3,553	31	37
Spinosa	2,039	45	35
Laurenzana	7,665	7	8
Corleto	5,227	12	42
Guardia	1,082	85	53
Cancellara	3,004	..	1
Total in the Potenza District	123,464	9,123	1,063
Pisticci	7,569	..	2
Ferrandina	6,353	2	3
Salandra	2,720	1	3
Craco	1,998	3	..
Gorgoglione	1,723	4	4
Aliano ed Alianello	1,864	50	28
Grassano	5,372	1	1
Monte Peloso	5,855	..	1
Total in the Matera District	33,464	61	42

PROPORTION OF DEATHS TO POPULATION.

Return of the Killed and Wounded, &c.—*continued*.

Communes.	Population.	Dead.	Wounded.
Melfi	9,274	1	..
Bariello	4,905	2	1
Total in the Melfi District	14,179	3	1
Maralca	7,076	..	..
Castel Saraceno	3,123	127	136
Carboni	2,318	39	19
Sarconi	1,244	32	4
Turso	3,510	1	..
St. Chirico Raparo	3,351	5	..
Sonino	4,566	1	4
St. Martino	1,623	6	23
St. Archangelo	3,950	99	17
Castronuovo	3,012	11	5
Roccanova	1,940	83	27
Total for the Lago Negro District	35,713	402	237

SUMMARY.

	Population.	Dead.	Wounded.
Potenza District	123,464	9,123	1,063
Matera ,,	33,464	61	42
Melfi ,,	14,179	3	1
Lago Negro ,,	35,713	402	237
Totals for the Province of Basilicata	206,820	9,589	1,343

It will be observed, that these returns only refer to towns, in which personal injury or death occurred in each district, and hence convey but a very imperfect notion of the entire amount of injury of every sort inflicted.

If we take the total population of the towns of Basilicata in the preceding return at 207,000, and the combined deaths and injuries at 11,000, we have one inhabitant in every 18·82, or about 1 in 19 killed or wounded by the disaster;

or, confining the calculation to the deaths only, we have 1 in every 21·5 of the population destroyed.

These returns, however, only referred to the towns. The mortality and injuries in solitary houses and small outlying hamlets, seem never to have been collected, and the policy of government was in every case, systematically to underrate the destruction of life and property.

The population embraced in the preceding returns is not one-half that of the province of Basilicata alone. It is quite probable, therefore, that the total number of deaths alone exceeded 10,000, and that the number lamed or injured was above 2,000.

The total of both has been estimated, upon plausible grounds, as high as 19,000. I believe the numbers above given, however, are much nearer the truth. An appalling mass of human misery, almost the whole of which was preventable by the exercise of proper care in choice of the methods of construction of the houses in the earthquake region, and future repetitions of which might thus be completely avoided.

CHAPTER LIII.

METEOROLOGY AND ITS RELATIONS TO EARTHQUAKE.

The meteorological records of the Royal Marine Observatory at Naples, which are kept in a style that would do credit to any such establishment in the world, were furnished to me by the Director, Il Capitano Patrelli, of the (late) Neapolitan navy, for the years 1848 to the end of February, 1858. It would be useless to present, *in extenso*, this vast mass of observation. I have extracted from it, in the following synoptic table, the barometric, thermometric, and hyetometric, mensual means, from 1853 to February, 1858, inclusive, viz., up to the date of my leaving Naples. The data thus given are sufficient to show that there is no obvious connection between the meteorological conditions of season and weather, whether preceding, contemporaneous, or succeeding, and the occurrence of the earthquake, except probably in respect to the rainfall for the time preceding. It is observable that the month of the shock (December, 1857), has a mean barometric pressure of 10·76 inches *above* the mean for the same month in the preceding four years, and that the total rainfall, for the month of shock and that preceding, taken together, is greatly *below* the mean of November and December, for the preceding four years.

METEOROLOGICAL TABLES OF

Synoptic Meteorological Table, from the Records of the Royal Marine Observatory, Naples, giving the Monthly Means, at 9 A.M., for Barometer, Thermometer, and Hyetometer, for the Years 1853, 1854, 1855, 1856, and 1857, being that of the Earthquake, and of the four years preceding, with January and February of 1858.

Years	1853			1854			1855		
Months	B.	T.	H.	B.	T.	H.	B.	T.	H.
January	755·29	10·4	60·4	755·32	11·10	123·8	756·75	7·64	62·44
February	770·32	9·7	286·3	754·52	7·64	17·8	750·00	12·0	60·2
March	751·33	10·3	183·2	753·17	10·32	20·15	750·32	12·05	153·8
April	757·02	14·2	28·3	758·01	14·41	38·27	751·66	14·38	33·3
May	753·51	20·4	36·7	753·04	18·73	122·44	753·34	18·25	102·0
June	753·88	21·8	28·6	753·08	12·83	32·00	755·70	21·8	96·0
July	753·90	26·8	0·	754·37	25·34	43·90	754·88	25·6	0·
August	755·08	26·2	25·8	753·73	25·51	7·12	755·84	24·4	12·7
September	753·81	22·9	66·07	757·84	20·77	14·10	750·83	22·0	190·2
October	758·20	19·3	90·5	758·55	17·86	110·33	755·29	20·4	66·2
November	754·59	14·7	113·2	750·37	12·19	315·3	750·48	14·0	31·5
December	750·92	10·0	270·4	753·22	9·74	141·6	758·21	9·2	90·2
Means for the whole year at 9 A.M.	755·65	17·3	1169·1	754·77	16·4	997·7	754·11	16·60	1014·3

Years	1856			1857			1858		
Months	B.	T.	R.	B.	T.	R.	B.	T.	R.
January	753·54	12·1	73·4	747·18	8·1	293·5	760·47	6·0	42·8
February	758·10	10·4	77·9	760·66	8·8	15·4	755·77	7·9	100·)
March	753·85	10·5	77·3	752·67	11·1	107·1			
April	754·57	15·4	69·13	751·73	14·6	44·9			
May	754·01	18·0	118·3	751·61	18·3	35·65			
June	756·51	23·1	0·	753·50	21·3	41·7			
July	754·82	25·2	11·0	750·75	25·1	21·13			
August	754·70	25·8	4·6	754·30	24·8	93·4			
September	754·04	21·7	80·3	757·77	21·0	73·9			
October	760·18	18·5	66·1	765·14	18·7	186·7			
November	754·45	10·8	116·6	758·45	12·1	57·9			
December	755·74	9·7	186·25	755·28	9·2	11·3			
Means for the whole year at 9 A.M.	755·64	16·7	880·9	755·59	16·10	982·6			

NOTE.—The barometer is situated 79·911 metres above the sea. The readings are in millimetres. The thermometer is centigrade. The rainfall is in millimetres. In the last line the totals for each year are given.

The latter giving a mean of 158·17 m.m"., against 69·20 m.m". in 1857, or a rainfall, for the month and month before the shock, of 88·97 m.m". below the average (less than one-half) of the four years anterior; and this is not compensated by the rainfall of the first two months of 1858, although that for February is above the preceding four years' means, and so shows a tendency towards compensation.

The mean temperatures of November and December, 1857, are very near those of the preceding years.

At first sight, this large increment of mean pressure, and deficiency of rain, might induce the supposition that the perturbations are, in some way, directly connected, in the relation of cause and effect, with the earthquake; and a more careful discussion of the table leads to the conclusion that such a relation really may exist. On the 12th October, 1856, a shock of earthquake was experienced at the Marine Observatory, which is recorded by the director in the table for that month and year. It was sufficient in power to stop one of the clocks, and the direction of wave-transit is stated to have been in a path from W. N. W. to E. N. E., but was most probably in the contrary direction. The precise meteorological conditions were observed immediately after the shock, which occurred at $1^h 58^m$ A.M. Naples mean time, and are given; but present nothing remarkable as to the epoch of occurrence.

If we examine the annual means of rain, however, we shall find that these earthquake years, 1856, 1857, present a decisive deficiency.

The mean of the rainfall for the years 1853, 1854, 1855, is = 1070·4 m.m'. The rainfall for 1856 is but 880·9 m.m'., and for 1857 but 982·6 m.m'., or nearly *one-fifth below the average* on each year. If we take the rainfall upon the last six months, July to December inclusive, of the five years, reduced to the mean for a month, we find a large falling off for the last three years; thus—

		Millimetres.	
	1853 .	94·32	mean fall per month.
	1854 .	105·44	,,
	1855 .	64·13	,,
Earthquake in October,	1856 .	77·47	,,
,, December,	1857 .	74·05	,,

But if we look at the table, we shall see that the deficiency *prior to the shock* of October, 1856, was still more remarkable; for during the four preceding months up to the 1st of October, 1856, only 95·9 inches of rain fell altogether, and there was none at all in June. The last six months of 1857 were actually dryer than those of 1856, in the ratio of 74 to 77½; and if we compare the total rainfall of 18 months, from 1st July, 1856, to the end of 1857, with that for the corresponding 18 months, 1st July, 1853, to the end of 1854, we find the numbers are—

$$\text{Eighteen months ending December, } 1854 = 1503\cdot 67$$
$$\text{,, \quad ,, \quad } 1857 = 1447\cdot 45$$
$$\text{Difference} \quad . \quad . \quad 116\cdot 22$$

Again, in 1857, November and December were both unusually dry, but the latter month, which is that of our earthquake, *unprecedentedly* so; the rainfall for this month only being for the five years—

		Inches.
1853 .	.	270·40
1854 .	.	141·90
1855 .	.	90·20
1856 .	.	166·25
1857 .	.	11·30

or, as compared with the mean for the month of the preceding four years, only as 11·3 inches to 172·19 inches, or less than one-fifteenth of the usual quantity.

Admitting, as we must, the identity of the explosive power at the vent of volcanic action, and of the originating force to which earthquake impulse is due, and that both (through whatsoever intermediate train of action) act immediately, by the development into steam, of water finding its way below the surface, and taking full account, for the important part that sea water undoubtedly plays, in such percolation and evaporation; still as we have proof undeniable, that fresh water (that of rain and snow, &c.) finds its way thousands of feet below the surface of every portion nearly of the world's dry land, we may be prepared to receive as highly probable, that seismic activity within limited distances from active volcanic vents may be more or less influenced by the supply of rain penetrating to the heated foci beneath the surface. Whatever be the source or mode of reaction, from which the supply of heat there, may be derived, the temperature at any given point is kept down, in proportion to the volume of water evaporated and discharged as steam, at volcanic vents, solfatare, &c., or in a liquid state by hot springs; the enormous absorption of heat becoming latent in the steam, being, in fact, the grand cooling agent. Under given circumstances of volcanic action, therefore, as respects the supply of heat, the energy, of explosive or impulsive or seismic action, is a question of limits as regards the supply of water. If there be *no* water, there is no supply of steam; if the supply of water be unlimited or excessive, the temperature is greatly reduced, enormous volumes of vapour, may be evolved, but the tension is small. At some determinate and intermediate rate of supply, the volume and tension together, in a given time, must be a maximum, and at that rate of supply, the impulsive energy, whether at the open volcano's mouth, or closed over and covered, as in the earthquake, will be most violent.

We may, therefore, well conceive it probable, that a large reduction in the supply of rain, especially when falling over a highly porous, loose, and fissured country, such as South Italy is, may sensibly increase seismic action beneath, by permitting the temperature of the pyrigenous "couches," to rise, and the tension of the steam, whether pent up or escaping in regimen, at neighbouring volcanic vents, to rise in proportion.

The anterior duration of drought at the surface, necessary to produce this effect to its greatest extent, would depend largely upon local conditions, chiefly geognostic. Under given circumstances, of rock formation, &c., a particle of water penetrating at the surface, takes a determinate time to reach the depth of the igneous foci—greater as the depth is so—and as the filtration is performed through finer channels, and through deeper beds of material, surcharged with water. Such surcharged beds, are the immediate magazine of supply for evaporation, they measure the capacity of "the boiler"—and if the "feed-water" from the surface, be cut off by drought, the larger such capacity, the longer before, by the reduced supply of water, the tension of the steam shall arrive at its maximum. It may be a period of many months, or only one of a few days, or it may be insensible altogether, if nullified by a constant and abundant supply of sea water, in addition to that from rain, &c.

In *very dry countries*, such as Asia Minor and Syria, (where they have long popularly connected the occurrence of shocks, with derangements in their annual rains), it follows from what has been stated, that a continuous and great *increase* in the usual rainfall, may be equally productive of increased seismic action; so that the conditions may be such, that either great drought, or great wet, may probably herald earthquake.

In so far then as the supply of rain is related, to the barometric pressure, to the direction of the wind, and to the temperature of the air, at a given point of surface and of time, and in so far as the supply of rain reacts upon the temperature of the air, by lowering it; in so far I think we may consider it highly probable, that future and more extended observation in volcanic and seismic countries will establish this connection, between meteorology and seismology; and that in such regions, unusually dry or wet seasons, may be found, (under geognostic conditions such as have been sketched) to prelude the earthquake, and if so may even ultimately give the means of attempting the prediction of its return.

The point here brought into notice, (so far as I am aware of for the first time,) of a distinctly observable relation between earthquake and rainfall, though on too narrow a base, to warrant as yet the assertion of its generality, is one altogether distinct from, the innumerable fancied connections between disturbance of a meteorological character, *close to* or *along with* earthquakes, in point of time, which form the subject of popular belief in all seismic countries, in one shape or another, as *causative* events. Most of these have been long since discussed by Von Hoff and others and disposed of.

It is equally distinct from any questions, as to meteorological phenomena or perturbations, resulting from the earthquake itself, as a cause, such as the unusual light mentioned in this report, &c., some of which have an undoubted reality, and have been discussed by several writers, as well as by myself ('Reports, Facts of Earthquakes, British Association Transactions') at a former period.

The probability of a connection, between rainfall and earthquake development, rests however, upon a wider base, than that of the facts adduced respecting the shock of December, 1857.

A like connection, though not with the evidence due to accurate meteorological tables, has been recorded in reference to several other earthquakes of this region. Thus, Grimaldi, in his account of the Calabrian shock of 1783, describing the weather of the year before, says: " L'esta nella Calabria ulteriore fu *Secchissima*, e calda fuori del solito, l'autunno fu molto pluvioso: ma la terra si ritrovava talmente arida, que assorbiva le aque in una maniera straordinaria." ('Discrizione de Tremuoti Accad. nella Calabria nel 1783. Opera Postuma di Francesco Antonio Grimaldi, p. 3, 8vo., Napoli, 1784.')

The very best account that has been given of the Melfi earthquake of 1851 is in a small paper by Signor Arabia, a physician of that city. He says: "La state dell' anno, 1851, fu in questi luoghi ora descritti notavole per *istraordinaria mancanza de aqua*, sendo che dalla meta del Marzo piogge abbondanti non erano cadute." ('Relazione storica del Tremuota de Basilicata nell' anno 1851, letta nella tornata del 14 Dec. dell' Accademia Pontaniana dall Socio Residente Francesca, Sav. Arabia,' p. 9, 8vo., Napoli, 1852.)

In a small pamphlet narrative of the Calabrian earthquakes of 1835 and 1836, by Rossi, he says (p. 10): "Ivi ne' mesi de Juglio e de Agosto le piogge in tanta copia caddero che le ricolte de'campi furono tutte perdute." After this: "Seguito ne' primi giorni del vegnente Ottobre *calore excessivo*, tal che agli 8 di quel mese un' ora dopo il mezzodi il termometro de Reaumur segno il grado 27, &c." ('Storia dei Tremuoti di Calabria, negli anni 1835-1836,' di Achille Antonio Rossi, 8vo. Napoli, 1837.)

Rossi also communicated his account in the 'Annali Civile,' fascia xix and xxiii, Naples. The first shock was on the 12th October, 1835, and there was periodic commotion up to April, 1836. The winter between, it is right to add, was wet and unusually cold. Were I to digress into earthquake narratives in other countries, similar evidences might be greatly multiplied.

I HAVE only now to add, to the facts recorded in the second part of this Report, those embraced in the Appendix to it. Of these, No. 1 is a translation of a local account of the shock of December, 1857, by Signor Raffaele Battista, a resident of Basilicata, and contains some interesting facts, though full of gross flattery as to the imaginary acts of paternal solicitude and beneficence of the late tyranny. No. 2 is a translation of the second part of the Report, of Professors Palmieri and Scacchi, on the earthquake in Basilicata of August, 1851, the analogies of which, with that described in the present Report, it is desirable to study; and No. 3 is a translation of all the meagre notices that are to be found of the events of this earthquake, in the successive numbers of the 'Giornale Reale,' the only newspaper in the years 1856-57 of Naples; many of the statements therein are very unreliable. I have omitted all notices of the "Royal Benevolence," &c., which, however impotent, were well paraded on the occasion, and limited the translation, to the statements made of the physical facts.

APPENDIX TO PART II.

No. (1.)

Translation of a Local Account.

' Il Terremoto de Basilicata, Relazione de Raffaele Battista, Segretario perpetuo della Reale Società Economica di Basilicata.' Potenza, 1858, dai Torchi de Vincenzo Santanella a spese dell' Autore.

THE EARTHQUAKE OF BASILICATA,

16th December, 1857.

I.

BEING obliged, by reason of my office, to write as accurate an account of the earthquake which recently convulsed the kingdom of Naples, and occasioned such ruin and mourning in unhappy Basilicata, as my ability and circumstances would allow, in order that civil history and natural science should possess the elementary facts, I see how difficult it is, to treat this subject in such a manner as shall present useful instruction to future ages, and throw some degree of light on the system of modern physics. Yet in the hope that some of the things I have to narrate may become a germ of foresight and humanity, or a caution for the future, I shall endeavour to describe the terrible and memorable event, the very thought of which, affects every fibre of my heart and renews my terror.

The whole subject may be regarded under two heads. The first is a simple narration of facts, which every one has been more or less able to observe for himself, or of which he has heard from others. The second consists of a few remarks, and scientific reflections which the learned may excuse, since I only put forward what I have learned from them, and the ignorant not despise, for, according to Cicero, they who illustrate and exalt the inventions of others, effect no less good than they who invent a science.

2.

On the 16th December 1857, which was preceded by a series of fine days, at a quarter past five, Italian time, a vertical shock of earthquake, lasting about twenty seconds, succeeded by an undulating shock of greater intensity and duration, excited the terror and occasioned the flight of the inhabitants of Potenza, who, at that hour, were almost all asleep. We say that the first shock was vertical, and the second undulating, because so they appeared to us and others; but many affirm the direct contrary, and the truth may lie with both parties, for the same contradiction is manifested in the reports of the other communes in the province, and in places still further distant, for it is impossible accurately to describe sensations at such a time of confusion. However, it is certain that the undulation was so strong and violent, that in some rooms objects were whirled round, or at least it occasioned a dizziness which led persons to fancy that they beheld everything in motion.

Signor D'Achille Bosica, Intendant of the Province, Counsellor in the Supreme Court of Justice, (although he had escaped with difficulty, and undressed, his house falling and the doors incapable of being opened from the sinking of the walls,) displayed a courage on that night equal to the occasion. He hastened first to the prison to quell the disturbance there, and provide for the public safety. The Royal Attorney-General shortly afterwards arrived with the same intention, so that the Intendant was at liberty to proceed to the hospital, where he was the means of relieving eleven women who had been buried beneath the ruins. He next addressed words of consolation and encouragement to the assembled crowds, and his gentle affability, the more acceptable in time of misfortune, was of great use in calming their minds amidst the general consternation. We had to deplore the death of but twenty-two persons, among whom Paola Catenazzo, who, to save her infant, and atone for having forgotten it, courageously ventured into her falling dwelling, and was returning with the beloved pledge, when the house suddenly fell and crushed her and her child. The devastation and destruction of the capital partially observed that night, became more apparent with returning day, and in proportion to the interior examination of the public and private buildings. Although, at first sight, a palace or house seemed outwardly uninjured, or but little damaged, within it was found so much so as to render it dangerous for habitation.

Besides the palace of the Intendente, the churches, and especially the cathedral, were rent open, destroyed, or shaken; also the courts, the monastery of Chiariste, that of the Reformed Fathers, called S. Marin, the Royal College, the House di Itami Riuniti, the prisons, the civil and military hospital, the prison hospital, the gendarmen barrack, and that of the reserved battalion, the telegraphic office, and the Mansion House. The damage was incalculable; in a word, the traveller who contemplates Potenza from a distance, sees the same outline and image, but when he approaches the town, he learns how true it is that we must not judge by outward appearance. However, several houses escaped almost uninjured. It is much to be lamented that this city, frequently destroyed from the same cause, as we learn from ancient chronicles, and just beginning to rise in the scale of civilization and improvement, under the influence of the estimable Intendente, should again be prostrated by such a calamity; at the very time, too, that improvements and decorations for the benefit of the citizens were in progress. The foundation of a new theatre had been laid, the new Royal College was commenced, and the project of a new street and sewerage, a work requisite to the sanity and cleanliness of the town, had been started. Whilst all were employed the next day, building sheds in the open spaces, away from the houses, messengers arrived from the different communes of the province, bringing sad intelligence to the Intendente; and within a few days it was known that on that night, and at that hour, every commune had suffered from the earthquake, or, at least, had strongly felt the shock and vibration. It would be tedious and useless to enumerate particular losses. But the great ruins of

Tito, Marsico, Paterno, Calvello, Viggiano, Brienza, Tramutola, S. Angelo le Fratte, Saponara, Guardia, and especially Montemurro, where upwards of 5000 perished, cannot be passed over in silence. Many were disinterred alive, but, for the most part, bruised and mutilated, and some even after eight days. The cries of many others were heard, who perished beneath the ruins, time and labour being insufficient to excavate them; and it may easily be believed that this miserable fate was not confined to the inhabitants of Montemurro. After the enumerated communes of this district, the communes of Castelsaraceno, Santarchangelo, Sarconi, and Carbone in the province of Lagonegro take rank with regard to extent of injury and number of deaths. The provident and indefatigable Intendents appointed commissioners of various kinds in Potenza, and in every commune, to arrange all affairs and relieve distress; he despatched the Secretary, General Cavalier Sanfelice, Counsellor Arillo, engineers, and physicians, to the most afflicted communes, and arranging everything in the capital, which demanded the largest share of attention, he sent everywhere, even to Melfi, for planks and beams, and a staff of workmen, to aid in building the sheds, and pulling down the falling walls. Afterwards he went himself to the desolated regions, in order to carry out, even at the risk of his own life, the rest of his benevolent plans, leaving Counsellor Cassillo in Potenza as his delegate and representative. However, it is needless to mention the many judicious expedients to which he had recourse in order to revive the public administration, trade, and social life; but we must not omit a circumstance which occurred on the evening of the 18th. Some prisoners who had either conspired to escape or were seized with an instantaneous determination to try, fell upon one of the turnkeys, who had entered their room on his usual visit of inspection: a companion hastening to the spot gave the alarm, and the attempt was immediately quelled by the prompt measures taken by the Counsellor of the Supreme Court of Justice and the Royal Attorney-General. A large concourse of people assembled to assist the military authorities, and the public force. The next day, after due deliberation with the Commissioners of Police, the heads of the sedition were exemplarily, but humanely punished.

We must also record that the Royal Attorney-General, D. Gennaro Sanchelli, having employed several of the prisoners in the public service on his own responsibility, exhorting them to diligence and honesty, and promising to recommend them to mercy, bestowed alms on the most distressed, and even remunerated the prison guards, and forty-one of the prisoners soon after received the royal pardon.

Great calamities afford generous hearts an opportunity to relieve their fellow-creatures, and the official journal fails not to record many instances of beneficence, and chiefly the royal bounty exerted in favour of all the communes of this province and Principato Citeriore, which were sufferers in this calamity. The Lucanians must always gratefully remember his Majesty's kindness in sending tents, clothes, and covering, together with engineers, surgeons, nurses, and companies of soldiers, and pioneers, with tools and implements, &c. His Majesty also dispensed thousands in the relief of the distressed, and his noble example was generously followed. It would be an useless repetition of well-known facts, were I to enumerate or praise the charitable actions of home and foreign benefactors, whose names are indelibly engraven in the hearts of the grateful, and recorded in the books of God.* To return to our subject: we assert that not only on the night of the 16th December many slight shocks, both vertical and horizontal, were felt in Potenza, and in almost all the other communes, but that they are still of such frequent occurrence, day and night, as to render the enumeration difficult; and it is likely that they will only cease with time, as happened after the celebrated earthquake of Melfi and many others. On this account, and owing to the want of safe houses, a great many families determined to pass the severe winter under sheds and thatched cabins; and as yet there are no attempts at rebuilding, all being employed in propping, or taking down the dangerous parts of every dwelling. It is enough to say that one room on the ground floor, and a shed, form the actual residence of the first authority of the province; another shed serves the Secretary, and the Royal Attorney-General and

---

* All this praise of Royal and Intendente bounty and humanity must be received cum grano salis. The writer had, no doubt, his own hopes or fears of the powers that—were.

the President of the Criminal Court are reduced to still smaller quarters. The magistrates, functionaries, and officials are suffering a similar or greater degree of discomfort, and yet amid this penury of habitation there are two large well-constructed sheds, suitably fitted up, in which the poor are gratuitously lodged. It is pleasant to record that at such a time of confusion the people of Potenza passed these days of affliction and distress, solely occupied in acts of devotion or humanity, whilst in two other communes of the province, which were the most desolated and afflicted, sordid avarice prevailed over piety. In Potenza it was delightful to observe the multitude which collected round the altars and portable chapels, erected in the square (*largo*) before the Intendente's house and other places, hearing the divine offices, and praying like the early Christians; and to this we must attribute the strength of mind which they evinced amid scenes of distress and mourning. On the 23rd January, a prisoner from the province of Salerno was brought into the chapel condemned to death for the murder of his sister; the scaffold was erected, the rites of religion about to be administered, and the brethren of the congregation were begging for masses for his soul, when Monsignor D. Michel Angelo Pieranuro, a man of great learning and kindness of heart, perceiving that the duty of intercession devolved upon him, communicated by telegraph with the King, and a message of pardon was returned, confirmed, on the following day, by the arrival of a courier, bearing the royal command.

3.

Of the Signs which preceded and accompanied and followed the Earthquake.

Many affirm that before the occurrence aërial sounds were distinctly audible; but during past years I have frequently heard similar noises which were not followed by an earthquake, and which were attributed either to Vesuvius, or to discharges of cannon, the echo of which, when the air is still, or when only a light breeze prevails, extends as far as Potenza. Noises and explosions subsequent to the earthquake were heard in Matera up to the early part of January, and by me and my family on the 8th and 29th of the same month in a small house in the environs of

Potenza. The 'Giornale' describes similar, or perhaps louder noises occurring in Principato Citeriore, and they are still audible in the most injured places of Basilicata. Some of those who left their houses at the first shock, saw at the second convulsion, over the wood of Ariosa, a mountain near Vignola, visible from Potenza, from which it is but a few miles distant, a beam of fire which disappeared in a moment. This meteor was seen, not only by the inhabitants of Potenza, but also by those of Vignola. In Potenza, some persons who were in the open space before the residence of the Intendente, observed a sudden darkness, followed by vivid flashes of lightning, springing from the ground, and darting through the air, and others saw the palace itself and other houses rise and fall with the ground, like reeds shaken by the wind, and the walls in the alleys knocked against each other. I need not mention the falls and staggering of the people. Another fact, which is apparently of greater importance, is that mentioned by the Syndic of Salandra, that for a month before, a gaseous exhalation, about sun heat, was observed to rise every morning from a cavity or aperture excavated for a watercourse, and that a similar exhalation was seen in the neighbourhood, both of which disappeared on the 22nd December. But this isolated fact may be ascribed to phosphoretted hydrogen gas, as in the burning quiescent fountains (*fontane ardenti e tranquille*) described by naturalists, and we are consequently of opinion, that it had no connection with the earthquake; but we must add that the Chancellor of the Commune assured us, that the exhalation was warm, having applied his hand to it, and that he considered it true smoke, as the side of the drain from which it issued with an earthy smell, was dried up and almost blackened. He added that the soil was cretaceous. The Syndic of Bella relates that half an hour before the earthquake, a suffocating smell of sulphur was perceptible, accompanied by a loud subterraneous noise; and that at the moment of the shock they who were living in cellars, perceived, besides the smell, a light sufficient to show the movements of the people in the room. The royal Judge also affirms, that a similar smell was perceptible, before some of the slight shocks, especially before that which occurred on the 11th January at dawn. The Syndic also speaks of large and deep fissures, from ten to thirty span. in a perimeter of about 600 tomoli of ground. It is known that a tomolo line measure is equal to 5·88 moggia of legal measure. Similar fissures have been discovered in the mountain of Ariosa before mentioned, and in other territories of different communes: it is no unusual effect of earthquakes. One circumstance excited great astonishment, viz., that in many wells in Potenza, and the adjacent communes of the province, a month before the earthquake, the accustomed volume of water was most remarkably diminished, and several wells were completely dried up. This phenomenon frequently serves as a salutary warning to the people residing in the vicinity of Vesuvius; with us it did not excite a shade of suspicion, for every one accounted for the failure of the supply, by imagining the usual known or unknown causes, without investigating the matter any further; and being considered of slight importance, it did not become a subject of public discourse. Amongst others, one well which, to my certain knowledge, was full of water in September, and increased by the heavy rains in October, was dry in November. If we consider that these wells have no channel through which the water could be dispersed, it is evident, that only a remarkable increase of caloric in the strata beneath could occasion this, either by evaporation, or absorption (which appears to me the more natural) of the strata. Another opposite fact is the increase of spring water subsequently to the earthquake, observable, among other instances, in the public fountain of Potenza and the water of the adjacent river. This is a manifest difficulty. If the water has been absorbed, and decomposed by a subterraneous fire, how can it afterwards return more impetuously and abundantly than ever? I shall venture an opinion at the risk of being excommunicated by natural philosophers, who explain the phenomenon in a different manner, and will say that when the water fails, it has been absorbed by *aspirazione* from above, and by the porous earth beneath; and when the water increases, a contrary force (*l'impulso*) urges it to flow back again. If these forces have been observed by Franklin and more modern philosophers in hurricanes, tempests, and whirlwinds, without their being able to account for them, my conjecture might at least serve to classify, under the same rule, a phenomenon which does not admit of complete explanation. And if electricity does not exert a direct influence over hurricanes, why do we not observe in whirlwinds (*trombe*) luminous masses, smoke, and jets of flame, in short, a smell of sulphur, and a hailstorm?

A worthy friend of mine, P. Raffaele of Tito, formerly Provincial of the Franciscan Friars, communicated to me some phenomena of still greater singularity. He told me that animals in general, but especially pigs, (a circumstance also observed by some in Potenza,) manifested marks of suffering and increasing uneasiness, for ten days previous to the earthquake. There were three hogs in a sty, close to the convent kitchen, and after supper, hearing an unusual grunting, he went out to see what was wrong, and found them rabidly excited, biting each other like dogs. The explanation given by philosophers of similar events is notorious; Virgil's, in the First Book of the Georgics, may suffice for all. On the evening of the 16th, at three o'clock, Italian time, my friend standing at the window of his room, which looked to the west, saw a great belt of fire and smoke, with a globe in the centre. This sight alarmed him, by recalling to his mind the fire and thunder of Sinai, when God gave the law to Moses. He pointed out the meteor to some of the fathers, who also observed it, and predicted some impending disaster. He says that the second shock was first vertical, and afterwards undulating, and rotatory. The air also was in motion, and as luminous as a lanthorn. Fiery meteors were observed all through the night, and some persons living in the country asserted that they saw a column of fire.

Dr. D. Raffaele Malvia told me that globes of fire were observed to fall upon the church, and that its destruction was attributed to them. Many heard an explosion previously to the earthquake, which was frequently repeated on a subsequent day. Father Raffaelo relates, that at the moment of the catastrophe, entire families were carried by the wind (*acremoto*) into the street, in their beds, and some from one house to another unhurt. He named, in particular, Pasquale Gatta and family, a son of Maronziello, and one Giuseppe Giaunotti, who, together with his wife, was whirled from house to house, falling in the street, thirty paces from his own dwelling. However, the woman was killed. He mentions similar facts, worthy of attention, especially mirrors and glass vessels being carried to a distance, without being broken. If these facts cannot be attributed to the violence of the oscillations, I maintain that they are the effect of a whirlwind (*tromba aerea*), a mysterious phenomenon to modern natural philosophers. Tito is known to possess sulphureous and ferruginous mineral springs, besides one, which from its colour is called white, but has not yet been analyzed. These, like other springs, were dried up for a short time, but are now flowing very copiously, but muddily, and the sulphureous springs are tepid, and leave more sediment. They also give off a very strong smell to a great distance. From the mountain called Peschi, situated at the side of the small crater, from which the waters issue, blocks of macigno have been precipitated into the stream; deep fissures have opened through the country; and towards Satriano, in a place called Kammotta, the earth fell in about the height of a man, and flames were observed to issue from it. That night slight shocks were repeated in Tito, upwards of twenty times. The manufactory (*i.e.*, of tobacco) was destroyed. The number of victims has been estimated at 280. Some strange and miserable cases occurred in this commune. One Nicola Mansione, precipitated from a third story into a cellar, with his relatives, who were all killed, succeeded in kindling a part of his dress, by means of a lucifer match, and perceiving some straw, lighted a fire, found bread and wine, and after three days was disinterred alive. One Nicola Spern was found suspended between two cross beams, holding in his arms his dead wife, and supporting his dying son on his shoulder. They were removed, but did not survive. A woman, named Arcaugiola Buena, was found dead amid the ruins, with her little children safe between her knees. A painter desirous of depicting maternal love, might profitably select this example. There are other deplorable cases of entire families being burnt, of a father who, being thrown on his son, and unable to extricate himself from the heap of ruins above him, crushed him to death. The wretched father, though bruised and mutilated, still lives. A phenomenon similar to that at Bella was observed in Viggiano, some days before the earthquake. The family of Spolidero saw, during the night, so strong a light in their rooms, that they could distinguish objects by it; and D. Girolamo, afterwards a victim of the disaster, fancying robbers were in the house, got up and called his sons to assist him in searching through it. A similar light was perceived on the night of the catastrophe. Oh! weak foresight of man! This wretched family, disinterred from the ruins of their own house, might have escaped this misfortune and saved their father's life. The faithful dog remained for several days motionless on the spot where his master perished, howling and refusing food. The creature would be worthy of a place among the celebrated animals of Signor de Rozan.

The crevices in the ground in this territory are very considerable, and an immense calcareous mass on the bank of a torrent denominated Casalo, was cleft in two, as if by lightning, and half of it precipitated down the declivity, destroying the olive and other trees. As yet the number of deaths is estimated at 60, but the true number cannot be precisely known. The land of the Æolian harp, once the delight of young and old, is now sunk in squalor and sepulchral silence! The estimable Signor D. Antonio Romania, of Marsico, informed me, that for a considerable time, that great valley (near which along the course of the Agri undoubtedly lay the centre of convulsion) was covered in the morning with a thick black mist, afterwards dispersed by the sun, the disc of which was dark, and the rays as intense as during the summer season; and that for some days previously to the earthquake, hollow sounds were heard in the air. These noises, too, preceded all the subsequent shocks. He adds that after the 18th, the rivers and springs increased very much, and some emitted, and are still omitting, exhalations, in which a strong sulphureous smell predominates. Large fissures have been observed throughout this territory from which a dense smoke, of disagreeable odour, frequently issues. Recent risings and swellings of the ground have been observed.

In Calvello, loud subterraneous noise and light, and whistling in the air were the precursors of the disaster; in the country the sky was vividly lighted up towards the south. During the night, fiery meteors preceded the repeated shocks. A few days afterwards, a fire, considered electrical, broke out of the ground in the district of S. Pietro, set fire to two large oaks, which were burning for three days, and crumbled a large stone (macigno) into powder.

Innumerable fissures have been observed. The courage and humanity of the citizens of this commune are highly laudable, and we must not omit to record the Christian example given by Judge Paolo Navazio: amid the applause and tears of 5000 inhabitants, he carried on his own shoulders the bodies of the poor people who had been excavated from their untimely graves. The Syndic, Signor D. Egidio Marco Giuseppe, who merited much from his unfortunate country, aided in the pious work.* With regard to Moliterno, I cannot do better than transcribe the contents of a letter which I received from the worthy young Signor D. Giacomo Racioppi, already distinguished by his literary and scientific works. "The 10th of December, like its predecessors, was mild and serene, the sun's rays warm, and the sky clear. No phenomena preceded the earthquake, or at least they were not understood or observed. On the 18th, a miller of Moliterno perceived that the usually pure watercourse which set his machinery in motion, was slightly muddy, and having ascended to its source, he found the spring greatly swelled and increased. Some days previously I had complained of the muddiness of the water brought to table; but as it was obtained from the most copious and clearest source, viz., the public fountain of Moliterno, I attributed it to the vessel which held it. Early in the evening of the 16th one of us fancied he saw the furniture shaken, but the rest in the room did not perceive it, and perhaps it was an illusion. The first shock occurred about five o'clock at night: after an interval of four minutes, (if time can be accurately computed in the agitation of terror,) the second ensued, severe, violent, and lasting thirty seconds. It was horizontal, vertical, and rotatory; men staggered on the pavement. Some plaster statues on the table were either thrown off, or shaken from their places. A cowherd going to his work at the fatal moment, observed that the atmosphere over the towns in the valley was lighted up and looked like a dazzling, moving band. Those who left their houses

* In the town itself (Calvello), on the 18th of January, an hour and a half before noon, a strong shock of earthquake was felt, preceded by a blast of wind and sparkling meteors, which described a parabola from south to west.

and ran into the country, perceived at the second shock a strong smell of bitumen and sulphur, probably issuing from the numerous fissures in their path.

These phenomena only (besides the straying away of gregarious animals) apparently preceded or accompanied the violent shocks. I shall add, on the chance of science discovering a relation between distant phenomena, that exactly a month before the earthquake—that is, on the 16th of November—long and loud explosions in the air were heard by the inhabitants of this valley, who ascribed them to the repeated echo of Vesuvius in eruption. We have frequently heard similar explosions since the fatal 16th, which were not always followed or accompanied by a shock of earthquake. During the night of the 16th till break of day, twenty or more undulations of the ground were perceived, often accompanied by a deep sound overhead. The sky was very clear, the temperature mild, and I saw hundreds of falling stars during the night. On the succeeding days the springs appeared to give forth their water most abundantly and clearly. A little stream, called Al Varco di l'ourzio, disappeared for some days, but burst forth again on the 3rd. The water in the river Sciara and Moglio flowed most copiously but muddily; the sky maintained its serenity. From that time to the present a continual clucking of hens has been remarked, such as usually occurs at a change in the atmosphere. I have also been informed that dogs barked hoarsely before the shocks subsequent to the 16th, and that on that fatal night horses were observed to raise their mane, and pull away from the halter, and that a mule was observed to roll on the ground with terror at each of the shocks on that night."

As to the phenomena observed in Montemurro, owing to my office of Inspector of Prisons, I had an opportunity of questioning at my convenience a large number of prisoners (not all of the lower class) belonging to that commune imprisoned soon after the earthquake. They all agreed in saying that circles of fire were seen in the air some hours before the great disaster; one man affirmed that he had seen similar meteors several evenings before the 16th. They added that these lights appeared at the time of the shocks, and also on the following days. A cowboy told me, that shortly before the earthquake the cows under his care, lowed in such an unusual manner, that he went to their stable to see if they wanted hay, but could not account for their disquietude. Large fissures, like those which we have already mentioned, have been observed in this territory. These are certified to me by letters from P. Lettore Guglielmo from Castelgrande, who also speaks of the noises which were heard, and adds that a month before the deplorable event, travelling with some others through the valley of Marsico, he was surprised to hear subterraneous and aërial noises, like those produced by cannon. He informs me that in Montemurro, or, to speak more correctly, that in the place where Montemurro was, individuals were excavated alive, after nine days' interment in deep holes, and mules and fowl after twenty. In Saponara, besides the noises in the air, those who lived in the country observed the whole atmosphere enkindled at the second shock, when the town was destroyed. It is also related that one Giuseppe de Cilla was lifted off his feet and thrown to a higher place than that he occupied; and that another man was raised up twice in the air, falling back twice to the ground. D. Giambattista de Canto, priest (whose house was thrown down, and his two sisters killed), was carried, without knowing how, about a quarter of a mile, to a declivity separated from other ruins, when he found himself on his feet and unhurt. Near the banks of the Agri, which flows through this territory, a great gulf four or five feet in diameter was found, close to the ruins of an ancient bridge, broken to pieces by the shocks. The water in this river increased greatly. We must not omit a circumstance already famous, viz, the conduct of the Cistercian heroine of this commune, Maria Margherita Ceramelli di D. Lelio, who, having extricated herself from the rubbish which covered her, endeavoured, with a courage and strength superior to her sex, to excavate the other sisters, pulling the quilts in which they were wrapped with her teeth, and drawing them out from the pressure of material with which they were laden. She succeeded in saving ten, and then hastened to her father's house, when she found that her younger sister had performed no less wonders. This young girl, safe and uninjured in the falling of the house, detached a basin in the roof of a small room, and obtained entrance, then removing a heap of stones in the adjoining room, dragged out safely her mother, three sisters, and a little brother. The father and elder brother were fortunately absent. They are still more fortunate to possess such heroic relatives. The deaths in this unfortunate city, which recalls to us the ancient Grumentum, amount to 2,500. Many rare and precious relics of antiquity possessed by private individuals were lost. In Carbone a very slight noise, heard only by a few, was the precursor of the fatal event; an electric illumination followed, with frequent explosions, and occasional flashes of lightning. The shocks were vertical, undulating, and rotatory. Other minor phenomena similar to those we have already mentioned were observed. New springs of water burst forth, and the estimable Signor D. Francesco Paolo Castronuovo, who has kindly given me much information, adds that the subsequent shocks invariably corresponded with the lunar phases and changes. On the evening of the 5th January a band of fire redder and brighter than lighted coals, appeared in the south-west.

Dr. D. Gaetano Arcieri di Latronico, a man distinguished for learning and talent, favoured me with observations worthy of his genius and diligence, and proportionate to the friendship with which he honours me, and I am grieved to say, that owing to urgent haste, I have scarcely time to put a few of them together for the press. He made several meteorological observations with the barometer and thermometer after the earthquake. He found the magnetic needle irregularly attracted, but was unable to observe electrical phenomena from the want of apparatus. He alludes to facts similar to those we have already detailed; viz., noises, falling stars, increase of water, especially at Sinni; increased heat of thermal springs, sulphureous smells, fissures, trees knocking together, stones rolled from the peak of Seluci, crevices, dense fog for several days, which did not affect Saussure's hygrometer, and must be considered a dry mist. On the 17th, an aëriform smoke was exhaled from a fissure in the rock Dorga, warm to the touch, and smelling of sulphuric acid gas. This has disappeared. The bells in Latronico were set in motion by the convulsions of that fatal night, and the sacred bronze, which should inspire sweet sentiments of religion, became the cause of greater terror. In the aberrations of nature, the mind also lost its equilibrium. A young man in this vicinity, being awakened by the first sounds, thought he was attacked, seized a pistol in the dark, and fired at the servant, who hastened in terror to him. The pistol did not go off: he rushed at the man with a dagger, and had wounded him slightly, before he discovered his error, when he burst into tears of agitation, and thanked God for having saved him from a double danger. Returning now to Vignola, where, as I have already mentioned, a luminous phenomenon was observed, we are informed that for some days before, the pigs in the pastures of Ariosa were restless, and ate little. On the 14th and 15th, the dried leaves were whirled round in a circle, producing an alarming, crackling, whistling sound, the air being quite still at the time. After the second shock, a charcoal-burner who had been dreadfully shaken in his hut, ventured out, and observed a column of rushing noisy wind coming from the south-west, causing the trees to knock against each other. The water in the springs and rivers increased. Crevices more or less deep and wide, even wider than a man could leap, were observed in this mountain, and a landslip of four to five tomoli in extent. I am indebted for this information to a friend of mine, Signor D. Michele Tucci, landowner and physician in this commune. Lastly, we must record, in attestation of the signs given by animals, that in Accettura, several observed on the evenings of the 15th and 16th an unaccountable disquietude among dogs and cats, an unusual howling and moving, leading them to foresee the melancholy event.

I do not know whether, besides the phenomena which I have succeeded in collecting, any more, either permanent or transitory, have been observed. Time and study are necessary to complete this imperfect compilation; these at some future day I hope to devote to it, and once more resume the subject.

4.

As philosophy, according to Cousin, is a sea without a shore, so natural science presents to man a series of facts, more or less numerous, which he arranges in groups according to the resemblances which he perceives among them, until from new observations, he is obliged to change his opinions, and give a new arrangement to the same facts.

Among the modern systems of geology, there are two as old as the study of nature, which appear to dispute for precedence, while the minor systems have reference, and can easily be reduced to them. One is, that the earth was originally in a state of igneous fusion, which is gradually cooling, and becoming covered with water. The other, that it was originally water, which, by absorption, is gradually forming a solid mass. These systems seek to explain every geological fact and natural phenomenon on different principles. But facts multiplying with observation, and being incapable of explanation, if we adhere exclusively to either system, what can be more natural than a mutual toleration of opinion? If a metaphysical disquisition would be considered fantastical, unless its principles agreed with facts, how should we regard a physical disquisition which should treat of colours, sounds, heat, cold, the motions of bodies, &c., without making use of sense, instruments, and various experiments? By the aid of observation and palpable facts, naturalists and geographers enumerate upwards of 300 active volcanoes upon our globe, the names and situation of which it is superfluous to mention; and according to the more or less vast extension of territory over which they exercise their sphere of activity, five volcanic zones have been defined; the accurate reasoning of Ferdinando of Lecca upon this subject is well known to the scientific world.

The kingdom of the Two Sicilies, that is to say, Vesuvius and Etna, (not to speak of other volcanic regions, and Vulture, which appears extinct, and perhaps is not,) forms a portion of one of these zones. The existence of these fire mouths, scattered for the most part at great distances over the surface of the globe, leads us reasonably to conclude, that a great fire exists in the interior, or, to speak with the Vulcanists, that the nucleus is in a state of incandescence, or that it has not yet cooled down from its primeval state of igneous fusion. To this we must add, that by the repeated experiments made by philosophers, the thermometrical temperature beneath the strata is found invariable, and has continued so for years, increasing with depth in a remarkable manner. In general, there is an additional degree of heat for every 25 or 30 metres, and if this ratio continue, the heat near the centre of the earth must be greater than we can possibly conceive; nor could we otherwise account for the origin of thermal waters, which spring up with the temperature of boiling water.

But if the existence of fire, or at least of excessive heat in the depths of the earth admits of no doubt, it is no less certain that another different and opposite principle exists in its cavities which are often converted into great reservoirs of water. Whether we attribute the origin of springs to precipitations of atmospheric vapour, to the melting of ice, to filtrations of sea water, which by means of capillary tubes may be raised to great distances, or to subterraneous vapours, which in cooling become liquid; the water sometimes erupted from volcanoes, the sudden and terrible inundations of mines, the floods which disappear for ever, the mountains suddenly swallowed up by immense lakes, force us to acknowledge (according to Malte Brun), the existence of great subterranean cavities, full of water. If these volcanoes possess within themselves the power of propagating their fires, and producing dreadful eruptions every time that they are furnished with new food and material, it would appear, on the other hand, that subterraneous water must extinguish, or at least quench and diminish these fires, and occasion the preponderance of the system adopted by the Neptunists. We shall not exclusively embrace either system, but content ourselves with philosophizing in the style of the ancient Academicians, and approving solely of that which appears probable, endeavour to show that volcanic principles in connection with aqueous, are capable of producing the phenomena of earthquakes and eruptions.

If you take, for example, 30 lbs. of iron filings, and 30 lbs. of sulphur, knead them into a paste with water, and bury them in a lump in a trench in the open country, you will shortly see smoke issuing from the spot, with very great heat and convulsion of the ground to some distance, and finally flames.

Now the materials of which volcanoes are composed are pyrites, or sulphurets, that is, sulphur combined with metallic substances, mixed with chalk, clay, marl, alabaster, quartz, slate, spar, and other rocks. These sulphurets being frequently moistened with water become decomposed, and produce the phenomena; for modern chemistry has taught us, that water contains $\frac{88}{100}$ of oxygen gas (pure air), combined with $\frac{12}{100}$ of hydrogen (inflammable air). The first of these gases is also combined in air which consists of $\frac{27}{100}$ of oxygen, and $\frac{73}{100}$ of nitrogen (that is not vital), and $\frac{1}{80}$ of carbonic acid gas; but this is not always the proportion, for reasons too complex to mention. Oxygen gas is necessary to combustion, and from what we have said, it is easily understood how it can exist in the interior of volcanoes, and in the depths of the earth, whither air and water can penetrate by the many known abysses on the globe. Alum also, and other salts, contain oxygen in great abundance. Now it is evident, that earthquakes and volcanoes are closely connected, or, in other words, that subterraneous or pre-existent fire, whether kindled by the combinations already mentioned, or by similar ones, may cause the earthquake. For let us suppose a decomposition of substances, not on a small scale, as in the proposed experiment, but to an immense extent, including that of water into oxygen and hydrogen; the necessary consequence is the development of aëriform fluids, which from their nature are incapable of being confined by the pressure of the earth, and in order to escape from imprisonment, exert all their power against the surrounding obstacles. Hence the earthquake.

To this we must add, that electric fluid, of which the earth is a vast reservoir, (in fact, man and the electric machine alone do not furnish us with electric phenomena,) acts in these cases like lightning and thunder in atmospheric regions. Among the ancients, Pliny perceived the resemblance between the tremor of the earth and the atmosphere. Even prior to him it had been observed by Epicurus, by whom fire was enumerated as one of the probable causes of earthquakes, (as we collect from Seneca's valuable book of Natural Questions). A fire, he says, *fulmini similis*, capable of throwing down and overturning all obstacles, *magna strage obstantium*. This is confirmed by the fact, that many earthquakes have been felt at very nearly the same instant, in places hundreds and perhaps thousands of miles distant from each other; and we are not aware of any other fluid, but light, and electricity possessing the power of instantaneously traversing space; nor can we attribute such force and destructive power to any other body in nature. But here another question very difficult of solution arises. Earthquakes, volcanic eruptions, and electricity, usually occur together or are separated by very short intervals in varying order of succession. Ought we then to attribute the earthquake to the volcanic eruption, or to electricity, (elettricismo), or to both?

The last opinion will not be admitted, by one who has considered the famous sentence of Maupertuis, that nature only exerts her least strength, or, to use Aristotle's words, who was the originator of the sentiment, "She does not do with more, that which she could do with less." I can see into what a circle, into what an abyss, that mind will fall, which wants to reason here *à priori*, or by creating hypotheses. To say that the earthquake may be occasioned by volcanic combinations, arguing from such analogy as occurs on a small scale, and the fact that earthquakes have either preceded or followed eruptions is surely not absurd, but very reasonable. Nor can we tell how far human knowledge, with regard to natural facts, would extend if we abandoned induction and analogy. But arguing in this way, and from various electrical experiments, remembering the nature of the fluid, which tends always to diffuse itself equally; the meteors which preceded or followed this earthquake of which we are treating, we might ascribe this phenomenon, at least from its visible effects, different from those of that which desolated Calabria in the past century, to electricity, which appears to us as inexhaustible as the light from the sun. Therefore, in my opinion, we may reasonably conclude that the electric fluid has displayed its power in the numerous and different degrees of affinity which various subterraneous substances bear to this fluid.

Among the correlative and subsequent phenomena I have not mentioned the earthquake which took place in Rodi on the 15th of December, nor the fog which enveloped Paris on the 19th of the same month. These circumstances, or at least the second one, may have had no connection with our earthquake, although it is remarkable that in 1783, when a hundred cities of Calabria were destroyed by earthquake, and Iceland at the same time convulsed by the eruption of its volcano, a dry fog extended almost all over Europe. It is important to note that after the 16th, the sky remained clear for eight days, then very fine rain fell, followed by heavy falls of snow, and on the evening of the 17th of January, and during the 18th, a violent and tempestuous north wind prevailed. On the 21st and 22nd, it blew still more fiercely from the west, leading us to fear that the buildings shaken by the earthquake would be still further rent and destroyed; however, the north wind returned again with wintry severity. In conclusion, the meteors and other phenomena here enumerated as having preceded, accompanied, or followed the earthquake, are positive facts, which I willingly submit for judgment to those who profess these sciences.

NOTE.—So far as the speculative part of this somewhat hazy piece of philosophizing is concerned, it must be taken for what it is worth. The style is one very prevalent in publications having a certain pretension to profundity and popularity of matter in Southern Italy at present, when treating of *official* phenomena. The Inspector of Prisons' statements must be taken with due allowance—such other facts as he records are the sole residua of value.

No. (2.)

Translation of Part II. of the Report to the Royal Academy of Science of Naples, by Professors Palmieri and Scacchi, on the Earthquake of 14th August, 1851.

Della Regione Vulcanica del Monte Vulture e del Tremuoto ivi avvenuto nel de 14 Agosto, 1851, relazione fatta per incarico della R. Accademia delle Scienze, da Luigi Palmieri ed Arcangelo Scacchi. Parte Seconda ; Storia del Tremuoto.

HISTORY OF THE EARTHQUAKE.

Melfi, 14th August, 1851.

FROM the past summer season, up to the moment in which we are writing (February, 1852), the earth has been frequently convulsed in several of the countries of Europe. All these earthquakes have had distinct centres of action, and a different intensity and extension.*

It is our province solely to speak of that which with reason has been denominated the earthquake of Melfi, not merely because this unfortunate city suffered the most in the death of its inhabitants, and the ruin of its buildings, but because the cause of these calamities was felt in the surrounding countries, the ground on which this ancient and illustrious metropolis of Puglia is built having been the centre of convulsion, as we shall presently demonstrate. Journeying

* The earthquake of Melfi was the signal for many others. Earthquakes occurred in Hungary, France, Albania, Calabria, &c. In the last region they were felt in the month of January, 1852, but not with the usual degree of intensity ; they lasted many days, and the shocks were so frequent as to compel the inhabitants to sleep out of doors. The shocks in Calabria had no connection with those in Melfi, which are still perceptible.

from Naples to Melfi by the Salerno and Valva road, almost two entire days are occupied alone in crossing the Apennines; and after a long and painful ascent the traveller at last reaches an eminence from whence his eye might range over the vast plains of Puglia, where the view is only broken, at the outskirts of the Apennines, by a solitary and majestic mountain; testifying by its configuration that its origin was very different from that of the mountains he has been contemplating for two days. This mountain, with its numerous ridges and deep valleys, with beautiful and fertile declivities, is Monte Vulture, at the base of which, built over the volcanic formation, stands first of all Atella, rich in historical associations, but now poor in inhabitants, owing to its unhealthy atmosphere; next Rionero, a new and populous city, probably owing, in part, its prosperity to the emigrations from Atella. Along the east side of the mountain the next town is Barieli, a large borough of Albanian origin; then Rapolla, an ancient episcopal seat, dating from Norman times; and, lastly, a little to the north of Vulture, Melfi appears, built on a gentle eminence formed of loose and incoherent volcanic tufa, covered with incompact and almost scoriaceous lava. To the right of the beaten track, the last of the Apennines appear to change into low hills, some of which are formed of fuvoid clays, and on the side or summit of these hills stand Ginestra and Ripacandida, and further on Venosa, Lavello, Maschito. Beyond, to the north, runs the Ofanto, and from thence Puglia is a level plain, presenting a lovely landscape from many points; but the best view is obtained from the highest ridge of Vulture, whence the prospect extends to the Adriatic. The chain of the Apennines stretches on from the west side of Monte Vulture, presenting the same low hills, on which Monteverde, Carbonara, Candela, &c., are situated. The rest of the region in which the earthquake was more or less felt is marked on the map.

On the 14th of August, 1851, the ground being dried up by *long want of rain*, the weather sultry, the sun shone out palely, as if covered with fog. Towards noon the sky was cloudless, and the atmosphere clearer, but at twenty minutes past two P. M. a sudden shock of earthquake occurred: a gust of wind was observed by those in the country, and some also saw a light vapour or cloud pass rapidly over the towns, which fell with a dreadful noise, and heard a deep subterranean report, which was more distinctly perceived in the many repetitions which followed the first agitation of the ground. In all those districts which suffered much injury, the shocks were first vertical and then undulating: the motion was communicated to a great distance, but with decreasing intensity, and simply undulating from north to south, about ten seconds in duration, as was observed in Naples. At the first convulsion of the buildings, men and women, old people and children, were buried under the ruins, some killed and some disabled by wounds, and not a few who had gained the street in which the walls of the adjacent houses were falling, perished in the act of escape. Some were safely sheltered under doorways where walls were left standing, whilst the roofs had fallen in. The survivors fled into the open air, and just as they were collected together, and were beginning to recover from their terror, and inquire for friends and relatives, half an hour after the first shock, another subterraneous report was heard, with new shocks, differing little in intensity from the first, and causing fresh ruin to the buildings left insecure and tottering from the recent convulsions. The people beheld this scene of ruin in the open air: in Melfi, Barieli, and Rapolla they were left without a roof to shelter them, without food, clothes, or furniture. But if this repetition occasioned new damage, it did not create new victims, for all were already out of doors; and to some, perhaps, it may have been salvation, because, already buried under the ruins, they were partly disinterred by the new convulsion, and, safe or wounded, reappeared among the living; while others, doubtless, who had been buried alive, perished at that moment. Before evening there was a third shock, and during the night which followed the earth was convulsed about eleven times. In the succeeding days slight shocks occurred, once or twice during the day: afterwards they became less frequent, as was the case in September, when we visited those regions; and at the moment in which we are writing they are still perceptible, but occasion no injury to the buildings. At the first shock the inhabitants did not observe any sign attending the coming calamity, but afterwards they perceived that each shock was preceded by a mysterious foreboding among animals, almost always accustomed to announce certain phenomena, which man with his intelligence often cannot foresee. Asses everywhere were the first to predict, by their frequent and unusual braying, that the earth would soon tremble. Next in order we may reckon the barking of dogs, the grunting of pigs, and an unusual disturbance amongst poultry. In some places—as in Foggia—an increase of temperature was observed at the moment of the shock, and an ascent of the barometer, which subsequently fell to 28 inches and 2 lines: this last, however, may have been caused by the vertical motion. We have no other observations, near Melfi or in Melfi itself.

In some places the failure of water in wells was remarkable, in others, springs spouted out with force, and then disappeared for a while, and some affirmed that the water was much discoloured. There is in Melfi a very abundant spring, which floods the valley with its stream, but no phenomenon of this kind was observed. In one of our ascents of Monte Vulture, on the 22nd of September, we visited the Fontana di Piloni, which owes its origin to two *distinct* springs, although very close to each other; and a few days afterwards (on the 3rd of October) we observed that the water in one had fallen one-half, and in the other one-fifth. The herds who frequent this place assured us that they had perceived the diminution six or seven days before, and that within their memory a similar failure had never before occurred. On the 16th August there was a storm with frequent thunder, large hailstones, and heavy rain; the wheat crop was completely destroyed, and the vines injured by the hail. In September and the beginning of October we saw frequent lightning at night, and in November the thunder and hail returned with greater vehemence. Melfi, Barieli, and Rapolla are almost destroyed. Next comes Rionero, one third of which is ruined, and the rest more or less damaged. Atella, Venosa, Lavello, Ascoli, Canosa, and Candela, rank next with regard to injuries, and then the other villages marked on the map.

In Melfi not a single house was left uninjured. The rage of the earthquake did not respect the best-constructed buildings, which were certainly the Bishop's palace, a vast and spacious edifice, in which a council had been held by Pope Nicholas II.; and the castle, with its superb towers, the famous seat of the Normans; the spire of the cathedral, which had resisted the earthquakes of 1348 and 1456, and, above all, that of 1694, which desolated these regions, as we learn from several documents, lost its summit. The dome, which had been thrown down by the last-mentioned earthquake, and rebuilt in another style, was once more destroyed; the college, the other churches, the monasteries, and convents, were thrown down, and the nuns were obliged to remain for many days in a log hut erected expressly for them, from which they were removed by the royal command to another convent near Avigliano.* The rest of the buildings, mostly ill constructed, could not stand when the best fell. The rock itself on which the city was built, being naturally incoherent, was split, fractured, or opened, so that in many places you could see to the foundations of the houses. At Porte Calcinara the ground opened more than a metre and a half in diameter, and shortly after the walls of the gate were swallowed up. On the south side of the hill, portions of building belonging to the foundations of the houses were seen rolled together with the dislodged tufa. Similar fragments of tufa and lava were observed in other places, both in Melfi and its environs: for instance, near the fallen Church of Madonna di Macera, three miles north of the city, and on the Rendina road, near the Ponte del Pesso. The ruins of the desolated city of Melfi show evident signs of the vertical shock: for example, pillars broken at the base, or at the joinings of the stones, while they still retain their upright position; chimneys lifted up and replaced in a somewhat different position. This has been erroneously considered by some a sign of rotatory motion, but we found no trace of the kind.†

* Melfi had seventeen churches, large and small, comprising those of the P. P. Osservanti, commonly called Capuchins: of these, three, besides the cathedral, formed parishes; all were destroyed, or rendered dangerous. At this present time some are being repaired through the liberality of the king, who, with paternal solicitude, hastened to visit his distressed subjects.

† Signor D. Francesco Granata, of Ilicurto, to whom, as well as to the brothers Catena we beg to express our gratitude, told us, that, being seated at table with the Bishop of Melfi, on the 14th of August, he observed that his Grace's snuff-box was several times thrown up and down on the table with great violence.

The extensive ruins in Melfi, the evident signs of strong pulsatory shocks, the fissures and rents in the ground, and the subterraneous noise which always accompanied the shocks (sometimes preceding them, sometimes simultaneously with them) prove that this city, as we have already affirmed, was the centre of the terrible phenomenon; and all who at the moment of the earthquake chanced to be in the open country agree in stating that they observed the country houses fall one after the other, according to their distance from Melfi. But if Melfi must be considered the physical centre of the earthquake, it does not equally represent the geometrical centre of the affected region, on which subject we have some important observations to bring forward. In the first place, the earthquake was felt with more intensity on the volcanic formations. Consequently Ginestra and Ripacandida suffered incomparably less injury than Barieli and Rionero; and yet the last town is in a direct line, further from Melfi than Ginestra. Secondly. The impetus of the earthquake decreased rapidly when it came in contact with the Apennine limestone, and extended more on the hills of sub-Apennine rock and Macigno formation, on which the towns of Venosa and Lavello on one side, Montoverde and Carbonara on the other, are built, than over the plains of Puglia. As you approach the summit of the Apennines, looking for the villages and towns that are built on the compact limestone formation, you soon perceive, from the houses, that some power must reside in these mountains to weaken the earthquake, or resist its influence. Lastly, Ruvo and St. Fele are distant from Melfi in a direct line, the same as, or even less, than Ascoli, and yet this place suffered much, while the former towns show no trace of the earthquake, except the terror of their inhabitants. And to look at St. Fele, perched on a rock or steep ascent, you are inclined to judge that at the slightest motion it must be precipitated into the ravine below. Thus, too, Calitri, Bisaccia, Maschito, Florenza, Avigliano, and Muro, built on the inclination of precipices, were untouched, or nearly so, in comparison with Ascoli, Candela, and Canosa, which were greatly injured. But without multiplying instances of this kind, we shall enable the reader to judge for himself, by showing how the towns may be classed with regard to the intensity of the earthquake, so that by glancing at the map which delineates the region in which the earthquake was most felt, he may compare these data with the distances from Melfi:—

1. Melfi.
2. Barieli and Rapolla.
3. Rionero.
4. Atella, Ginestra, Ripacandida, Venosa, Monteverde, Lavello, Ascoli, Canosa, Candela, Carbonara.
6. Towns difficult to classify, as Trani, Barletta, Cerignola, Lavologna, Bisarcia.
7. All the remaining places marked on the map suffered scarcely any injury, and in some of them no trace of the earthquake remains, except the recollection of terror, in the minds of the inhabitants.

From this scale, and from inspection of the map, it is evident that the shocks of the 14th of August (the only ones which really did any injury, the others being of slight intensity) must have been propagated with greater force on the line of the Ofanto so as to affect Canosa, very distant from Melfi, and to arrive still vigorous on the coast of the Adriatic, injuring Trani and Barletta; but we must remember the other earthquakes which occurred in September and October, in Terra d'Otranto, which extended to the province of Bari, giving new shocks to those places which had partially suffered in the earthquakes of Melfi.

A shock of earthquake was felt in Canosa, on the night of the 6th and 7th of September, which was not perceived in Melfi, Barieli, Rapolla, Rionero, &c. The earthquake which destroyed Vallona and other cities of Albania, with the loss of 2,000 human beings, was strongly felt in Terra d'Otranto, and extended also, although weakened, through the province of Bari. We affirm these facts without positively denying the possibility of the propagation of earthquake waves in one way more than another, even in a plain like that of Puglia, of the same geological formation, at least on the surface. But this greater elongation of force towards the Adriatic, does not weaken the observation relative to the decrease of power along the chain of the Apennines, a fact which agrees with others of the same kind in various places, as recorded by Humboldt.

Returning now to the ruins of Melfi, as no building, even among the strongest and best, escaped uninjured, we cannot say whether the earthquake had more power in high or in low places; yet we are of opinion that houses built on a declivity must have fallen sooner than those built on a level surface, and in general we remarked this in all endangered districts. Houses built on a level surface, with a square or rectangular foundation, not much longer than wide, of a moderate height, especially if provided with beams and iron chains (i. e., chain bars built into the walls), at least allowed egress to their inmates, and although injured were for the most part left standing. The house of Signore Calvino is an apparent exception to this rule, it being the only private house in the district of Venosa which buried any person beneath its ruins, and yet it is recently built on a large, level, and almost square foundation; but on attentive examination we find that its devastation must be attributed to faults of construction, for the roof had no tye-bars, whilst the floors were covered *a volta a vela* with a very weak arch very thin at the top; the quoins were made of hewn stone, wretchedly bonded into the rest of the fabric, so that at the occurrence of the earthquake, the front wall, by the motion of the arches, was easily shaken from its vertical position, and then some fragments of the roof falling on the arch of the upper story, which had already lost its equilibrium by the displacement of one of its abutments, caused it to fall on the story beneath, burying all the people who were in it. We take this opportunity to state that the inhabitants of Vulture, availing themselves of the lava, which is sufficiently porous and capable of taking a good bond with cement, built their walls of unhewn stone of lava rubble-work; and as the cement which they use is not very good, owing either to the small proportion of lime which is mixed with it, or the want of selection of the Pouzzolana, it does not, as good cement, harden with time, but loosens, and crumbles into dust, so that the walls do not offer much resistance to the convulsions of the ground. The ceilings are also made of lava, and are easily destroyed by the vibration of the walls. In Melfi little skill is displayed in uniting the fragments of lava; we have seen a wall, the inner side of which was left standing, while the outer had fallen, clearly showing that it had been formed by the two sides being simply laid together, but not bonded.*

Generally speaking, houses built on a declivity, when not thrown down, are found injured on the side next the hill (*dal lato della costa*), which proves the utility of giving a contrary inclination to the foundation, as is usual in the analogous case of counterscarps (*contrafforti*) or revetments, and it was certainly to this circumstance that the monks of the monastery of St. Michael, in Monticchio, owed their safety; the building being partially ruined by the shocks, and menaced by the stones which were detached from the lofty overhanging rock, would surely have been precipitated into the lake beneath, had not the foundation been so judiciously built. When the amazed inhabitants of Melfi, who had escaped death, were collected together in the open air, and somewhat recovered from terror, they turned to the wreck of their native place, and endeavoured to seek out their homes, frequently rendered inaccessible, and set to work, looking for persons and furniture, beneath the ruins of overthrown buildings; they were speedily assisted in their search by people sent by the mayor of the province. Many were found dead, many wounded; the former received Christian burial, the latter were conveyed to hospitals erected at the most convenient places, and maintained by the charity of the survivors, and the care of government, with the aid of the medical men of the district, and the hardworking Sisters of Charity. The excavations being continued

---

* Solidity is indeed no protection against the rage of the earthquake; yet it is also true, that good buildings are not the first to fall, and that they at least allow the inhabitants time to escape. The episcopal palace was greatly injured; but still it is almost entirely standing, and there is scarcely any room fallen in: the square porch, with pillars and arches, constructed in an artistic manner, with hewn stones and good cement, permit the traveller still to behold this superb edifice, and to ascend and admire the room in which the council was held. We may say the same of the castle, which, with its rent sides, does not yet yield to the rapacity of centuries and the violence of nature; but still recalls the memory of its past grandeur. The steeple of the cathedral has, it is true, lost its summit, but it has resisted many earthquakes, and, lopped as it is, stands erect amidst the general ruin, three stories higher than the other buildings. We have seen another steeple, of Norman architecture, built of hewn stone, which stood erect beside the fallen church. The unhappy Acquilecchi was scarcely saved beneath a doorway in the midst of a heap of ruins, which buried all his family, for under the decorative exterior of his house old and badly-built walls were concealed.

for some days, they had the happiness of finding many persons alive, who had been supposed dead. For instance, on the 17th, a living, but orphaned sucking child, of eighteen months, was found, named Filomena Palmieri, whom we afterwards saw, and Manro Faroli, a boy of five years, was disinterred alive on the 20th, although with a bad wound in the head, which was not perfectly healed on the 27th September, when we saw him. We learned from the father, that he was found nearly insensible, and suffered from intense thirst, which was not diminished for four or five days after, but that he did not show much desire for food. In reply to our inquiry he told us that he found urine but no excrement, where the child was discovered, and that he had fever for several days after. The boy was unable to tell us anything, either from bashfulness in our presence, or want of intellectual development, although well grown and strong in body. Our illustrious predecessors who described the earthquake of Calabria, in 1783, have recorded several cases of more prolonged fasting, but in individuals much older than these children. We are unable to say how many suffered from illness, induced by terror, but cases of cure of some diseases, by the earthquake, or by its terror, are not wanting; for instance, a man who had been confined to bed for many months, with articular pains, suddenly acquired the *painless* use of his limbs. The man's name is Tiberio Gallelli, and the circumstance was related to us by Signor D. A. Paradisi, of Bariele.*

We must now speak of the losses of each city, borough, or village, to which the scourge which we are briefly describing, extended, for it would be useless to enlarge on the ruins of Melfi, few houses there, being left standing, and all being badly injured, reminding us of the aspect of disinterred Pompeii, with the addition of the heaps of stones blocking up the streets, the walls inclined or tottering, here a beam supporting part of the roof, there a piece of framing (*congregnazione*) broken in pieces, standing in the

---

* Signor D. Vincenzo Cavalo wrote from Barletta, on the 16th of August, to Cav. Gussone: "The earthquake has destroyed me. I was asleep on my back, and at half-past two o'clock the vertical motion jerked me up in such a manner as caused an acute pain in my loins, and as yet I cannot hold myself straight. The horizontal motion from N. E. to S. W. did not at all affect me."

most picturesque and strange position, while in the midst of the desolation, men and women, old people and children, wander in silence squalor and misery, depicted on their countenances, and all wearing some mourning garb, for they are fathers weeping for their children, brothers for brothers, wives for husbands, children for their mothers, &c.

The appearance of Melfi, although we had already seen Atella, Rionero, Bariele and Rapolla, affected us with indescribable emotion. The reader can acquire an idea of its ruined condition from the faithful sketch of Signor Flauti, junior;[*] but who can describe the sorrow legible in the countenances of those poor creatures, who are wandering round the walls of their former homes, no longer possessed of their domestic hearths, relatives, or friends? How resist the thought of the misery of the poor apothecary, who had lost his all beneath the stones, and was reduced to beggary? Here was the small proprietor, whose sole fortune consisted of a few houses; there, close to the ruins of a café, its former master, deprived of bread and hope. Such was the picture presented to us when we had already wept over the fate of other districts more or less afflicted. Alas! the sole comfort which the mind can feel amid such misery, is the consideration of the clemency of the prince, and the sympathy of those persons who contributed to the relief of the unfortunate people. The victims of Melfi exceeded 700; among these were several prisoners killed by the fall of the prison; others were pardoned by our monarch on his arrival in this region, blessed and thanked by the people for his wise arrangements and liberal succour. Little different from that of Melfi was the fate of Rapolla and Bariele; it is true, that a greater number of buildings were left standing, but if closely observed, they are found with fallen roofs, or tottering walls, or such injuries as render them unsafe, and dangerous. The rock on which they are built is the same, that is, volcanic tufa. About Bariele, many caves are excavated in the rock, the first habitations of an Albanese colony which settled there, and which now serve as a shelter to the houseless. Both these towns stand partly on the summit of hills, or rather hillocks, at the base of Vulture, and partly on the declivity. The houses on the heights are the most injured, perhaps owing to their greater

[*] Copper-plate to original Report.

age. Rapolla, though nearer to Melfi than Barile, appears at first to have suffered less, but when the matter is more closely investigated this is seen to be an illusion, owing its origin to the circumstance that some of the walls, especially of the houses in the environs, are yet standing; in reality, it has suffered greatly. Among the fallen buildings in Rapolla, the cathedral, a structure in the Norman style, especially attracted our attention; its steeple had been partly destroyed in the earthquake of 1694, and afterwards restored, as an inscription still legible on the wall attests. We subjoin an accurate sketch of this church, one among the many destroyed by this earthquake, made by Achille Flauti, architect.

Barile, although more populous than Rapolla, possessed no remarkable monuments, except a beautiful altar, with corresponding marble balustrade, in the fallen Church of Madonna delle Grazie, which has been taken away and restored in another place, by order of the Commissioners, appointed by the king, to inquire into the injuries of the churches, to provide for the necessities of the population, and procure them the divine comforts of religion. The earthquake here, as at Melfi, was first vertical, and then undulating. Some observed at the moment, an unusual light in the rooms, occasioned, probably, by the alternate opening and closing of the walls, for a hen was found on a terrace with both her legs locked between the joints of the pavement which had opened, and closed again, like the ground at P. M. Acanzio, in the earthquake of Calabria, in 1783. There were about 120 deaths in Barile, exclusive of those who were dangerously wounded; and about 70 in Rapolla.*

Rionero, also situated at the base of Vulture, on a gentle declivity, about four miles distant from Melfi, in a direct line, lost with some of its churches, nearly the third part of its houses; the rest also were more or less injured. It is remarkable that in some places the ruins are crowded together; this is mostly observable in the low part of the town, the region of deaths. The victims of Rionero were 64, exclusive of the wounded. Here, too, the earthquake was first vertical, and then horizontal: and from the 14th of August, to dawn on the 15th, quite as many shocks were perceptible as at Melfi.

* The population of Barile is 5000; that of Rapolla, 3200.

Atella, situated at the very outskirts of Vulture, almost at the limit of the volcanic formation, about six miles from Melfi, and a mile and a half south of Rionero, having declined in prosperity, as we have already stated, contained but 1,000 inhabitants. The earthquake was felt here with a force sufficient to destroy some buildings, and greatly injure others. The ceiling of the Church of St. Lucia fell in, and upon a wall which had been covered by a recent building, a fresco, the work of no common artist, was found: it probably belonged to the seventeenth century, although some attributed it to the fourteenth, and some to a still earlier date; but from the dress of the people represented, and the manifest allusion to a past calamity similar to the present disaster, we are inclined to think that it is a record of the earthquake of 1694, in which it appears Atella suffered greatly. In this picture, the Deity is represented as about to let loose the thunderbolts of his justice, on a people seeking refuge beneath the cloak of the Virgin, at whose intercession the thunders are restrained. It justly attracted the attention of our august sovereign, who visited this place to relieve the wants of its terrified population, and who not only commanded its safety until the repair of the church, but desired the renowned fresco-painter, Pompeiano Pasquale Abate, to proceed to Atella and make a correct copy.

The nuns of Atella were able to remain in their dwelling, although it was greatly injured, and were not compelled to emigrate like those of Melfi.

Proceeding from Rionero to Bariele, the east side of Vulture terminates in a ravine through which the small river Olivento flows. The Macigno formation reappears on the opposite bank, which rises with a considerable slope; here stand Ripacandida opposite Rionero, distant about a mile and a half in a direct line, and Ginestra opposite Bariele, at about the same distance. Both these towns suffered not only less than Bariele, which was destroyed, but much less than Rionero, and perhaps also than Atella. This is proved not only from the smaller number of dwellings which were injured, but from the less number of perceptible shocks on the 14th of August, and following night. In fact, the shock of the 14th instant, felt by all in Rionero, was but just perceived by a few in Ripacandida. In Rionero, as in Melfi, eleven shocks were enumerated during the nights of the 14th and 15th; but in Ripacandida only five, of which I was assured by Father Giacinto Schiro among others. The highest part of this townland suffered the most; two houses, two stories high, were shaken down. It was necessary finally to throw down one-fifth of the buildings, amongst which was the Convent delle Teresiane. The rest escaped with slight injuries. In this village of 2,500 souls, there was but one victim—a woman. Ginestra, a small territory near Bariele, suffered even less than Ripacandida, owing probably to the small elevation of the low tenements. No death occurred, and two houses only were found in a dangerous condition. The rock on which it is built is sandstone, while Ripacandida is built on large pebble conglomerate.

The inhabitants of this village describing the horizontal motion, compared it to the opening and closing of the ground. At Monteverde, all unanimously agree that the earthquake commenced with a loud noise from west of north, followed immediately by the vertical and then the horizontal motion. A fifth of the buildings suffered much injury; amongst these the cathedral, but many of the edifices were previously in a bad state. A mother escaping with a child in her arms, was struck by a stone, which caused her to let fall the child, and as she stooped to raise it, a wall fell and buried both beneath its ruins. A hill to the north of Monteverde, called Lavagna, formed of large pebble conglomerate, was deeply rent on the east side. The losses in Carbonara were somewhat less than those in Monteverde. The cathedral, a beautiful building, was opened in two places in the roof. None perished in the ruins. We were assured that for more than a week the sparrows were not seen or heard, chirping round the walls. Monteverde stands on a steep hill of Macigno formation, Carbonara, on sub-Apennine marl, and large pebble conglomerate. On a lovely hill of the same formation covered with vines and olives, about eight miles east of Melfi, stands Venosa, the birthplace of Horace, reminding us how justly that famous poet doubted, whether he should call himself an Apulian or Lucanian, for truly, Venosa as well as Lavello appear to be cities of Puglia, the warm breezes moderating the climate of all that part of the district of Melfi on which the earthquake exerted its baneful power, and causing it to abound with exquisite fruits, grapes, and olives. At the foot of the hill on which Venosa stands, flows the ancient Danao, now called Fiumara. The earthquake of the 14th of August did much injury to this famous and ancient city of 9,000 souls. The public buildings, churches, university, Episcopal Palace, and Mansion House were all thrown down, left tottering, or greatly injured; and the traveller beholds with especial sorrow the injuries of the Church of the Holy Trinity, which belonged to the old Benedictine monastery, whose rich abbey passed into the hands of the Knights of Jerusalem.

In this church is the tomb of Roberto Guiscardi, and his wife Aberada.*

In the tomb of Guiscardi, opposite Aberada's, the ashes of William of the Iron Arm, Drogone, and some others are inclosed, as we learn from a half-effaced inscription:—

> "Drogone comitum comiti ducum duci hu-
> jus sacri templi instauratori Guilielmo
> Regi Roberto Guiscardo Normanno
> Restauratori fratribus, ac eorum suc-
> cessoribus quorum ossa hic sita sunt."

Next to it the Fathers had commenced a splendid tomb of large hewn stone, (taken, perhaps, from the amphitheatre at Venosa,) which they had not time to finish, but which, incomplete as it is, awakens the admiration of the traveller, who beholds an important work of art of the fourteenth century. A painting on one of the pillars in the nave of this church, represents the pope giving the benediction, and beneath is written—

> "Papa Nicolaus
> Hoc sacrum Templum consecravit
> Anno Domini MLVIII."

The Castle of Venosa, built with great solidity, suffered no important injury. It is a work of the age of Alphonso of Aragon,

---

* On the tomb of Aberada is the following legend:—
> "Guiscardi Conjux Alerada hac conditur arca
> Si genitum quæris hunc casaninus habet."

and was built by Pirro of Balzo, who, according to Fontana, taking part with Ferdinand, the son of Alphonsus, opposed the Duke of Tarento, who fought against the former.*

The private dwellings in Venosa suffered considerably, but only four persons were killed, two in the house of Signor Calvino (before mentioned), one monk, and one student.

Lavello, as well as Venosa, is built on a hill of large pebble conglomerate. This hill terminates on the east and south in a precipice and abrupt descent.

The losses of Lavello may be compared with those of Venosa. The largest church was partially thrown down, and the others, S. Antonio, S. Maria del Principio, S. Anna de' Cappucini, and S. Giovanni were either thrown down or greatly injured.

The suburban church of Madonna della Speranza is greatly injured, and another named of the forest (*detta della foresta*) is completely ruined. A great many houses have been more or less damaged, and the injury has been estimated at 30,000 ducats. Three of the buildings fell on the 14th of August, but it was necessary to pull down fifty. A young girl aged eleven years perished under the ruins. The country-houses, in the district of Lavello did not escape devastation and ruin. In one denominated Cozzetto, about two miles from Lavello, four persons from Rionero perished. With the losses of Lavello we may compare those of Canosa, Ascoli, and Candela, and avoid the repetition of fallen churches and ruined dwellings.†

* The accomplished professor in the College of Venosa, D. Raffaelo Smith, collected much information for us relative to the history of this city and its monuments; but we do not like to deviate from our intention of giving a simple narrative of facts which solely concern the earthquake.

† In Canosa attention is especially attracted to the injuries inflicted on the cathedral, an important memento of mediæval art, not a little remarkable for the circumstance that the remains of Boemondo are interred there.

No. (3.)

Translations of all Notices of the Earthquake of 16th December, 1857, and of those occurring soon after, which are to be found in the several Numbers whose dates are given, of the " Giornale del Regno delle Due Sicilie." Published at Naples.

No. 35.   Naples, 17th December.

LAST night about ten minutes past ten o'clock this city was visited by two severe shocks of earthquake, a brief interval occurring between them. God be praised, we have sustained no injury. Terror urged the greater portion of the population to assemble in open places, but there was no disturbance of public order. We have received the same account from Caserta, Nola, Aversa, Pozzuoli, Salerno, and Avellino, in which places, except the alarm of the inhabitants, we have no disasters to deplore, nor have we heard of any breach of order.

As to the Principato Citeriore, Eboli and Campagna experienced the shocks with greater intensity, and a house has been knocked down in the latter, but no personal injuries are reported. The telegram from Salerno adds that no answers have been received from Sala, Lagonegro, or the Calabrias, notwithstanding the repeated inquiries from that station. But whatever may be the cause of this interruption we have learned that even in Paola the shocks were felt and were harmless. In Castellammare two persons of the lower order escaping by a ladder from an apartment where they were sleeping with others, fell, and received some slight injuries. The telegraphic despatch is here interrupted.

We have just received the following letter from the director of the astronomical observatory of Capodimonte:—

"Naples, 17th December.

"Sir,

"I hasten to inform you that last night at ten minutes after ten o'clock, French time, a shock of earthquake took place which lasted about four or five seconds; two minutes afterwards another shock of much greater intensity occurred, which lasted about 25 seconds. They were both ondulatory, and proceeded from the south to the north. The severity of the second shock was apparent from the circumstance that two pendulum clocks belonging to this observatory, which were oscillating in the direction of the prime vertical, were stopped, but three others were not affected. The foundation of the tower in which our equatorial instrument is placed also sustained injury. We were also conscious of three successive, but slight shocks, at three and at five in the morning, lasting about a second."

December 13.—To continue the sad report which has just reached us from Principato Citeriore relative to the earthquake. We must repeat that the telegraph from Eboli to Sala has been interrupted, and that the accounts which have reached us from the second of these communes are most distressing. Trusting that the facts are exaggerated, we shall communicate them as we have received them; and it is our painful duty to state that three deaths have occurred in Sala, and that the district prison, the barracks, and other buildings are injured; in Atena, half of the houses are shattered; in Padula, more than a hundred houses have been injured, and the number of deaths is unknown; in Polla, the disasters are immense, and the victims numerous, among which the brigade of gendarmes, the belfry and church of Saldina, near Salerno, are injured; two ladies killed. In Campagna many houses are destroyed, including that of the Sub-intendant.

We have this moment received a telegraphic despatch from the Intendant of Basilicata, informing us that much damage has been done in Potenza, many houses being thrown down, and an unknown number of people buried beneath the ruins. We have learned that two shocks were felt in the city of Bari, and but one, and that harmless, in Campobasso. The telegram from Bari is incomplete. It runs thus: "The greater part of the inhabitants are——." The passengers who arrived this morning in the "Duke of Calabria" assure us that the earthquake was felt in Calabria, but no injury sustained. We rejoice to add that this holds good of Cosenza and all Calabria Citeriore.

December 19.—The despatch from Bari this morning informs us that the two shocks of earthquake caused no other damage but the injury of the police barrack, and the terror which makes the greater portion of the inhabitants spend the night in the open air. From Foggia, Trani, Manfredonia, and Lucera, we have the same comforting assurances.

To the sad details of the deplorable disasters which have occurred in the district of Sala, we add those which have arrived of a less serious nature from the district of Campagna. Ricigliano appears to have suffered the most, for two deaths are reported, besides the fall of ten poor houses, from the ruins of which five or six persons were saved. Two more were saved in S. Gregorio and two in Duccino. In Caposelo a man had his leg broken, and a child in Penarchia met with a similar accident. In many other communes of the district, injured buildings and churches are reported, and in S. Gregorio the cupola of the choir fell in. The return of the earthquake is everywhere dreaded. A second despatch from Potenza informs us that the telegraph is adjusted; shocks are still felt there, but less frequent and less hurtful. The injuries are very serious.

We have just heard that two harmless shocks of earthquake were felt in Salerno this morning, one at six and the other at ten A. M.

We had written so far when the details of the sad disasters which have befallen the unhappy city of Potenza, where no house is uninjured, arrived. The palaces of the Intendant and the tribunals, the civil and military hospital, the quarters of the gendarmerie, the college, the churches, the cathedral have received such injuries as render them totally unsafe. All were employed up to the date of the official report, the 17th instant, in excavating the interred, the number of whom was unknown. The population who had passed the fatal night in the open air are seeking shelter in the sheds which have been hastily erected. Most distressing are the reports from other communes of the province. Tito, Maricconnuovo, Laurenzana, and Brienza are almost destroyed. Two-thirds of the inhabitants of Vignola have perished, and the rest are badly hurt. Melfi, which suffered so much before, has no deaths to lament, nor Avigliano. The injuries in Viggiano, Calvello, Anzi, and Abriola are great, and the terror and despair of the inhabitants still greater.

A telegraphic despatch from the Calabrias informs us that the earthquake was almost imperceptible in Cantanzaro and but little felt in Reggio.

No. 279.   Naples, 21st December.

Dark, beyond all description, are the particulars of the disasters which have occurred in the two provinces of Principato Citeriore and Basilicata, where the destructive violence of the earthquake of the night of the 16th and 17th of this month appears to have been concentrated. With the deepest grief we continue to relate them in the same order and manner in which they reached us, careless of everything but the manifestation of the simple truth. First of all, we grieve to state that up to the 18th instant, nineteen dead bodies had been disinterred at Potenza, and it is feared that many more are beneath the ruins. Three hundred have been exhumed in Polla. Il Caporale di Gendarmeria Montefusco, was taken out alive. In Sapouara, the Royal Judge—thanks to the prompt assistance of his colleague, of Moliterno—was disinterred alive, but the unhappy man is left to mourn his wife and two sons, buried under the same ruins from which he had been extricated, bruised, and lamed. Lagonegro experienced three shocks in the space of seven hours. None of the inhabitants perished, but the greater portion of the buildings, both public and private, were more or less injured, and three of them destroyed, among which are the church of P. P. Cappuccini and the electric station. The shocks continued until yesterday, but infrequent and slight, and the entire population was assembled under the sheds which had been hastily erected in the great plain which surrounds the town, whither all had fled on that disastrous night. In the Commune of Carbone twenty-one dead and seventeen wounded are reported, as well as serious injuries to the dwellings. Castelsano is almost levelled to the ground, and 400 persons have perished. Sarconi is almost as bad, except that there are but thirty dead. The buildings in Chirico Raparo are destroyed, and four dead are reported. Maratea is partly destroyed, but only one death ascertained. The other communes of the district of Lagonegro, which have sustained injuries to the buildings, particularly to the churches, and where no deaths are reported, are Maratea, Lauria, Castellucio, upper and lower, Rotunda, Vigianello, Sant' Arcangelo, Calvera, San Martino, Castronuovo, and Senise. We have as yet learned nothing of the other communes in the same district. With these sad details we have also received a report of the efforts made by the local authorities to alleviate, as far as possible, the effects of this shocking calamity. L'Intendente di Potenza, with a zeal, activity, and foresight deserving of every praise, although compelled to work in the midst of ruins, has made without delay all the arrangements which necessity requires, among which we must mention the establishment of a central commission at head quarters, and other commissions in the various suffering districts to provide for every need. The first of these commissions consists of the Intendant himself, the bishop, &c. &c.

A similar commission has been appointed by the Intendant in the uninjured districts, to collect such offerings as the humanity of the well-disposed and generous will supply for the relief of the sufferers in this calamity. These offerings will be promptly and prudently used for the construction of temporary shelter for the wounded, the demolition of tottering buildings, the clearance of the streets, &c. And the sub-commissions are enjoined (if necessary) to have recourse to the central commission for supplies, and to pay and support their operatives.

No. 280. Naples, 22nd December.

The mind recoils from the enumeration of the calamities which now move all hearts; and we the more abhor our task as the new reports exceed beyond measure those already received. We ascribed the mournful sum of deaths in Polla to the inaccuracy which confusion entails, but a telegraphic despatch from the Intendant of Salerno, who has gone there, confirms the fatal intelligence, and asserts that the number amounts to upwards of 2000, and that the men are still engaged in disinterring the victims of this awful scourge. After Polla the communes of Pertosa, Atena, and Aulotta have sustained the greatest injuries. The first two and Polla are completely destroyed, and the last is little better. Padula and San Pietro occupy the third grade in this mournful division, and Sala, Diano, Sassano, Montesano, S. Arsenio and Supri the fourth. The entire number of deaths in these districts is 2600.

To moderate the consternation which these particulars must excite, we hasten to add that when the large bounty of our pious sovereign was announced to the unhappy survivors, an unanimous " Viva il Re" burst from them. Sheds have been erected everywhere to receive the unfortunate individuals who had passed nights in the open air, and who would have suffered greatly but for the mildness of the weather. Buildings have also been constructed for offices, and the celebration of divine service, which till now has been performed in the street or under unsuitable shelter. Ovens have been built where required, and it is consoling to learn that besides the relief bestowed by his Majesty's command, the communes have assisted each other by that law of Providence in virtue of which men are more charitable in time of misfortune. Physicians, nurses, and the consolations of religion are to be had everywhere. The wounded and ill, the bruised and lamed receive supplies of blankets, linen, and medicine. Provisions abound, thanks to the generous charity of the sovereign, so that yesterday many barrels of flour, as well as leeches and medicine, were in readiness to proceed from Principato Citeriore to Brienza, in the Commune of Basilicata. To these necessaries were added prepared meal, cheese, and other comforts. A means of relief of the highest importance, owing to the inclement season, is about to be sent to the aid of the unfortunate. Within a very few hours all those who are unsheltered will receive the bounty of our adored sovereign, who has commanded all the military tents to be forwarded to them.

Two thousand tents are on the way for the relief of two thousand families.*

With respect to the lesser disasters of the Basilicata, we have learned that in Melfi a child perished under the ruins of a stable; the half-dilapidated tower of the Church of S. Augustin was thrown down; the Casa Communale, and the house of the Sub-intendant, with almost all the buildings, were injured; one house and a great many walls fell, and the Agrarian Institute and the Meteorological Observatory were disfigured.

In Bariele many houses were shaken, and two deaths and two wounded men are reported; in Atella the greater number of the houses are shattered; and in Venosa, the roof of the Church of S. Francesco, and one of the castle towers were destroyed. As to the Principato Citeriore, the lesser injuries are those of Vallo, where the small belfry of S. Catherine fell, and many buildings were disfigured, and a physician and his wife injured by the fall of a wall. The prison at Matera was slightly injured, and many houses greatly disfigured. No deaths ascertained in Majori and Minori. In the latter, many buildings were destroyed and a house fell. In Tramonti, a man and his daughter were found dead under the ruins of an old house, notwithstanding the rapidity with which they were dug out. Official reports have arrived from the province of Terra di Bari relative to the damage occasioned by the recent shocks of earthquake. The districts of Barletti and of Altamura have only suffered from the terror occasioned by the earthquake; in the former, the oratory of the Arciconfraternita del S. S., erected in S. Pietro, and in the latter, some more ancient edifices fell. The most deplorable disasters occurred in Canosa, where five persons were excavated from the ruins after life was extinct; but thanks to the activity of the local authorities, many others were saved. Several churches have sustained slight injuries.

The Province of Principato Ulteriore has not suffered positive damage, except the injuries to the buildings in the different communes. In Serino a lady, escaping from her house, had her leg broken by the fall of an old ruinous wall: the belfry of a church was also thrown down. In Solofra and S. Michael the greater

* It is impossible to avoid saying that by far the greater part of these statements are absolute and audacious figments.—R. M.

number of the churches were injured. The province of Abruzzo Ulteriore Secondo, where the earthquakes of the night of the 10th were felt with diminished violence, is, God be praised, uninjured. The same comforting assurances have reached us from Capitanata, Molise, and the Three Calabrias. In the district of Taranto some private houses are reported injured, in particular the church of P. P. Domenicani and the Seminario Arcivescovile. The Church of the Cappuccinelli, the palace of the archbishop, and the Chiesa Madre in the Commune of Acquaviva.

No. 263.   Naples, 20th December.

Although we have received numerous accounts of the calamities of Potenza, and the communes of that province, they are still incomplete and unsatisfactory, partly because the attention of the authorities has been occupied in relieving the unfortunate survivors, and preventing further accident from the fall of tottering buildings, and partly because accurate details cannot be obtained at a time of general agitation, when every day develops the extent of desolation and adds to the number of disinterred victims. Therefore, instead of repeating with some difference the particulars we have already given, we shall confine ourselves to matters that have not yet been spoken of, and for the benefit of history and science, state that in Potenza the two shocks felt upon that fatal night were of equal duration, and that the first was preceded and accompanied by a fearful noise, whilst the sky was clear and the air tranquil. The first shock was undulatory and up and down (*sussultorio*), but that which followed about three minutes after (as far as the time could be ascertained, when every second appeared a century), added, to more violent undulations and upheavings, a rotatory and jerking motion; for the walls were thrown upside down, and the heavier furniture moved from its position and tossed about as if in a whirlpool, whilst lighter articles, kitchen utensils and crockery, were thrown to a distance. The great projectile force (of shock) is known to any who have read the descriptions of the earthquakes of Lisbon, Murcia, Valencia, and Guadaloupe, but especially that which devastated Calabria in 1783, destroying in a moment more than a hundred communes, with the loss of upwards of 30,000 people.

The reader can imagine the fate of all the buildings in Potenza at the second shock of earthquake, during which the tottering habitations were falling against each other. We have already mentioned the principal injuries done to the public buildings; we now add that the victims (twenty-one according to the last official report), all belonging to the labouring classes, people who were unlikely to be awake at the hour the catastrophe occurred, especially in the provinces. From what we have said of Potenza, it is easy to conceive what must have been the shock, and the noise, in such places as are entirely or almost destroyed. We shall give the remaining details in catalogue form.

Brienza.—The earth opened along the market-place; the buildings were greatly injured. Up to this date a hundred people have been taken from the ruins.

Picerno.—The greater part demolished; eight dead; the houses still left standing are much disfigured.

Pietrafesa.—Many houses thrown down; a few wounded; none dead.

Abriola.—A few huts destroyed; some houses disfigured; one dead and two wounded.

Vignola.—Many buildings disfigured; a great many houses thrown down; others injured; number of deaths unknown.

Marisiconuovo.—About two-thirds of the dwellings destroyed; a large number of deaths, amount unknown.

Calvello.—A heap of ruins; many victims, all not yet disinterred.

Viggiano.—Almost all levelled to the ground; a fire, as in Laurenzana, increased the horrors of the earthquake.

Tricarico.—A few injuries to buildings; no deaths.

Bariele.—Many houses in ruins; two dead; some wounded.

Rionero.—Slight injuries to the buildings.

Montemurro.—Entirely levelled to the ground; a few survivors, and these injured.

Tramutola.—All the dwellings destroyed; a large number of deaths, amount unknown.

Balvano.—Great damage. No deaths.

Moliterno.—All the houses more or less injured, some thrown down; no deaths.

Saponara.—Dwellings entirely destroyed; a few survivors, some of whom are wounded.

Tolve.—A great number of houses disfigured; no deaths.

Bella.—Some damage to the Campanile, the top of which falling injured the church. Fissures in two other churches and some private buildings.

Atella.—Much damage, but no deaths.

Guardia.—A hundred deaths and more wounded. Churches, chapels, and dwellings thrown down.

Matera.—Slight injuries.

Corleto.—Injuries to the buildings; nine dead and more wounded.

Sareoni.—The greater part of the houses thrown down, the rest disfigured. From twenty to thirty deaths already ascertained.

Castelsaraceno.—The greater part fallen. The number of victims great, but unknown.

Montemilone.—Great injuries to the houses and buildings, especially to the church, the roof of which is half destroyed; no deaths.

Muro, S. Fele, Castelgrande, and *Pescopagano* escaped with some damage to the buildings.

Matera.—By permission of the Archbishop, the seminary is dismissed as the building is injured. The nuns of St. Lucia have gone to the Convent of the Annunciation for the same reason; the penitents, especially those who have no friends, have taken refuge in the monastery of S. Chiara.

Ferrandina.—About fifteen houses destroyed, also the town clock, and the roof of the cathedral; injuries more or less severe in the other houses and churches; four deaths.

Salandra.—A few houses destroyed; three deaths; churches and houses injured.

Craco.—Damaged. No death.

We now give the particulars from the Principato Citeriore:—

Cava.—The town hall almost a ruin. No death.

Baronissi.—The prison is injured; the old houses, and especially the churches, have suffered. No death.

Oleverno.—Injuries to some old houses.

S. Arsenio.—A few houses destroyed; two persons have perished.

Ottati.—Very slight injuries to almost all the houses.

Nocera, infriore and superiore.—Many houses falling, also the churches. No death.

Pagani.—Scarcely perceptible damage done.

S. Giorgio, Siano, and *Bracigliano.*—Considerable injury to the churches and houses.

Amalfi, Vietri, and *S. Valentino.*—Uninjured.

Pertosa.—Seventy bodies have been disinterred, and it is believed the victims amount to 300. Forty have been taken out alive from the ruins.

Sacco and Piagine Lottane.—Escaped with the fall of a wall or two.

Laurino.—In the mountain of Vesalo, four miles from the town, a large boulder (*macigno*) fell and killed a man who was asleep in a rick and injured his companion severely.

Torreoruoja.—The walls of two houses fell, also a portion of the belfry.

Mojo.—The roof of a house fell, carrying away part of a room and a child who escaped uninjured.

Borgo.—Village of S. John at Piro. The roof of the recently built parish church fell. The walls are standing, but are all split.

No. 284.   Naples, 28th December.

The consoling news of the safety of the inhabitants of the Capitana has been confirmed. The public and private buildings only have been injured.

The communes of Cagnano, Montesantangelo, Casaltrinita, Pictra, Scoina, and Vicsti have only suffered from the terror of the double shock. In Itcali Saline no house is demolished, but many are injured.

In Orta, also, the royal parish church and that of the Purgatorio are injured.

As to the province of Bari; in Trani, the house of the Procurator-general is injured. In Gioja, the (Tempio di Patronato Communale) Church of the Patron Saint, the Church of the Franciscans, and that of the Purgatorio are injured; the roof of the latter is much split. The barracks also have suffered. In Spinazzola many old uninhabited houses fell, others were injured, especially the barrack.

In Altamura, Gravina, S. Eramo, a few houses suffered damage, especially the barracks of the two first communes.

In Nori, the town hall was injured.

In continuation of what we said of the commune of Canosa, we add, that besides the five deaths there were eight wounded; 155 houses greatly injured, and twelve thrown down. Among the churches which have suffered are the convent and church of S. Francis, and the Chiesa del Purgatorio.

No. 286.   Naples, 30th December, 1857.

Saso.—Thirty houses demolished and 100 injured; only three deaths; eleven persons have been taken out alive from the ruins.

Spinosa.—Few houses left standing, and those are tottering and injured.

Gallicchio.—Sixteen deaths, a great many wounded, and several with broken bones.

Genzana.—A part of the church called Le Grazie has fallen; two houses slightly injured.

Trivigno.—Some houses demolished.

Ruoti.—The belfry fell and much injured the church. Some small chapels fallen.

Vaglio.—The church is partly *fallen* and partly *falling*. Many private houses are demolished.

Ilaragiano.—A few houses have fallen and others are injured.

Salvia.—Slight injuries to the church and belfry.

Latronico.—Much damage, but no deaths. The church is falling.

Stigliano.—Several houses fallen and others injured. A woman was taken out alive, but hurt from the ruins; a child bruised.

Anzi.—Much injury to the houses, both in the town and in the country. One death.

Pietrapertosa.—The cathedral, the other churches, the campanile, and the houses much injured. Enormous stones split, and detached themselves from the mountain.

Ferrandina.—Fifteen houses entirely demolished. Churches

and more houses injured. Two people were killed, and two children suffocated in the confusion.

Aliano.—Many injuries and eleven deaths.

Alianello.—Completely destroyed. Forty-two deaths.

Craco.—The buildings injured. One death.

Montemurro.—We have already said that this place is but a heap of stones. More than a thousand people have perished. We have the consolation of knowing that some were taken alive from the ruins eight days after the fatal night.

Marsico.—Entirely destroyed. It is computed, at present, that 400 have perished.

Castelsaraceno.—The houses have all fallen. The church and monastery are tottering. The deaths exceed 400. A lady and infant were saved from the ruins, a young girl of fourteen years, and several others.

Sarconi.—The number of deaths does not exceed thirty; but the buildings are levelled to the ground.

Maratea.—A great number of the buildings demolished.

Lauria, Castelluccio, &c.—Great damage to the public and private buildings.

Sacco, Licusati, &c.—The buildings more or less injured, but no deaths.

Matera, &c.—More or less injury to the houses, but no deaths.

Salandra.—Forty houses demolished; the rest more or less injured and falling. One body has been disinterred. The Syndic reports that for about a month a gas was observed to issue from a ditch filled with running water, about two miles from the town. The gas was of sun heat. A few days ago at twenty paces distant, the like gas was observed to exhale from a similar ditch. It was only perceptible in the morning hours, and disappeared during the rest of the day. On the 22nd instant this exhalation entirely ceased. It is believed that a spring of thermal waters has its issue here.

Grassano.—About 100 houses fallen; all the other buildings are more or less injured. A young girl of fifteen years of age was killed, and a lady had her leg broken.

Grottola.—Some houses fallen; the rest injured badly. One death.

No. 287. Naples, 31st December, 1857.

Sorrowful details arrive every day from the regions of this calamity. In the district of Sala, the shocks continue, less severe during the day than during the night, and each is preceded by an alarming noise. On the 28th, at 0 P.M., and on the 29th, at 0 and ½ past 7 P.M., three strong shocks of earthquake took place, each of from 10 to 12 seconds' duration, and followed by others less intense. At Potenza, also, on the evening of the 20th at 0¾, a strong shock of undulatory earthquake was felt, followed by others less severe during the night. They were all harmless, but at the first the people who were in the houses, fled out into the open spaces.

No. 1. 2nd January, 1858.

In continuation of the accounts relative to the effects of the earthquake of the 16th December, we state that on the 23rd two ladies and two children were taken alive from the ruins in Montemurro, having been buried seven days.

In Muro, Rionero, S. Fole, and Castelgrandine, no positive damage is to be deplored, only injuries to private dwellings. In Pescopagano one house fell; but no death occurred.

We have received the following particulars relative to the disasters in Canosa:—

The number of buildings entirely destroyed, is eleven: of those injured and falling, ninety-six. In a house in the Strada S. Giacomo two children were disinterred, one dead, the other alive.

In another house in the Strada Carozzo, six were extricated alive, one perished. In another house in the same street, three were taken out badly hurt, two perished. A woman was killed by the fall of a house in the Strada Forte.

Ruvo suffered no injury. The Syndic reports that on the morning of the 7th of December, about 13 o'clock, Italian time, a report like the explosion of a mine in a closed place was heard by all the inhabitants, the greater part of whom were yet in bed; a momentary shock of earthquake followed.

No injury occurred in the communes of Castellabate and Castelnuovo (Principato Citeriore). The buildings in the environs of Laurino suffered.

In the commune of Bella, about two miles from the town, in the district Carlotta d'Isca, the earthquake of the 10th December levelled hills, upturned ground, formed valleys. Half an hour before the shocks, a light like that of the moon was observed in this region, and a fetid vapour smelling like sulphur was perceptible. The double shock was felt here, and the noise heard, and the next morning an area of about six hundred moggia of tilled land was found surrounded by a furrow from ten to thirty palms in depth and the same in breadth.

No. 2. Naples, 4th January.

From the last accounts of the district of Castellammare, we find that in the island of Capri alone was the earthquake not felt; that in the commune of Gragnano, a great many buildings were injured; and in the village of Sigliano, some houses were partly thrown down, and a young man endeavouring to escape, by jumping from a wall was hurt, but not severely; that in Pimonte the roof and façade of the cathedral were injured, and the house of one Antonio Donnarumma in falling, buried him, his wife, and two children, who were all disinterred alive and unhurt. By a report of the same date, we learn that in Ottajano, the church of S. Michael was greatly injured, and that of S. John the Baptist slightly so.

We have received from the Intendant of the province of Terra d'Otranto the following particulars relative to the effects of the earthquake of the 10th December, in the communes of that province, in which, by God's mercy, we have no deaths to deplore. In Taranto, considerable injuries to the façade of the church of S. Domenico, to that of Mount Olivet, and of S. Antonio outside of the city. Several other buildings received injuries. The private buildings in Palagiano have received insignificant injuries; the church suffered slightly. The same in Castellaneta. In the communes of Laterza and Ginosa the shock was more violent. In the first, the church belfry was so shaken, that had it not been secured for some time with iron chain bars, it would surely have fallen on that disastrous night, and occasioned great loss of life. Many houses have suffered considerably. In Ginosa the injuries were more important; twenty-six private houses were more or less destroyed. The town hall, and the residence of the royal judge, suffered not a little, several of the chambers being rendered uninhabitable.

No. 7. 11th January.

Nothing in this number of the 'Giornale' except the incidental mention of 200 people having been taken alive from the ruins of Polla. The columns are filled with an account of the "Royal beneficence" for the relief of the sufferers, &c.

No. 48. 4th March.

The unhappy survivors at Montemurro, were alarmed on the 26th of last month, three hours before dawn, and again at daybreak, by so strong a shock of earthquake that they fled in terror from their sheds. They were a prey to greater consternation, when they learned from some countrymen, that the earth had opened and closed again, during both shocks. No bad news, except terror, which, however, is a great misfortune to people who have suffered so much. At the first of these hours (three hours before dawn) a severe shock was felt at Viggiano, when some walls fell, but no other damage occurred.

Balvano also experienced a slight shock on the 23rd, and on the same day, just as night was setting in, two subterranean reports like those of a cannon of great calibre, were heard in Saponara, on interval of thirty seconds between them. The inhabitants fled from their sheds in great alarm, and assembled in the chapel to pray. After these remarks, it is unnecessary to mention the slight shocks which have been felt in other places of the Basilicata, not excepting Potenza.

No. 62. Naples, 9th March.

On the night of the 6th March, three somewhat prolonged but harmless shocks of earthquake, were felt in Lagonegro. On the following day, at 3 P.M., two much more violent shocks each of from nine to ten seconds' duration occurred; another shorter one at 8 p.m.; and at 5 a.m. on the 7th, another more severe shock of from five to six seconds' duration. Although the buildings suffered no little damage, we have nothing to lament but the consternation of the people.

No. 55. Naples, 12th March.

Two undulatory shocks of earthquake were felt at Salerno, the first at 50 minutes after 2 p.m., on Sunday the 7th instant, and the second after midnight on the following Monday: both harmless, like all those which we have noticed during the last few days.

No. 57. Naples, 15th March.

About an hour and a quarter after midnight, on the 7th instant, another shock of earthquake, at first susultatory, and then undulatory, was felt, slightly at Potenza, but severely enough in many of the other communes of that province. In Tramutola it completely demolished the buildings, before tottering, but occasioned no death. In Montemurro, the shock was felt an hour earlier, but there are no new victims to deplore.

No. 60. Naples, 19th March.

We are grieved to announce that the shocks of earthquake still continue, in the province of Principato Citra. After the very severe one of the night of the 7th at Salerno, which we mentioned in the journal of the 12th ultimo, another, still more severe, took place about half past 20 or 21 o'clock, Italian time, that day, and terrified the inhabitants of the different communes of that province, who considered it equal in intensity, to the second which occurred on the night of the 16th December. Many slight shocks followed, during the night, especially in the two communes of Vibonati, and Sapri. These shocks were all preceded by fearful noises. Sapri, Casaletto, and Vibonati, have suffered more or less damage, especially the two first, where several houses were demolished. In the first of these communes, a young girl and a child were injured, by the falling of the beams of a building, but their recovery is hoped for. The population ran to the churches to implore Divine aid.

and the authorities are zealously engaged with the necessary repairs.

No. 66.   Naples, 27th March.

On the 23rd of this month, about 2 o'clock P. M., four shocks of earthquake were felt at La Sala, but all harmless. On the same day, and at the same hour, shocks were felt in Potenza, preceded by a slighter shock at 10 A. M. These shocks have been so frequent, (sometimes susultatory, and sometimes undulatory,) in the two provinces, that one can scarcely say that they have ever ceased, since the day which was so disastrous, to them. On the 17th, they affirm that the earth trembled incessantly, although not alarmingly or destructively.

No. 82.   Naples, 17th April.

On the morning of the 10th instant, about 8, 9, and 10 o'clock, three shocks of earthquake, were felt in Reggio, the two first, brief and slight, the other, longer and more severe. In Palmi, a commune of the same province, at a quarter past 11, and at half past 13, Italian time, of the 8th instant, two brief, but rather severe susultatory shocks were felt. They were all harmless. A slight shock, preceded by a loud noise, was felt in Rodi, in the province of Capitanata, on the 13th March.

No. (4.)

To his Excellency Signor Bianchini, Minister of the Interior, &c., Kingdom of Naples.

Naples, 3rd March, 1858.

MON SIGNORE,

It is an object of high importance to the advancement of terrestrial physics, to determine with rigid accuracy, the extent of elevation or of depression, which large tracts of land are thought to undergo, when, as in the kingdom of Naples, exposed to volcanic influences from beneath. Nowhere in Europe, do circumstances so favourable for such observation, and so precious to science, exist, as around Naples and especially at the Temple of Serapis, already the subject of much investigation in this respect. Unfortunately, however, nearly all determinations of level hitherto attempted in this region, are comparatively valueless, because the only fixed datum possible, as that whereby changes of level in the land should be determined, has been the assumed mean level of the tide, in the Bay of Naples. But from the very small rise and fall of the tides here, and the great perturbations to which they are liable from changes of direction and force of wind, &c., such affords no certain fixed datum whatever, from which to measure changes of level.

To establish, therefore, in their stead, a fixed datum, which should become the standard to which hereafter all scientific levels could be referred, (and to which, also, all levels of public works might be referred, if thought proper by Government,) would be a work, at once worthy of his Majesty the King, highly promotive of European science, and valuable hereafter, even for civil purposes, within the kingdom of Naples.

I take leave to suggest for this end, that his Majesty the King, should cause a line of instrumental levelling, to be carried along the high road, from Rome to Naples, with the necessary care to insure accuracy, starting from the sill of the great door of St. Peter's Church at Rome, as the nearest presumably fixed and invariable point of level, and ending at the Palace of Naples, or at some other determinate point, in or near the capital, and there, as well as at intermediate points, to be permanently marked upon blocks of stone. To this line, or to some of its intermediate points, the changeable levels of Serapis, and the levels of every other place in the kingdom could, by easy and known methods, be referred when required, and with absolute certainty. The operation itself, of effecting this, would be very inexpensive, and could be performed this present spring season, by either his Majesty's Corps de Génie, or by officers of the Ponte o' Stradi, if appointed for the purpose. Not more than six or eight weeks need be consumed in this work, which, when completed, would cause his Majesty's name to be renowned throughout Europe, for the promotion of science, by a work so important. This datum, once established, should be made to correspond, in his Majesty's kingdom, to the "Ordnance Datum" of our British national surveys.

In these suggestions, I know that I should be supported by the opinion, of all the greatest of European geologists and physicists, as also, I have no doubt, by those of his Majesty's kingdom.

Should his Majesty graciously sanction, the commencement of this work, I should be happy, before quitting Naples, to confer personally with the executive authorities, who may be intrusted with its execution, and to convey to them my views, as to the precautions and conditions necessary, to insure to the result its just value to science.

I have the honour to be,
Signor Commandatore,
Your most obedient Servant,
ROBERT MALLET, F.R.S.,
Mem. Inst. Civil Engineers, of England.

PART III.

DEDUCTIONS AND CONCLUSIONS.

CHAPTER I.

OF THE SUPERFICIAL POSITION OF THE SEISMIC VERTICAL, OR OF THE POINT ON THE SURFACE VERTICALLY ABOVE THE FOCUS.

The two preceding parts, have been necessarily tedious and lengthy, as describing not only the development of a method, but the numerous facts elicited with a view to its application; the colligation of these facts, and the generalizations and conclusions to which they lead, may be more briefly given. I purpose treating them under distinct heads, and first, of the point on the surface vertically above the focus.

Referring to the seismic Map A, transcribed from Zannoni's great map of the Two Sicilies; this map, embracing the whole of the observed country, is laid down upon Mercator's projection, to a uniform scale both in parallel and meridian, of 0·64 inch English, or 0·162 metre French, to the geographical mile, and is divided into squares of ten geographical miles on the side each, and numbered consecutively from Naples Observatory as Zero. The original map by Zannoni was produced between 1809 and 1812, from trigonometrical survey of the chief points, and is generally of great accuracy, and from its large scale (more than half an inch to the English mile) admits of very exact angular protraction and distance measurement.

Upon the seismic Map A, I have laid down, the outline of the coasts, the positions of all the principal towns and villages, distinguishing all those at which seismic observations were made. The isoseismal curves—first, second, third, &c.—are marked respectively, by broken lines, in which the number of consecutive dots, fixes that of the curve it designates. The chief mountain ridges, or summits of chief elevation, are lightly marked in, and lastly, the whole of *the wave-paths*, observed in direction upon the surface, have been *marked with red lines* from each town or place of observation respectively.*

It became necessary in the protracting of these lines of wave-path, which were all observed by the prismatic compass, to have regard to the magnetic declination. The observations made, upon the local declination at various points, and given in Part II., showed that over the whole observed area of country, it did not differ anywhere more than one or two degrees, from the mean declination at Naples; except at one or perhaps two spots, where there appeared to be great local disturbance.

As the most convenient arrangement, therefore, and one

* The reader who is actually engaged in seismic research, should examine the original large charts in possession of the Royal Society, and also compare Zannoni's map, of which one copy is accessible at the Royal Geographical Society, London, and for the use of which the author has to acknowledge having been indebted to the Council of that Society. The necessity of limiting the expense of illustration of this work involved several changes from the originals in the reproduction of these maps, and owing to the great reduction in scale and the methods of colour-printing, some inevitable slight errors have been introduced not to be found in the large charts, all of which make the Maps A and B less demonstrative than the originals, or than the author desired.

not productive of any sensible error in result, all the observed wave-paths are reduced to the true azimuth, from one equal western declination of 14° 30′, and are so laid down.

It was found by trial, that a difference in declination of 1°, would not make, at the mean distance of the places of observation from the seismic vertical, a change of half a mile upon the superficial position of any one of the latter.

It will be obvious at once that the great mass of the wave-paths radiate from Caggiano, or close about it, and hence that from some point beneath the neighbourhood of this village the impulses that produced the earthquake were delivered. In protracting the single line of wave-path marked red, from or through any given point of observation, where more than a single direction had been there observed, the most probable mean direction was adopted. I have taken *the mean* of the extremes, of *observed* angles of azimuths, when equal probability attached to all the observations, *i.e.* when the whole divergence, might be assumed as error of observation; but I have adopted *the most probable*, single wave-path, where obvious and à priori reasons existed for concluding, that local disturbance, due to physical configuration of the adjacent country, or other such causes, had produced partial or secondary waves whose paths should be eliminated. To the circumstances affecting such cases I shall refer again.

Outside the third isoseismic curve, and between Salerno and Naples, a number of wave-paths will be observed, which do not connect themselves directly with the seismic vertical or focus at all. These, due to waves of reflection and refraction of the direct shock, we shall pass for the present also.

GENERAL TABULATION OF

It will be convenient to tabulate here in one view all the separate local observations, of wave-path azimuths, before pointing out what they lead to by the aid of the map.

Wave-Path Observations at all the Stations observed by Compass.

Naples, City	N. 8° E.	
	N. 13° E.	
	N. 6° E.	
	N. 20° W.	} Pausilipo Tunnel.
	N. 38° W.	
Torre del Annunciata	S. to N.	
Castellammare	N. 6° 30' E.	
	N. 12° W.	
Sorrento	S. to N.	
Resina	S. to N.	
Amalfi	N. 133° W.	} And orthogonal.
Atrani	N. 133° W.	
La Cava	N. 15° 30' E.	
	N. to S.	} And orthogonal.
	N. 17° W.	
La Trinita Monastery	N. 16° 15' W.	And orthogonal.
Salerno	N. 53° W.	
	N. 34° 30' W.	
	N. 60° W.	
	N. 67° W.	
	W. to E.	
Pæstum	N. 90° W.	
Eboli	N. 66° W.	
	E. to W.	
La Duchessa	N. 74° 30' W.	
	E. to W.	
Taborna d'Urma	N. 81° 30' W.	
Castelluccio	N. 70° W.	
Chiesa d'Incoronata	N. 80° 30' W.	
Auletta (House), one mile from	} N. 90° W.	
Auletta Town	N. 90° W.	
	N. 115° W.	
Villa Caramo	N. 100° W.	

Portosa	N. 116° W.	
	N. 120° 30′ W.	
	N. 84° W.	And orthogonal.
	N. 69° 30′ W.	
	N. 120° W.	
Campostrina	N. 15° E.	Lateral gorge.
	N. 140° W.	
	N. 157° 30′ E.	
	N. 69° E.	
Polla	N. 12° E.	
	N. 160° 30′ W.	
	N. 157° 30′ W.	And nearly orthogonal.
	N. 165° W.	
Polla	N. 17° E.	Sluice House.
St. Pietro	N. 142° W.	
St. Arsenio	N. 144° W.	
Diano	N. to S.	
Atena	N. 165° 30′ E.	
	N. 177° 60′ E.	
	N. to S.	
La Sala	N. 171° W.	
	N. 157° W.	
	N. to S.	
Chiesa de la Trinita, one mile from La Sala	N. 108° E.	
Padula Town	N. 155° E.	
	N. 167° E.	
	N. 15° W.	
	N. 17° W.	
	W. to E.	
Cortona, Monastery of Padula	N. 136° E.	
	N. 116° E.	
	N. 165° E.	
	N. 136° E.	
	N. 115° E.	
	N. 41° 30′ E.	
Sassano	N. 137° E.	
Lago Negro	N. to S.	
Lauria	N. to S.	

Montemano ..	N. 150° E.	
	N. 160° E.	
Arena Bianca	N. to S.	Nearly.
Mulitorno	N. 140° E.	
	N. 145° E.	
	N. 154° E.	
	N. 155° E.	
	N. 125° E.	
Sarconi	N. 175° E.	
	N. 149° E.	
	N. 145° E.	
Saponara	N. 150° E.	
	N. 120° 30′ E.	
One mile from Saponara ..	N. 140° 30′ E.	
Spinosa	N. 134° 30′ E.	
Montemurro	N. 143° E.	
	N. 134° 30′ E. }	Also nearly vertical.
	N. 7° to 8° W.	
	N. 38° W.	General path.
Viggiano	N. 136° E.	
Chiesa, St. Clementina, Piano Viscolicol .. .. }	N. 130° E.	
Tramutola	N. 150° E.	
	N. 163° 30′ E.	
	N. 144° E.	
	N. 162° 30′ E.	
	N. 120° E.	
	N. 152° 30′ E.	General path.
Taberna Vigilliano (Salvi- tello) .. .. }	N. 135° E.	
Viotri di Potenza	N. 47° 30′ E. ⎫	
	N. 45° E. ⎬	And orthogonal.
	N. 49° 30′ E. ⎭	
Picerno	N. 45° E.	
	N. 68° 30′ E.	
	N. 90° W.	
Tito	N. 74° 30′ E.	
	N. 87° 30′ E.	
	N. 59° 30′ E.	
Potenza	N. 47° 30′ E.	

THE WAVE-PATHS.

Potenza	N. 45° E.
	N. 77° E.
	N. 22° E.
	N. 80° E.
	N. 92° 30' W.
	N. 100° E.
	W. to E.
	N. 119° 15' E.
Drindisi	W. to E.
Tricarico	W. to E.
Vignola	N. 80° W.
	N. 70° W.
	W. to E.
Signor D'Errico's Station, Monte Poloso	N. 90° E.
	N. 45° E.
	N. 103° E. True path.
Avigliano	N. 45° E.
Atella	N. 45° E.
	N. 45° 30' E.
	N. 55° 30' E.
Rionero	N. 45° 30' E.
	N. 25° W.
	S. to N.
Spinazzola	N. 85° E.
Canosa	N. 50° E.
	S. to N.
Monticchio Monastery, Monte Vulture	N. 38° E.
	N. 67° E.
Barcille	N. 35° E.
	N. 35° E.
	N. 25° E.
	N. 45° 30' E.
	N. 55° E.
	S. to N.
Rapolla	N. 45° 30' E.
	N. 24° W.
	S. to N.
Melfi	N. 30° E.

Molā					N. 40°	E.	
					N. 30°	E.	
					N. 37°	E.	
					N. 45°	E.	
					N. 45° 30'	E.	
					N. 16°	W.	} E. and S. E. side of city.
					S. to N.		
Ascoli	..	..	..	..	S. to N.		
Polla	..	..	,,	..	N. 25°	E.	
					N. 25° 30'	E.	
Moro	..	..		..	N. 16°	E.	
					N. 16° 30'	E.	
Laviano	..	..	..	..	N. 20°	W.	
Laviano	..	..	..	..	N. 82°	W.	
					N. 84°	W.	
					S. to N.		Statement of the priests.
Valva	..			..	N. 25° 30'	W.	
					N. 46°	W.	
Oliveto				..	N. 44°	W.	
					N. 45°	W.	
Capua	,,	..	..	..	S. to N.		
Calabrito	..	..	..	..	N. 45°	W.	
St. archis	..	..	..	..	N. 45°	W.	
Capaccio Nuovo			..	..	N. 97°	W.	
Castel Saraceno	..		..	..	N. 135°	E.	
Alta Mura	..	..	..	..	W. to E.		
Barragiano	..	..	..	..	N. 45°	E.	
Buonabitacola	..		..	..	N. to S.		
Sapri	..	..	..	..	N. to S.		
Laurino	..	..	..	..	N. 135°	W.	

In all, one hundred and seventy-seven observations, made at seventy-eight different places, situated in every part of the circumference round the seismic vertical.

Referring now to the wave-paths as laid down in *red lines* upon the Map A, it will be found that *sixteen* of them, pass through the same focal point, or within a circle of five hundred yards' radius around it.

These are the wave-paths of the following places, going round the local point from east to west by the north, viz.:—

Salerno	Diano
Oliveto	Sassano
Muro	Sapri
Bella	Campostrina
Barragiano	Polla
Potenza	Villa Carusso
Sarconi	La Duchessa
Tramutola	Castelluccio.

It will also be found, that *thirty-two* of them, pass within a circle concentric with the preceding, of one geographical mile radius, round the focal point, and *including* the preceding stations, viz.:—

Eboli	Tramutola
Salerno	Moliterno
Oliveto	Atena
Buccino	Certosa at Padula
Valva	Sapri
Laviano	Sassano
Muro	Diano
Bella	Polla
Salvitello	Campostrina
Vietri di Potenza	Pertosa
Barragiano	Auletta
Picerno	Villa Carusso
Potenza	Chiesa d'Incoronata
Vignola	Taberna D'Urma
St. Clementina	Castelluccio
Sarconi	La Duchessa.

We further find, that *sixteen* others, *exclusive* of all the preceding, fall within a concentric circle of 2½ geographical miles' radius, and outside of the last of one mile radius, namely—

Senarchia	Tricarico
Melfi	Viggiano
Barielle	Castel Saraceno
Canosa	Padula
Avigliano	Montesano
Alta Mura	Laurino
Monte Peloso	Castelluccia
Tito	Sisignano.
Brindisi	

And outside of this again, there are found *twelve* wave-paths, all converging within a concentric circle of five miles' radius, and whose divergences are accountable for.

Beside all these, we have the separate system of reflection, &c., of Salerno to Naples, &c.

Now it has been shown p. 18 (Part I.), that the point of intersection upon the surface, of *any two wave-paths*, is geometrically sufficient, to fix the position of the seismic vertical. Here we have *sixteen*, or eight pairs, (any one of which may be taken indifferently as intersecting with any other,) all passing through the same point, or within 500 yards around it. If therefore, we were to put out of view all the others, the evidence from these alone is irresistible, that we have obtained the real position, of the place upon the earth's surface, vertically above that one beneath, whence the shock emanated.

The focal centre of impulse, in nature, it will be remembered, is not a mathematical point, but a subterraneous region, possessing determinate, and perhaps often, very large dimensions; and whatever be the nature of the impulsive force, or however it may operate, whether by producing the sudden rending of rock, or production of an enlargement of an existing cavity; the wave of impulse, as propagated outwards, passes simultaneously, or almost simultaneously, from many points about the actual focus, widely distant from each other. The direction of impulse, being everywhere necessarily normal to the surfaces of impact, the wave-path at the moment of starting at widely separated points, is in part determined, by the size and figure, or contour, of the focal cavity. Hence the wave-paths, on starting at such distant points of the focal cavity, if produced inwards, would not necessarily be found to meet or intersect in a single point, and hence no actual observations of wave-paths made upon the earth's surface *could* be found mathematically converging to a single point. The terms seismic vertical, and seismic focus, are strictly and alike applicable to every separate wave-path, each really having its own; but for our purpose, the terms really mean, the points upon and beneath the surface, through which a vertical passes that intersects the centre of gravity of all the partial foci referred to an horizontal plane, which is the focus of all the separate partial foci. Or, again, the collocation of all the partial seismic verticals, from the separate wave-paths, may be employed, to trace out the form and extent of the focal cavity, from which they unitedly spring, as we shall see further on.

A certain amount of divergence, then, from radiation from a single mathematical point of the wave-paths is to be expected, and is true to nature, and within certain limits (the second circle of 2½ geographical miles' radius round the focal vertical for example) arises from—

1st. The actual spread or dimensions, of the focal cavity of impulse.
2nd. Errors of observation, or rather of determination, from the observed effects at the several stations.
3rd. Errors introduced, by protracting all the wave-paths, (determined by magnetic bearings at each station,) to a *common mean* magnetic declination.
4th. Actual small changes of direction, due to refraction, or reflection, or both, in any given path, during the propagation of the wave outwards, due to change of formation, &c.

The three last causes of divergence are small, the two last very small. The amount of divergence of the wave-paths grouped round the seismic vertical, from a common emanation of impulse therefrom, is therefore mainly due to the size and form of the focal cavity, and hence *the diameter of the focal circle that equals such divergence, becomes an approximate measure of the horizontal dimensions of the focal cavity itself*, whether it be, a rent, or suddenly blown out chamber, or whatever else.

The most distant stations of wave-path observation (for unreflected waves) were from the seismic vertical; Cunosa, N.E., 47 geographical miles; Salerno, west, 35 geographical miles; Lauria and Sapri, south, 37 geographical miles, nearly. But the mean distance of the greater number of stations, was from 12 to 15 geographical miles from the seismic vertical, which is one more favourable to obtaining exact results than any, either much greater or much less. The more distant the station, the less the second cause, and the more the third cause, named, of divergence, affects the observed and protracted wave-path, and *vice versâ*.

Apart from the perturbations that may arise, from the physical features of the surface or from the nature of the formations traversed, the indications from the most distant stations, should be the best, but the effects presented to observation from these are also the feeblest; while at the stations that cluster, very close above the focus, the phenomena, though well pronounced, are more perplexed by the violence of their production, and entangled with effects produced by the transversal movements of the wave. It may be remarked, then, with respect to the Map A, that the great preponderance, of our very best observations, as regards distance of station, give wave-paths, falling within the circle of $2\frac{1}{2}$ geographical miles round the seismic vertical.

We have thus ascertained, the point of the surface vertically above the seismic focus, which we find to pass nearly through Caggiano, a village 59 geographical miles east of Naples, and $10\frac{1}{2}$ geographical miles south of it. We therefore now proceed, by means of the angles of emergence observed, to determine the *depth of the focus* itself, beneath the surface.

CHAPTER II.

OF THE MEAN AND EXTREME DEPTH OF THE FOCUS BELOW THE SURFACE.

When the distance, upon the surface, from any station to the seismic vertical is known, it is obvious that a single angle of emergence of the wave-path will determine the depth of the focus, the seismic vertical itself, being in fact, the other of the two wave-paths; and if the earth's surface be viewed as a plane, which, as will be shown, we may consider it, without introducing sensible error, for a seismic region within our limits; then calling r = the distance from the seismic vertical to the station, the emergent angle at which is = e, we obtain the depth,

$$d = \frac{r, \sin e}{\cos e},$$

of the focus of that particular wave-path, below the horizontal plane passing through the station. In that way the various values of d, have been calculated, and plotted upon the Diagram Nos. 1 and 2, for the following twenty-six stations in every azimuth around the seismic vertical.

In this Diagram, in both figures, the strong horizontal line marked .0. represents the level of the sea. The fine

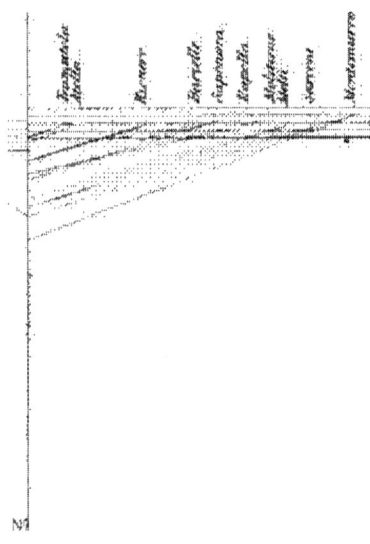

lines parallel to and over it, are at levels respectively of 1000 feet English above it, and above each other, and the seismic vertical, is the strong perpendicular black line. All observed stations, to the *eastward* of the meridian passing through the seismic vertical, are arranged to the *right* of the latter, and at their respective radial surface distances from it, and all the stations to the *westward* of the same meridian in the same way, arranged to the *left* hand of the seismic vertical; and all at the nearest approximation to their true levels above the sea.

In No. 1, the two fine lines drawn from each station, are those of the least and greatest emergences there observed, while in No. 2 the mean depths along the seismic vertical taken *from each pair*, (or for each station,) are deduced and plotted, as also shown by the fine lines, which form, with the horizon, the angles of *mean depths*; and, finally, from all the latter is deduced, the *general mean focal depth*, or that point which represents *the mean depth of the centre of effort*, or mean of all the partial foci.

STATIONS FOR EMERGENCES, &.

Stations.	Elevation above the Sea.	Observed Maximum and Minimum Values of ε.	
	Feet.		
Salerno	Sea level	13°	10°
Eboli	327	21° 30'	18°
Laviano	1,637	28° 30'	21°
La Duchessa	1,441	35°	24°
Polla	900	57° 53'	35°
Auletta	880	45°	
Villa Carusso	1,000	64°	60°
Portosa	880	75°	65°
Vietri di Potenza	700	79° 30'	64° 15'
Salvitello	1,500	50°	48°
Atena	1,100	47° 30'	

Stations for Emergences—continued.

Stations.	Elevation above the Sea.	Observed Maximum and Minimum Values of e.	
	Feet.		
Tito	2,100	33°	30°
La Sala	1,768	27° 10'	24°
Chiess della Trinita	800	25°	
Polenza	2,580	27° 7'	
Padula	900	25° 30'	20°
Avigliano	3,308	25°	20°
Francescani, Padula	700	20°	18°
Tramutola	2,000	18°	17°
Atella	1,800	18°	15°
Rionero	1,957	16° 30'	16°
Dareille	..	8°	4°
Saponara	2,300	16°	12°
Rapolla	1,800	12°	
Moliterno	2,090	13° 30'	11°
Melfi	1,000	16° 20'	15°
Sarconi	2,000	10° 25'	
Montemurro	2,700	20°	15°
Naples	Sea level	6°	

Naples and Darielle I have eliminated, the first as belonging to the separate system of waves of reflection, and both, because, as stated in Part I., the determination of the angle e, becomes uncertain when so very small.

This Diagram is plotted to the same scale, as the Maps A and B, and to what is called "a natural scale," *i.e.*, the vertical and horizontal scales are equal; so that the wave-paths in No. 2, represent to the eye very nearly, the precise paths of the emerging shock, at every station, as if seen in vertical section by an observer.

The greatest distance, from the seismic vertical, of any station (marked), is that of Salerno, 35 geographical miles, the next greatest being, Melfi and Sarconi, both under 27 geographical miles. The earth's sphericity, therefore, at these extreme stations, is 816 feet for the former, and 186

DEPTH OF FOCAL CAVITY FOUND.

feet for the latter; and as both these are far within the limits of surface inequality of level, the method, which assumes the surface as a plane, introduces no error in depth worth consideration; especially when it is remembered, that two contrary and mutually corrective errors are produced; the direct effect of sphericity becoming evanescent being, to *depress* the observed depth of focus; but as the angle *e* is always measured from the horizon of the station of observation, so also sphericity will *throw up*, the line of the wave-path along the seismic vertical.

Referring now to the Diagram, No. 2; it will be found, that, *out of twenty-six separate wave-paths, twenty-three start from the seismic vertical, at a depth of above* $7\frac{1}{2}$ *geographical miles, or of 43·284 feet*. The *maximum depth* is $8\frac{1}{4}$ geographical miles, or 49·359 feet, and the *minimum depth* is $2\frac{3}{4}$ geographical miles, or 16·705 feet.

Eighteen of the wave-paths, start from the seismic vertical, within a vertical range in depth of 12,000 feet, and having *a mean focal depth of* $5\frac{3}{4}$ *geographical miles, or of 34·930 feet, which may be taken as the depth of the focus*; all these measurements being from the level of the sea. The extreme vertical range, between maximum and minimum depth, is 32·654 feet. On examining the Diagram, however, having regard to the points in the seismic vertical, whence the wave-paths start thickest, it will be apparent that *the probable vertical depth of the focal cavity itself does not exceed 3 geographical miles, or 18·225 feet, at the outside.*

CHAPTER III.

OF THE FORMS AND AREAS, OF THE MEIZOSEISMAL AND ISOSEISMAL CURVES, AND THE POSITION OF THE SEISMIC VERTICAL THEREIN.

The determination of these areas, and of the curves that limit them, must always be, to a certain extent, arbitrary, because we have no sufficient means of comparing, the total mechanical effort at the surface, along the successive points of any coseismal line; and as it is certain that, apart from the perturbations due to physical configuration, this effort must be different, at every different distance, from the seismic vertical, so, strictly, an *isoseismal area* is impossible. In order, however, to make comparison, and to obtain some clear notion, of the relative distances of propagation of equal seismic effort, in different radii, from the seismic vertical, we must attempt to sketch out, the form and boundaries of equal effort, upon conventional principles.

I have hence divided the total area, of the vast region within which the shock was in any way perceptible, into four, more or less concentric areas, each marked by a determinate though arbitrary limit, of the seismic effort that acted within it. The innermost and smallest of these, (as shown in Maps A and B,) is that within which, the greatest seismic effort has been exhibited, in boundary: it is marked thus ———— —. This is the *meizoseismal area*, within which the greater portion of the *cities and towns were perfectly prostrated*; they are marked by black dots ● thus.

The *first isoseismal* outside the last is marked thus ——————— and defines the boundary of the space within which, *large portions* of the cities and towns were *thrown down, and persons killed* and wounded by their fall, as in the preceding. All such towns are marked thus ◉.

The *second isoseismal*, the last marked upon the Maps A and B, is defined thus ——————, and marks the boundary of the space within which, the effort was chiefly limited to the *production of fissures*, and slight dislodgments in the buildings, and in which *no loss of life* occurred. The towns within this area are distinguished thus ◉.

Lastly, upon the Map C (as the large scale of A and B did not admit of it) I have marked the *third isoseismal* thus ——————, being the boundary of the area at which *the shock* was *perceived* at all *by the unassisted senses*, and all the towns, &c., at which it was observed are marked thus ◉, so far as such are shown on Maps A and B. Beyond this, a portion of a *fourth isoseismal* is marked in Map C by a dotted line thus ——————, being the *probable* boundary at which the wave was *sensible, even to the instrumental delicacy as a seismometer*, of Padre Secchi's floating barometer at Rome. Within the meizoseismal, and first isoseismal, a few towns will be observed marked thus ◉ in place of thus ●, and between the first and second isoseismals a few will be found marked thus ●; to these I shall refer again, when remarking on the effects of physical configuration, &c. In the Map B the principal mountain ranges, with the river courses, constituting the chief physical features of the shaken country, are shown. Upon this map the *observed directions alone* of wave-path at each station, are marked with their azimuths in figures, the protraction of the wave-paths themselves to their intersection about the seismic vertical being reserved to the Map A only, and marked thereon in *red* lines.

The more important applications of the Map B will occur further on, when referring to the effects of physical configuration of surface, upon the forms of the isoseismals, &c. On both Maps A and B, all the towns that were affected by the system of reflected and refracted waves only, are distinguished thus ◆.

On examining the forms, of these closed curves, it will be perceived that they are very far from circular, or symmetrical, or similar to each other; and that the seismic vertical, is very far from being situated in the centre of figure, with respect to any of them. In fact, viewing each coseismal line as an irregular ellipse, the vertical through the centre of effort, is very nearly in one of the foci. This is, however, probably quite an accidental circumstance, as very many conditions, and those of great complexity, but chiefly comprehended under the one expression, "want of homogeneity of medium, and of uniformity of surface," have concurred to produce the figures found. The operation of these distorting forces, which will be presently considered, proves how wide away from the truth, are those beautifully regular, circles and ellipses, by which Johnston, Berghaus, and, indeed, all previous describers of earthquakes, have limited the supposed fields of their action.

The superficial areas, within the several coseismal curves as thus laid down on Maps A, B, and C are as follow:—

	Area in Geographical Square Miles.
1. Meizoseismal* (orange) area; that of general total destruction of edifices and great loss of life	716
2. First isoseismal (red) area; that of great prostration of edifices and loss of life	1,685
3. Second isoseismal (blue) area; that of partial prostration and of universal fissuring of edifices, with partial or with no loss of life	4,976
4. Third isoseismal (yellow); area, within which the shock was distinctly perceived by the unassisted senses, and produced more or less alarm; and more or less fissuring and damage, towards the parts nearest the preceding isoseismal line	29,500
5. Fourth isoseismal (lilac); the area of which is unknown, and only partially marked, to the north-	

* These colours refer to the original maps in the possession of the Royal Society. Upon these, the totally destroyed towns are marked red; those partially overthrown are marked blue; those wherein the shock was distinctly felt yellow; those external to the third isoseismal are not coloured; and those affected only by the reflected and refracted wave system are coloured green. Economy in colour printing compelled the changes described in the reproduction of the maps. The original nomenclature is here stated, as the author suggests to seismologists, the desirableness of consulting the originals; the small scale of the published maps giving less palpably and clearly, the physical relations of the country, to the earthquake phenomena.

	Geographical Square Miles.
ward; being that within which the shock could have been easily perceived by instrumental disturbance	Area uncertain.

Each of these areas, includes those preceding and within it.

Upon the Map C, I have laid down for comparison, the *first* and *second* isoseismals, of the great earthquake of 1783, and those of the shock of Melfi of 1851, and the *second isoseismal only, of thirteen others*, of the greatest earthquakes upon record in Italy, with their dates.

These areas, with the exception of the two first, are only tolerable approximations, the scanty and incomplete accounts admitting of no more. On examining the several curves, it will be seen, that with the exception of that of 1783, this earthquake of December, 1857, has been probably the most formidable and wide-spread, that is known to have desolated Italy; and it is very doubtful, if the excess in the seismic areas, of that of 1783, as laid down from the best accounts, be not considerably exaggerated, for the meizoseismic area of the latter, certainly does not appear, to have passed much beyond, the Calabrian plain, opposite the Gulf of St. Euphemia; and hence this area of greatest effort, was not greatly larger, than that of the shock of 1857.

The only earthquake, whose first isoseismal (blue in the original) compares in area, with those of 1783 and 1857, is that of 1740, in the north, which is said to have extended with damage, from Volterra to Milan. The records of that, however, as well as of the one of 1672, on the Adriatic

shore, I believe to be much exaggerated, and hence the areas larger than they ought to be.

Seismal *area alone*, however, affords no test of comparative seismic energy. If the depth of focus were the same, the area would be, *cæteris paribus*, a measure of comparative energy.

The focal depth, however, in different earthquakes, in the same region, may, for anything we yet know, differ greatly, and either a very deep focus, with such a form of focal cavity, or such other conditions, as shall produce wave-paths, chiefly *emergent at very steep angles*; or a *very shallow* focus, although of equal intensity of original impulse, may equally result in great *limitation of area shaken*; and yet within it, or within its central portion, the destruction may be great or absolute. The former of these conditions, seems to have been in operation in the Melfi shock of 1851, whose emergence at and around Melfi, was extremely steep, and its destructive energy within the central region, tremendous; but the total area shaken, was very moderate, and the decay of energetic effort in passing out from the centre, extremely rapid.

In fact, the impulse in this case, seems to have been delivered upward, as through a funnel, formed by the volcanic formations about Melfi and Volture, encircled by the limestone and murgic rocks.

Each isoseismal area as marked, is in fact, the partial integration of the total seismic effort, for the space, and within the conventional limit as to effect, fixed upon for each; and distances proportional to the eccentricity of the seismal curve at any points from the seismic vertical taken along any radii indicate points of equal effort, (apart from any small causes of local disturbance); so that the *forms of the isoseismal curves, indicate* truly to the eye the relative distances in all directions around the seismic vertical, to which *the same degree of overthrowing force*, has extended *horizontally*.

If the impulse were the same, in all horizontal or emergent directions, and the earth were perfectly homogeneous, all radii for equal overthrow must be equal, and the isoseismal curves must all be circles. If the impulse be the same in all directions, but these curves be found, ellipses or ovals, then the longer radii indicate the directions, in which the conditions of the medium (the earth), have permitted it to transmit the wave furthest, with least loss.

If the impulse be greater, towards one or both opposite directions in some given azimuth, then even in an homogeneous medium, the isoseismals must be elliptic; and if both conditions concur—*i. e.*, preponderance of original impulse in one direction, and heterogeneity of medium,—then from both causes the curves will become distorted; and although still closed curves, and of the elliptic order, they may assume almost any form.

CHAPTER IV.

OF THE EFFECTS OF THE PHYSICAL CONFIGURATION OF THE SURFACE, AND THE FORMATION BENEATH IT, UPON THE PROGRESS OF THE WAVE.

That is to say, upon the *distance of its sensible transmission*, and irrespective of local or other conditions, changing its direction, or producing reflection and refraction, which will require separate consideration.

The conditions in nature that are most effective and frequent in modifying the distance of transmission of the wave, in formations of the same, or nearly the same materials, are—

> 1st. The existence of continuous mountain chains, and their direction with regard to the position of the seismic vertical, or origin of impulse.
>
> 2nd. The occurrence of great faults, or lines of dislocation, whether parallel or transverse, to the great chains, filled with loose, or with heterogeneous material, and their direction with regard to the origin, &c., as before
>
> 3rd. The existence of deep and continuous valleys, narrow in character, and with precipitous flanks, and their direction with regard to the origin, &c.

4th. The great prevailing positions, of the stratification and bedding of the formations, of the shaken country, whether highly inclined, with generally parallel anticlinals, or with these in many different azimuths; or with prevailing horizontal, or gently inclined stratification, extending over great areas.

The change of elasticity and density, between the rock of one formation and another, does not, so far as my observation has informed me, produce at all an equal extent of superficial modification, of the wave of shock, to that which is effected by these four causes.

Breach of continuity of medium, as I have long since shown, by the loss of *vis viva* that takes place at every surface of contact, is the condition, of all the most effective, in limiting the progress of the wave, and robbing it of its volume, up to extinction.

From the nature of the building up, of every mountain chain, of anticlinals, with strike more or less parallel to its axial line, it follows, that the mass of material, is most solid, the breaches of continuity, fewest and least, in the latter direction. The wave is therefore best transmitted "end on," by mountain chains; as well as by the formations reposing on their lowest flanks, and filling the valleys between parallel ranges.

Humboldt mentions, that the course of earthquakes in the north of the Asiatic continent and elsewhere, has been observed "to follow the courses of the great rivers," but he offers no explanation of the fact. It is not, however, in consequence of any connection with a river course, that the fact is so, but that the river marks the direction of the great continuous chains, and of the direction also, in which the valley formations are least broken and discontinuous, namely, parallel to the *alignment* of the flanking chains.

The same principles apply, in explanation of the fourth condition stated. The wave travels best "end on" to the strata, and not transverse, more or less, to them.*

When the wave-path is transverse, or obliquely transverse to mountain chains, on the contrary, everything tends to oppose its progress, and hasten its extinction. The surfaces of discontinuity are as numerous, as the multiplied beds that we should cross, in boring through the base of the range, to say nothing of fissures, or other casual breaches of connection. The planes of the bedding, are continually altering in direction, with reference to the wave-path, by which the wave suffers continual loss of *vis viva*, and is dissipated by dispersion. As the wave is transmitted from valley to range, and from range to valley, in perhaps many successions, it is continually passing from one formation into another, with a change of velocity in each, and therefore loss of *vis viva* at the junction. As we ascend, in the order, from the deeper to the more superficial formations, reposing upon the flanks of the ranges, we in general find

* The author has since shown, by experiments for the determination of the elastic modulus of the stratified and laminated rocks of Holyhead (North Wales), that although waves of impulse are best transmitted as above stated, "end on" or edgeways, through stratified formations in mass, they are best transmitted transversely through the lamination of solid portions of the same rock, i.e. the elasticity of the material is greatest in the latter direction, but the amount of discontinuity between the different beds more than neutralizes this, when the wave-path is transverse or oblique to both stratification and lamination. See Proc. Roy. Soc., 1862.

their density, hardness, and elasticity getting less and less; hence the wave, in whatever path, transmitted transversely, suffers continual refraction, as illustrated in Fig. 342; the general tendency being, at each parallel range to depress the wave-path, and reduce the apparent angle of emergence, the wave losing by partial reflection at every such change of direction.

Such changes of direction occur likewise, no doubt, whenever an emergent wave reaches the surface, in a path parallel or nearly so, to the axis of the mountain chain and valley; but the alternations are then much fewer, and the distances between the refracting surfaces of contact of the formations, are very much larger, and the loss, therefore, much smaller.

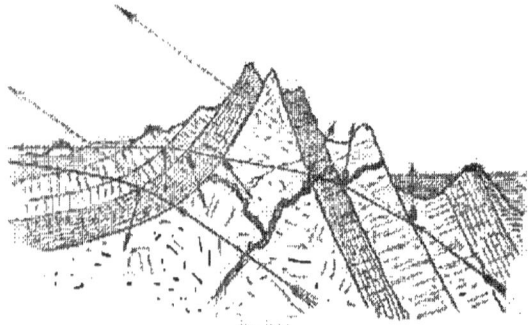

Fig. 342.

When the wave has emerged at the outgoing side, of a transverse mountain range, (the left-hand in Fig. 343,) owing to the curving and bending in direction, of the formations, it will emerge *at some points* of the outgoing flank, without any refraction, (when incident perpendicularly to the surfaces of formative contact); while at others, it will be refracted, and also partially reflected; and the refraction at different points may possibly be in contrary directions; hence great complication in the wave issuing along the slope, and loss of its energy.

When stratified formations repose conformably, upon the *in-going* flank of a mountain range, (as to the right-hand of Fig. 343,) and the angle of emergence of the wave at the base of the range is such, as to pass it nearly "end on" into such strata, (of newer beds for example reposing on older, and having no hold upon them); then the whole of the wave that enters these beds, will pass off at the free outlying surfaces of their upper extremities and be then extinguished;

Fig. 343.

the wave thus "breaking" upon the slope of the central formations, like a ripple upon a sea-beach; while such portion of it as passes deeper, and through the innermost axial formation, will emerge at the outgoing flank, (to the left,) after having sustained all the losses of *vis viva* and volume already described, by change of medium, refraction, and reflection.

Again, when loose and incoherent masses, (such as the gravel and clay deposits in valleys and river courses,) repose upon the gentler slopes of the bases, of the lower ranges, the wave entering such at a small angle of emergence, will be almost completely extinguished, by compression, and change of position of the particles, of the incoherent formations at the slope of the rock, at *a b*, (Fig. 344); nearly as if the sur-

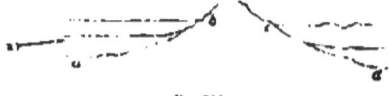

Fig. 344.

face of contact, was with respect to the loose material, a free lying surface. The same will be the case at the emergent side of the range, *c* to *d*, in converse order, for such portion of the wave, as at greater depth may have directly entered and passed through, the central rocky mass between *a* and *d*; there will, therefore, be in such a case, almost a complete extinction of the wave

The former case, that of Fig. 343, is mentioned as amongst the conditions which modified the great Carpathian shock, of Sillein, in Hungary, of 15th January, 1858, so well described by Herr Jeitteles, of Kaschau; (Sitzungbericht der Mat. Naturw. Classe der Kaiser 'Akade' Baude xxxv., s. 511,) and the latter has been already described where occurring locally in having cut off the town of Diano, from the shock, from north to south through the piano. (Part II., p. 330.)

The occurrence of the second condition, viz., great lines of dislocation where the fissure first opened, has to a great depth and for a considerable thickness, become filled in with loose material,—seems, from the results of my observations on this earthquake, to be competent to arrest at once almost the whole progress of the wave.

Its entire volume, or by far the greater portion that arrives at the first surface of contact, or wall of the filled fissure, at *a b*, (Fig. 345,) in the direction *e f*, is expended in compressing and altering the relative positions, of the clays,

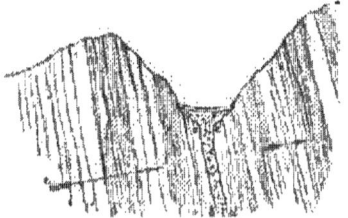

Fig. 345.

gravels, rock fragments, detritus, or whatever other loose and incoherent materials the fissure contains. Upon the width of the fissure, in proportion to the amplitude of the wave, at its entering the loose material at *a b*, and upon the *degree* of looseness, incoherence, and capability of being crushed and moved, possessed by the latter, will depend the residual unextinguished portion, that shall be transmitted on to the opposite wall of the fissure *c d*, and so into and on through, the solid rocks beyond. Where at the same time the rock at both sides, has been so tilted, that its bedding is vertical, and nearly parallel with the walls of the fissure, transverse to the wave-path, then the obstacles to the wave are the greatest possible; and where the plane, or various planes, of the fissure, are met obliquely, by the emergent wave-path, *e* to *f*, instead of perpendicularly, then we have, in addition to the foregoing, further loss by refraction and reflection, as already described. This effect of fissures, was presented upon a grand scale by the earthquake of December, 1857.

Lastly, deep and continuous valleys with precipitous sides, cut off and extinguish the wave at their free lying surfaces, upon which the wave-path passes off into free space at their emergent flanks. In this case the portion of the wave that passes on, beneath the bottom of the valley between, and through the lateral flanking range beyond, lies so deep, that its path is not emergent to the surface beyond, until after a distance horizontally, so great, that the energy of the wave is almost expended, or greatly reduced.

This will be understood from Fig. 346; almost the whole of the wave emergent in the direction $a\ b$, above the level of $c\ d$, is extinguished at the free lying surface $f\ r$; but the portion that passes on, below the level of $c\ d$, is not emergent at the surface until it has passed through the long distance to e, when its force has become decayed.

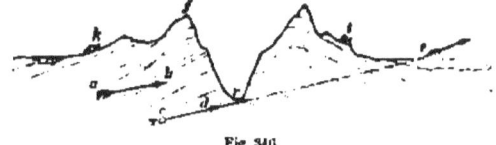

Fig. 346.

In such a case, a city at e, may be unconscious of anything, but perhaps some tremors, emergent in nearly vertical directions, while another city, a very few miles off, at k, may have been totally destroyed, by a shock nearly horizontal in direction.

In Part II., some local examples of this condition, acting upon a large scale, have been adverted to, as affecting the country upon the highest forks of the Tanagro, above Vietri di Potenza, and between Tito and Bella, &c. Before applying these general truths to the earthquake we are engaged with, we must consider the effects of the form and position of a focal cavity, upon the transmission of a wave of shock.

CHAPTER V.

OF THE EFFECTS, OF THE FORM AND POSITION OF THE FOCAL CAVITY, IN MODIFYING, THE DISTANCE OF TRANSMISSION OF THE WAVE OF GIVEN EFFORT, AND THE FORM OF THE ISOSEISMALS.

WHATEVER the nature, of the original impulse, if it were produced at a single point, or radiating from all points, of the surface of a spherical cavity, in a homogeneous medium, the isoseismals must be circles, and equal effort upon the surface, be transmitted at all equal distances, from the origin. The conditions are altered, however, when the focal cavity, from the *parietes* of which, the impulse, of whatever sort, is transmitted, has a different and less regular form. Every particular form, will give rise to a new modification of effects. It will be sufficient for illustration, to refer to one, and that the form, which no doubt, almost invariably occurs in nature, namely, where the focal cavity is a plate, or narrow fissure with considerable length and depth, and having some determinate position of its plane, with respect to the horizon, or surface. If *any impulse*, like that of suddenly accumulated, elastic pressure, be delivered forth from such a cavity, it *must leave its walls, at all points, in directions normal to their surfaces.* It is obvious that the impulse must produce its most effective effort, in the directions perpendicular to the general plane of the fissure, and in an homogeneous medium. The outward passage of *the wave*, at like points of the phase, will *not be in spherical but in ellipsoidal shells*, whose greatest axis, will be perpendicular to the plane of the fissure.

1st. If the *plane of the fissure be horizontal*, and at a considerable depth beneath the surface, this greatest axis will be vertical, and the main power of the shock will be expended within a very limited area of the earth's surface, and the wave within it will emerge steeply; while its decay in passing outwards from the seismic vertical, will be extremely rapid, and the form of the isoseismals, in a homogeneous medium will depend upon the horizontal contour of the fissure. The phenomena will be very much those, of the Melfi shock of 1851, modified by the actual heterogeneity of the earth.

2nd. If the *plane of the fissure be vertical*, (suppose, to fix our ideas running north and south,) then in a homogeneous medium, the greatest axis of the ellipsoid, will be east and west, and the horizontal distances, upon the surface of the earth, for equal effort, greatest in the east and west azimuths, and least in those north and south, so that the form of the isoseismals will be elliptic.

3rd. If the *plane of the fissure be inclined*, more or less, to the horizon, as ff, (Fig. 347,) $e\ e$ being the earth's surface, then the greatest axis of the ellipsoid will be inclined also, and in the direction $s\ e\ d$, which will be the direction of greatest effort, and *the overthrowing power of the wave will be unequal*, both from amplitude, and direction of emergence, for objects situated *at equal distances*, as at s and p, *from the seismic vertical* $V\ O$, *in the azimuth of the greatest axis*, i. e. in the azimuth of a plane perpendicular to the walls of the fissure and near it. Whence it results, that the isoseismals must, in this case, take the form of ovals or distorted ellipses, the larger and fuller end of the oval, of each one, being found towards the end at which the wave-

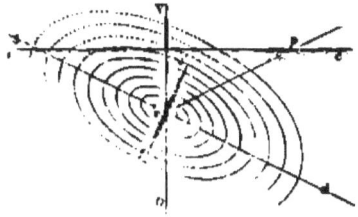

Fig. 347.

path *c s*, in the line of the greatest axis of the ellipsoid, is emergent, and the smaller and narrower end, being opposite. And inasmuch as the direction of greatest effort at the side *c d*, plunges into the earth, and is never emergent at all, we may adopt the felicitous expression of Stokes, for the analogous case of sound, and call all the localities in such a case, existing (to the right in the Figure), in the direction of *p*, from the seismic vertical, as *places in earthquake shadow*.

So far, we have viewed the medium as being the same and homogeneous, as to the opposite sides of the fissure. If this be not so, however, and that the plane of the fissure be situated, so as to have at one side of it, a dense, hard, highly elastic, but slightly compressible material; and at the other, a much less hard, but still elastic, and much more compressible, material; then a new cause will be added, to those preceding, for a still further distortion of the ellipsoidal wave-shells, and with them, of the form of the isoseismals.

This will produce its greatest effect, when the plane of the fissure is inclined to the horizon. There are two cases: *the plane of the fissure may be inclined so as to slope*, as in Fig. 348, *towards the less compressible medium*, lying to the side *d* of the plane of junction (and of fissure *k i*), or *it may slope from the less compressible medium*, as in Fig. 349, and

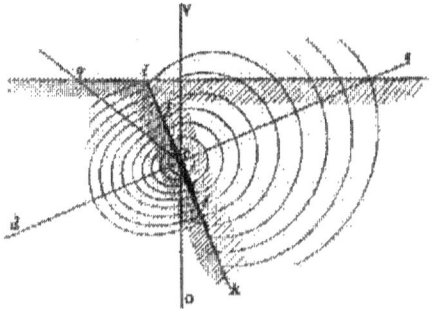

Fig. 348

towards the more compressible one at the side *d*, of the plane of junction, &c., as in the latter Figure, the same letters

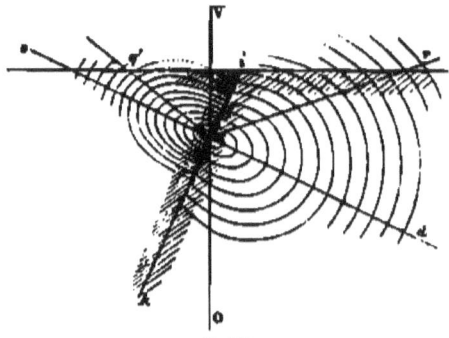

Fig. 349.

referring to each figure. In both cases, the greatest axis, of the two abutting and more or less distorted, semi-ellipsoids of wave movement, will be in the direction *d s*, perpendicular to the plane of junction of the media, and of the fissure. In the first case (Fig. 348) the wave-path in that axis, will be emergent at *s*, at the side of the more compressible medium, and in the second, at the side *s* (Fig. 349) of the less compressible medium. The wave, in the harder and more elastic medium, to the side *d* (Fig. 348), and *s* (Fig. 349), will have a faster transit rate, and probably a greater velocity of the wave particle, than in the less hard and elastic medium; but the amplitude of the wave at starting, will be much greater in the latter, and will continue greater; and unless its velocity be very low, in comparison with that in the harder medium, that is, unless the difference in elasticity between the media, be very great, the wave of greater amplitude, will carry furthest, before sensible extinction. Observing in the two figures, the relative directions, in which the ellipsoidal wave-shells emerge, in both media; it is obvious that, taking the three elements, of seismal energy, or overthrowing power upon the surface, together; viz., wave amplitude, velocity of wave particle, and direction of wave-path, at emergence; the distance of equal effort, from the seismic vertical *o v*, will be greatest, in the direction of the more compressible medium, and the difference most, where the wave-path in the greatest axis, of the semi-ellipsoid of greatest amplitude, is emergent, as in Fig. 348, and *vice versâ*.

So that in the former case, (Fig 348,) the distances for equal effort of overthrow, from the seismic vertical, along the greatest axis, may be at *q* and at *s*, and in the latter (Fig. 349) at *q'* and *r*; the larger and fuller end of the isoseismal oval passing through *s* and *r*, and the smaller and narrower through *q* and *q'*.

In the former case, (Fig. 348,) the difference between the observable angles of emergence, in the isoseismal curve, will be greater, (for equal overthrow,) between q and s' than between q' and r; and the difference, both in distance and angle, greater, as the difference in compressibility of the two media, is greater, and the elasticity of the less compressible, less perfect.

The phenomena may be illustrated to the senses thus:— If two large blocks—one of marble, and the other of caoutchouc—be laid in mutual contact; and in a cavity, formed equally, in the centre of the plane of contact of both materials, a small charge of gunpowder be exploded, its impulse will be almost entirely expended, in propagating a wave of movement through the india-rubber, the range of movement in which, will be far greater, than in the marble, although the rate of its propagation may be slower; but a loose body, laid upon the upper surface of either block, will be disturbed by the shock transmitted at a far greater distance, upon the caoutchouc, than upon the marble, &c., &c.

I have shown elsewhere ('Fourth Report Facts of Earthquakes, Rep. Brit. Assoc., 1858'), that in perfectly homogeneous media, the meizoseismal zone, or curve, depends upon the emergence of the wave-path at the surface being at the angle where the horizontal component is a maximum. The angle e has a meizoseismal value of $54°\ 41'\ 9''$, upon one assumption as to the law of decay of the wave, and of $45°$ upon another and the more probable assumption, that the decay is directly as the distance from the original; the radius of the meizoseismal zone (circle) being, in the former case, equal to the side of a square, whose diagonal is the depth of the focal point from the surface, and in the latter equal to this depth. What has preceded proves, that this does not hold good for unequal dimensions of focal cavity nor for heterogeneous media.

CHAPTER VI.

APPLICATION TO THE ACTUAL FORM OF THE ISOSEISMALS.

We are now enabled to combine the views stated in the three last chapters, and apply them in explanation of the forms of the isoseismals, the centre of effort not occupying the centre of their figure, &c., and to other facts of the earthquake. Upon the Map B the physical features of the shaken country are, to some extent, marked in. The greatest and most nearly continuous chains of the Apennines are shown; some of the subordinate elevations, and the river courses, which indicate generally the lines of elevation and depression of the surface.

Upon the (original) Map A, the axial lines alone of the great and more continuous ridges are marked in.* Referring to both these maps, it will be seen, that the three coseismals are crossed diagonally, by the nearly continuous ridges of the great Apennines; the one running west to east, from about Baronissi to Spinazzola, the other north to south, from the direction of Melfi down to that of Lauria.

* It would have been best this were so likewise in the Map as here reproduced. The reader will find it advantageous, if engaged in research, to consult the original Maps A, B, C, and D, in the Collection of the Royal Society, and to compare the surface as delineated on Zannoni's great map.

The meizoseismal curve, is almost a regular oval, whose longer axis is to the shorter, in the ratio of 30 : 12, and the seismic vertical, close to Caggiano, is very nearly in the focus of the minor or north end of the oval or about one geographical mile to the south and west of it.

What has produced this great distortion of figure, from a circle, with the seismic vertical in the centre? The maps show, that besides the great Apennine chain, passing through the area, at a small angle to the major axis, from between Tito and Potenza, on the north, to Lauria on the south, another great continuous chain, namely, that of the east flank of the Val di Diano, rises almost precisely at Caggiano (the seismic centre), and stretches down, nearly in a *right line, and almost parallel to the major axis*, as far as Tramutola, where it joins in with the former chain.

The impulse, from its very starting-point, was delivered "end on," along the latter chain, and so obliquely upon the first mentioned, as to produce much of its effect, longitudinally. These indicate, in brief, the main circumstances of surface configuration, that produced the very lengthened propagation of the wave, from the focus towards the south-east.

But other conditions conspired with these, to limit and shorten its propagation, in the orthogonal direction, or in that of the minor axis of the curve. To the north of the seismic vertical, rounding from Castelluccio and Buccino on to Avigliano, we have one of the extensions of the great east and west chain of the Apennines, opposed *transversely* to its progress, and at an average distance from the focus, of not more than six geographical miles. Again, from the same point (Castelluccio) we have, stretching thence along the whole length of the S.W. boundary of the curve, the continuous chain of lofty mountains forming the S.W. flank of Val di Diano, and going down to Sapri and Maratea. This range, from the northern end, twelve or fifteen miles in length, opposed itself *almost transversely* to the wave: as the direction of the wave-paths going further south, became more oblique to the range, the effect of the latter was not only *to bar the progress* of the wave, *across the ridge*, but *to conduct it "end on" along its own line*, and parallel, or nearly so, to the major axis of the mezoseismal oval.

Proceeding now to the first isoseismal (———————), it is crossed diagonally, by the great north and south chain, from about Avigliano on the north, to Lauria on the south; the north end curving round, from Lavinno towards Potenza, so that for the most northerly portion, of about fifteen geographical miles in length, *the chain presents itself transversely to the wave everywhere, and at a distance to the axis of not more than ten geographical miles.*

In a word, looking broadly at the Maps A and B, it will be seen that from Oppido, to the north, all round to the westward and south-west, by Avigliano, Buccino, Castelluccio, Petina, Sassano, and Buona Ditacola, the first isoseismal, is barred in, and absolutely surrounded, (except at the narrow gap of Castelluccio, valley of the Tanagro,) by *continuous transverse chains*, so that the seismic vertical, stands as it were, in the focus of a great amphitheatre of mountains, which barred the progress of the wave across them, and acted like a vast elliptic reflector, to deliver back the impulse, towards the east by south.

In the direction from the focus, of east by north, (Caggiano to Potenza,) the wave progress was impeded, by the transverse action of the north and south Apennines: but further south, the impulse, as already observed with reference to the meizoseismal area, impinged more and more obliquely upon the axial line of this chain, which, therefore, as it went further south, became a better transmitter in that direction.

But whence comes the enormous spread out, of the greater end of this coseismal curve to the south-east? It was explained in Part II. (in treating of the main and secondary shocks at Padula), that when a transverse, or, within certain limits, an oblique impulse, impinges laterally upon a continuous mountain range, two movements of vibration are communicated; the one, a wave transmitted along and in the line of the axis, the other a transverse wave, which causes the axial line to sway laterally, and transmit a *quam prox.* horizontal transverse wave, along from one end to the other; like the sinuous movement which travels along a long rope when, hanging suspended between two points at the same level, it is jerked suddenly at one end, transversely to its length. Such were the two wave movements, transmitted along the chain, southwards of Tito.

If a mountain range so vibrating laterally, be quite free at both sides, the lateral wave passes along, and is finally delivered out, at the free lying surface, of the end reached by the progress of the wave; but if a number of subordinate chains spring out from one side, a large portion of the transverse wave, will be in its progress, transmitted to those abutting mountain ridges, and *in succession delivered into them "end on."* The transverse wave itself, will therefore rapidly be robbed of its volume, and very little of it will reach the outgoing end of the principal chain. Now, this is precisely what has taken place here.

It was pointed out in our sketch of the physical configuration of South Italy (Part I.), and is indicated by the Maps A and B, and by the general direction of the watercourses delivering into the Gulf of Tarentum, that the main prevailing directions, of all the lower ranges of hills to the east, of the great north and south Apennine range, run in a direction nearly N. W. to S. E.; that is to say, in one, nearly parallel to the major axes, of the meizoseismal and of *all* the *isoseismal* curves, and all these hill ranges abut, with small but various obliquity, upon the great north and south Apennine chain. Hence the transverse vibration of the latter, was transmitted under, the most favourable condition to its propagation, to the S. E. "end on" through these lower ranges. But further, it was also pointed out, that to the east of the great north and south Apennine, the mountains become lower; the country is no longer truly mountainous, but rolling, with vast plains, whose formations are bedded, on the whole, nearly horizontally. These are conditions again favourable, in the highest degree, to the distant propagation of the wave to the south-east. As soon as it passed the great north and south range, it was delivered as it were into a wrinkled and corrugated, but still *comparatively level, continuous and unbroken plate, of hard and pretty uniform formations, whose main corrugations all run in the N. W. and S.E. direction, that is, in the same direction with its transit.*

At the S. E. end, the full swell, of the curve of the first isoseismal, will be observed, however, to be sensibly flattened, between Latronico and Tursi. Examining the Map B, it will be seen that here it runs close along by the course of the river Sinno, falling into the Gulf of Tarentum, and that the wave-paths, radiating from the seismic vertical, here crossed somewhat obliquely, the deep and continuous valley, and flanking ranges of the river course, and hence the wave here suffered a partial and sudden arrest.

These remarks will I hope, be sufficient to make clear, the great modifying causes (so far as surface is concerned), that have determined the forms of these isoseismals, and limited the areas of equal destructive effect, of this earthquake. The same principles of explanation will be found to apply to the second isoseismal (— ··· — ···). The great east and west chain of the Apennine, stretching across from Baronissi to Spinazzola, and at a direct transverse distance from the seismal vertical, of only about ten geographical miles, to the very axial line, opposed itself with all its parallel ranges, *transversely* to the propagation of the wave, to the north, and north by west; while the causes operative, in the meizoseismal and first isoseismal areas, as already described, were also so here, in extending the propagation of the wave towards the south, south-east, and east.

To the extreme S. E. end of the second isoseismal, the flattening of the curve, and narrowing of the band of country, between the first and second curves; is ascribable, to the wave having there reached the low-lying clays and other discontinuous littoral deposits, that skirt the shores of the Gulf of Tarentum. To a like reason is to be attributed, that its progress towards the south-west extended no further than the seaward slopes, of the great masses of the Monte Alburno range, leaving the deep clay plains of Pæstum, from near Salerno to Agropoli, almost untouched.

Had I been able to extend my survey, to the whole of the country between the second and third isoseismals,

(Map C), similar, though less marked phenomena, would no doubt have been apparent; of some such, I did obtain the facts. Thus Ascoli and Canoza were both badly shaken, and owed their pre-eminence in misfortune, the first, to the wave which was passed northwards, " end on," by the chain leading to beyond Melfi, and thence delivered into the plain of Ascoli, from its free lying, northern extremity: the second to the like action of the northern chains, that tail off from Palazzo to Minervino, at the east abasements of the great east and west chain of the Apennine.

It should be remarked here, that Canosa, Nocera, Senarchia, Moratea, and some other towns are marked on (the original) Map B blue, with a red elongated dot at one side, which signifies, that although most properly marked, as belonging to the blue class, or those of the second degree of injury, still lives had been lost in them, but under circumstances that did not warrant their being assigned the bad pre-eminence of the unhappy places marked (in red in original map), and by a black dot (●) on that here produced.

CHAPTER VII.

OF THE SEPARATE SYSTEM OF NAPLES CITY, AND THE TERRA DI LAVORO, OR OF THE WAVE OF REFLECTION AND REFRACTION.

It was recorded in Part II. that the wave-paths, as traced by me at Naples and around the Bay, were at an early period found to be irreconcileable with those of the interior of the country, and appeared to come from no common origin. This apparent difficulty vanished, however, when I discovered, that the shock at and about Naples was but a secondary wave, and due to reflection and refraction, of which it affords the most striking and beautiful example: the phenomenon itself, although predicted by myself elsewhere* upon *à priori* grounds as likely to be found, having *never before* (so far as I know) been *observed* as actually occurring, and doing so here, upon a very vast scale.

The impulse transmitted from the focal point (nearly beneath Caggiano) towards the N.W. and S.W., was obstructed, as has just been described, by *meeting transversely the great ridges—four in, quam prox. parallel succession*, to the N. W., viz., that from Bella to Castelluccio, that from Laviano to Conturso, that from Calabrito to Eboli, and

* 2nd. and A. 'Reports on Facts of Earthquakes.' Reports British Association.

that from Montella to two geographical miles west of Eboli; and nearly to the S.W., by five nearly parallel, though very irregular ridges, including the mighty double mass of Alburno. But by one narrow gap, as it were, the way was clear for its easy transmission in a direct line, from the seismic vertical, to Salerno and thereabouts. This occurred where all these transverse ridges sink down, and leave the outlet to the west of the great Valley of the Tanagro, reaching from within a mile or two of Caggiano, to the sea; and having a clear width at Eboli, between the hills to the north of it, and those on the left bank of the river Salaris, due south, of from three to four geographical miles.

Along this Valley, of the Tanagro and Salaris, the wave was transmitted "end on" to the general mass of *the formations of the valley itself*, and with small loss; so that from the origin divergent pencils of wave impulse in azimuths between 66° and 75° W. of north were transmitted, past this gate of Eboli, and debouching into the broken and hilly plain, between Eboli and Salerno, thus reached the southern flank, of the great range of Monte St. Angelo, between Baronissi and Capo di Campanello, opposite Capri, *in wave-paths very oblique to the axial line of this range*.

The mountains of this range, forming the projecting peninsula to the south side of the Bay of Naples, are but a prolongation of the great east and west range of the Apennine, with a depression about Baronissi. From about Teora and Caposele, westward of Capri, the axial line of the chain is nearly straight, and its direction not far from east and west by compass, with a slight inflection from a right line, at a point north of Atrani.

The *abstract direction* of the axial line is marked on Map A (original) by a red line; the wave-paths, as ascertained for Salerno, La Cava, Amalfi, and other places, to the south of the range, and also those for Naples, Capua, Ottajano, and others north of it, are marked, and the direction of transit shown by "arrow heads." And on Maps A and B, the *probable forms* of the isoseismals, of this separate reflected and refracted system, are marked in thus (——·····——·····——), that to the south of the range, which falls almost wholly in the sea, in the Gulf of Salerno, being only inferential.

The whole of the St. Angelo range of limestone mountains, as stated in Part II., is highly metamorphic, forming, as it does, the southern lip of the vast volcanic basin of the Vesuvian area. The wave from the focus, to near Salerno, passed through Apennine, and still newer, limestones, and calcareous breccias and loose deposits. Upon impinging on this mountain range, it reached at once, a continuous wall of rocks, of variable but greatly higher elasticity, and superior density; and at an angle of incidence (horizontally) of 56° to 59°, a reflected wave was produced.

The observed wave-paths at Amalfi and Atrani, &c., *prove* that this was so, the direction being N. 133° west, which gives the angle of their wave-paths, with the perpendicular to the mountain axis, = 59°, or the angles of incidence and of reflection equal. The wave, no doubt at a low level, in the base of the chain, passed through, suffering refraction twice, and crossed the Bay of Naples, beneath the sea, and was observed, as to direction of its path, at Pausillipo, N. 38° west. The directions of the wave-paths at Salerno and at Eboli, N. 66° to 67° west, which, as already stated, reached the range, with an angle of incidence, of 56° to 59°, passed through, therefore, with *an angle of refraction of 33°*; the direct wave-path having suffered an inflection to the extent of 26°, in passing through the mountain range, and in whatever harder volcanic rocks, if any, it met with, between that and the point of observation, at the north side of the bay.

But besides these reflected and refracted waves, transmitted by the elastic material, of the roots of the range at a considerable depth below the ridge, the mountain range itself vibrated laterally, by the transverse sinuous wave, before referred to (Part II., Padula) and Part III., Chap. VI., and hence wave movements, almost precisely normal, horizontally, to the axial line, were transmitted from it. These are indicated by the observed wave-paths, at Capua, Naples, and generally all round the Bay, to the north of the range, and at La Cava, La Trinita, &c, to the south of it.

The orthogonal wave-paths, observed at Amalfi and Atrani, in a direction N. 138° east, are rather uncertain as to explanation; it is observable that they are almost precisely in the same direction as the refracted wave at Pausillipo, and it is probable they were produced, by a second series of transverse sinuous vibrations, of the axial range, produced by partial reflection of the original wave, of that order, at the free lying surfaces, of the end of the chain, at Capo di Campanella, when reached by it; and so transmitted backwards, along the chain, (like a water-wave traversing forward and back from one end to the other, of a long trough, or as the same sort of sinuous wave produced by jerking a stretched rope, returns to the hand, after it has reached the fixed and remoter end).

The other wave-paths observed at La Cava and Salerno, in directions due east and west, were obviously the residual impulse, of the direct wave; obstructed by the north and south transverse ranges, north of Eboli, and at last transmitted in part, from the last of these, that between Montella, and a point two or three geographical miles west of Eboli.

We have now accounted for all the directions, of these *secondary wave-paths*; and it only remains to make a few remarks upon the peculiar forms of the isoseismals of reflection and of refraction to the north and south of the range. The local centre of effort in this separate system, was necessarily, at a point in the axis of the range, midway between Nocera and Minori, for this was about the place at which the full and unobstructed effort of the direct wave, arriving obliquely at the range, impinged upon it; hence, we should find the longest wave-paths diverging from this point to the northward, and the isoseismal where broadest opposite this: it is so in fact.

The greatest amount of destruction happened in the towns of the Terra di Lavoro, in and about Nola, and the line north of it. But the most striking and confirmatory fact, as to these complex wave phenomena, here, is to be found in *Capri Island having escaped*, (Part II.) without even having been conscious of any shock. Looking at the maps, and observing the wave-paths, and the forms of the isoseismals to the north and south of the range, it is obvious that Capri stands in a position where the energy of such of the waves as could reach it at all, would be the least possible; and where it is extremely probable, that by mutual interference, they destroyed each other totally. The local wave observed at Ottajano, will be referred to hereafter. The small spread of the isoseismal of Naples (———····——···——) to the north, between Frigento and Monte Freddano, &c., is due to the extremely broken, irregular, and *hummocky* nature of the mountains, about these spaces and down to Pagano, as well as to the obstructive effects of the transverse north and south ridges, in producing *earthquake shadow*, as already explained.

CHAPTER VIII.

OF THE SOUNDS THAT ATTENDED THE SHOCK.

A MORE exact and careful examination of the sounds, audible in earthquakes, than has hitherto been accorded to them, will (as the deductions in the present instance to be made prove), be hereafter found a most valuable auxiliary, in deducing the nature of the focal cavity, and, probably, many other conditions of subterraneous action as yet little thought of.

The occurrence of sound at all, necessarily infers *impulse* at the focus, of the nature of a blow, or a succession of them, either due to, fracture of hard and elastic material, the sudden separation or rending open further, of existing fissures or cavities, or the sudden rush out, of highly elastic steam, or its as sudden production or condensation, so as to produce a musical note like those due to the impulse of wind in an organ pipe, or explosion, more or less sudden, as from the rush from the tail of a rocket to the explosion of a shell or mine.

The character of the sound heard in the shock of December, 1857, however various at different points, was everywhere made up of sudden explosive reports, (one, if not more than one,) variously contemporaneous with rushing and rolling sounds.

It was not in superficial area, coextensive with the shock, but the form of the area within which it was heard, was closely similar to that, of the two first isoseismals generally, so that the same conditions, that were favourable, or the contrary, to the distant propagation of the wave of shock, were about equally so, to the wave of sound, but the latter was the feebler of the two, *ab origine*. Echoes, the disturbance of local noises at the moment, the uncertainty with which the ear judges of direction of sound, the evanescence of the phenomenon, and the difficulties inseparable from trusting to merely collected information of often incompetent observers, or unfaithful narrators, who observed under alarm, must ever deprive sound phenomena (except when heard by the physicist himself) of the unerring certainty of deduction, that belongs to the mechanical problems, presented by the phenomena left after the shock.

Still we shall find that sounds, are not without their seismic significance and response, and when more of their complex conditions shall have been submitted to careful *à priori* discussion, we shall be much better prepared to put the inquiries as to facts, that will be valuable in result.

No sound whatever, was heard to *accompany the shock*, except within a very limited portion of the central area of great disturbance.

The limits of surface, within which the *shock* was experienced, in its respective degrees of intensity, have been already given. Within the first and second of these (the area of great disturbance) sounds were heard, along with, or nearly along with the shock, over an area equal to more than 2500 geographical square miles, or within a space extending from Melfi to Lagonegro, north and south, and from Duchessa to Monte Pelosa, east and west.

The narratives of those situated towards the northern and southern *extremities of the sound area*, all described what they had heard, as a low, grating, heavy, sighing rush, of twenty to sixty seconds in duration, some thinking that it was also a sort of rumbling sound, but with none, a distinct, well-defined explosion, or several in succession.

Those who were situated towards the *middle of the sound area*, and towards its east and west boundaries, on the contrary, very generally described the sound, as something of the same character as to *tone*, but with more rumbling, using the words "rombo, rumore di carozzo," &c., more, and such as "fischio, sospiramente," &c., less; and as shorter and more abrupt, both in commencement and ending, and in duration.

These descriptions, aided by the expressive gesticulation and imitative powers of the narrators, conveyed a far more exact notion of the sounds heard, and of the relative times in which they were heard, than I can hope to transmit in writing. They were collected in my progress, and as they may be referred to in the narrative, without much idea of their leading to any very distinct or valuable conclusion. The result however now appears to support the conclusions arrived at, from the rigid methods of tracing the origin out from the wave-paths, in a manner as remarkable as it is satisfactory.

It will be seen that our wave-path lines on the surface, although they mainly point to one great focal point, do not do so absolutely, some pointing to an extreme centre, about 2¼ geographical miles north of the main focal point, and some to another, *nearly* 5 geographical miles south of the same; the length or distance along the right line connecting these extremes, and passing through the main focus, being about 7½ miles, and in a direction nearly 20° or 30° east of north. Many of the more southern wave-paths, at that extremity of this linear *locus*, are those from places such as Saponara, &c., almost parallel to the major axis of the meizoseismal area.

That the existence in *part* of this linear locus of *foci*, may be due to unavoidable errors of observation in the wave-paths, and to local changes of direction, of the wave-paths observed only at some points, there can be no doubt; but the length of this *locus* of *foci*, coupled with the facts recorded as to the sound, leave as little doubt, that the centre of effort was not confined horizontally, to a single, or a very small point of space, nor diffused horizontally, and equally, round the main focus, over a very wide one; but was limited to a surface, either in a vertical or highly-inclined plane to the horizon, which we shall see reason to believe, was a curved surface, which passed through the main focal point nearly beneath Caggiano.

Such conditions would be fulfilled, were the originating impulse due, to a great rent or fracture, suddenly produced, in the course or direction of this curved plane passing through the focal *loci*, and this is exactly the condition that will account for the sounds, so variously heard and described, at different points of the shaken area.

A rent or fracture produced under our conditions, must have commenced at a middle point in its length, *i. e.*, at the main focal point, for at this point, the forces producing fracture must have been most violent, and the fracture extended, or ran out thence with great rapidity, in both directions, viz., N. N. E. and S. S. W.; extending, at the same time, upwards and downwards, in height and depth, from the same point.

The noise, therefore, whether produced by the actual fracture of rocky strata, in the hard lower limestone, or in some still lower rocks, or due to the rushing of steam at high pressure, into the huge fissure as it opened along, or due, as most probable, to both united and together, could be heard *nowhere* upon the surface of the earth above, *as an explosion, but everywhere as a prolonged sound* of some sort; and the amount of prolongation, as heard by an observer at any given point, would be greater, in proportion as his station was more, *in directum* with the line of the rent, or with its chord, if curved, and his position further and further removed from the middle point of its length.

The *sound is produced*, at the point in the act of being rent, and into which, as it opens the fissure, the steam is rushing; it is therefore produced, *in succession along every point of the line of fissure*, from the origin or focus, to its extremities, where the rending force becomes evanescent.

Now if t = the whole time of rending the fissure, to any given distance along it, from the origin r, and d = the distance of the hearer upon the surface of the earth, from the same; v = the velocity of sound, in the masses fractured and transmitting it to the ear; and omitting all consideration of intermediate transmission, through small thicknesses of the atmosphere before reaching the ear, or of sounds produced simultaneously with the longitudinal rending, by that occurring at the same time up and down; then $T =$ the time of rending sound will be

$$T = t + \frac{\sqrt{d^2 + x^2}}{v}$$

when it shall reach the ear from x. Therefore, the whole noise of rending, from o to x, will reach the ear in the time,

$$T' = t + \frac{\sqrt{d^2 + x^2} - d}{v}$$

but x and t remaining the same for every station, and d being variable, this function diminishes rapidly as d increases, and at an infinite distance is equal to t. Hence the nearer the station of the hearer is to the middle of the length of the fissure, (as the above is true from 0 to x, in both directions of rending, from the centre or main focus,) in a line perpendicular to its plane, and the further he is off, provided he hear it at all, the more short, abrupt, and explosive like, will the sound appear to him: while, on the contrary, the more oblique, or nearly in the line of the fissure, he is situated, the more he will hear it, as a long rushing sound.

But as the fissure has considerable vertical dimensions, as well as horizontal ones, this is *pro tanto* true, for a vertical plane, as well as for the horizontal one; and hence, even were the fissure *instantaneously* opened, to its whole extent, as if by a single effort, no hearer could be so situated upon the earth's surface, as to hear the noise, however short and abrupt, as a single explosion, but must hear it as a prolonged sound.

In fact, it is quite analogous to standing a good way off, at the centre, of the front or rear, of a long line of troops, ranged up and down the slope of a steep hill, who fire in file, commencing at the centre, or standing at the same distance from one extremity of the line. In the former case, we shall hear the whole sound, in less time by nearly $\frac{1}{2}$: 1 than in the latter; while the explosive-like character and loudness will be nearly as 2 : 1, twice as much sound impinging on the ear in the same time.

It should be observed, that the same sort of continuous sound, variable in duration at different stations, could be produced, by a single sound or explosion, occurring simultaneously along the whole length, of a line such as that of our fissure; the sound from its different points, arriving at the ear in succession, as they came from a greater distance; the case being then analogous to the rumbling of thunder, simultaneously produced, along the whole length of the flash, so far as our senses can take note of it.

But to this view there are great objections—

1st. The sound in that case, could be *nowhere* "sospirantl;" it would be everywhere rumbling, and only vary in loudness, and in length of duration.

2nd. Bearing in mind the extreme velocity of propagation of sound in solids, as compared with its velocity in air, the assumption of a single explosion, must involve, the existence of a line of simultaneous rupture, of enormous and improbable length, to account sufficiently for the prolongation of the sound.

3rd. The physical conception, of any such simultaneous fracture, or of any force, or mode of application of forces, capable of producing it, is difficult, if not impossible.

It may therefore be concluded, that the sounds heard, in the earthquake of December 16th, 1857, were due to the rending, and probable filling with high-pressure steam, of a rent, commencing at or near the main focal point, and extending (as indicated by the wave-paths) about 7½ geographical miles in length. We shall see reason to believe, however, that the extreme dimensions of the rent, exceeded this considerably. The production of the rent, was the originating impulse of the earthquake, its repletion with dense steam or a further extension of it, probably, that of the second shock.

Had we precise observation, of the exact time, during which the rushing sounds were heard at each, or at two or more stations, and knew the exact velocity of sound, in the various solid or other media, between the fracture and the hearers, we should obviously be in a condition, to calculate the length of the fissure itself, assuming the depth of focus, to be about its mean depth: and such exact observation, which may be readily made by a Brequet watch, or other chronoscope, may be, upon the grounds above indicated, commended to future observers of earthquakes.

It is obvious, also, that the conditions which have been pointed out, are sufficient to account for, most if not all, of the phenomena recorded, of the *relative time of arrival and of duration, of the sound and of the shock, at given points*; while the fact, that the sound was heard at all only, within a very limited area of the total surface convulsed, by this earthquake, (an area equal to not above $\frac{1}{116}$th of the whole, within which the shock was distinctly felt by the unaided senses,) seems to point out, that the wave-pulses of audible sound, and those of shock, are different—differing not only in volume, but probably in velocity, and capable of propagation to very different distances, from the same origin.

A great deal of obscurity, as yet hangs over the way in which the sound from the earth, reaches the auditory nerves, whether by vibration, communicated from the earth's surface to the stratum of immediately superincumbent air, and by it to the ear; or directly from the vibrating surface of the earth, through the bones and other tissues of the human frame, to the ear. Upon this point, the remark made casually by one of the persons at Polla, that he heard the noise, come up through his body or legs from the earth, is not to be wholly lost sight of. The probability is, that the sound, from its starting-point, travels to the ear both ways; viz., through the earth directly and the human body, to the ear; and through the earth, (vertically, or nearly so, to the nearest points of air,) and thence through the atmosphere, to the ear: and as the rate of transit is very much more rapid, probably, in the solids, than in the air, this condition would add another, to the causes already assigned, for the continuity of the sound. (Compare 'First Report on Facts of Earthquakes, Reports Brit. Ass., 1850, cap. 23.')

One circumstance connected with the sounds of earthquakes, has hitherto received but imperfect explanation, namely, the arrival at a point distant from the origin, of *the sound, before the shock*. The fact, has been apparently sufficiently attested, as occurring occasionally, and some years since it was adduced, as one tending to cast some doubt, upon the general theory of earthquake dynamics, which, based upon the movements of elastic waves, has since been universally accepted. The phenomenon admits of simple probable explanation, and may be treated, along with that of the tremors before and after the shock, in the following chapter.

CHAPTER IX.

OF THE TREMULOUS MOVEMENTS THAT PRECEDED AND FOLLOWED THE SHOCK, AND OF SOUND BEFORE THE LATTER.

The shock, properly so called, that which shakes down buildings, &c., and the precedent and succedent tremors, are all waves of the same order, differing only in dimensions, and more or less in direction; the shock, being a wave of large amplitude, the tremors of small or very small; the latter also, in part, mixed with small transversals.

Whatever be the form, of the focal cavity, whether spherical, linear, or lamellar, we must assume it, suddenly enlarged in dimensions; either by its walls giving way at once, to a previously steady, or to a slowly increasing pressure from within, or by a sudden increase of that pressure, brought upon its *parietes*.

In either case, if the cavity itself is enlarged in volume, *by rending or fracture* of the material, composing its walls, *the velocity with which a rent or fracture can be propagated through any material* substance, however great may be the force producing it, can never exceed that expressed by the equation

$$V = \sqrt{2g(h)\frac{d}{D}}$$

in which d, and h, are the density of mercury at $0°$, and height of the barometric column, e the modulus of elasticity, and D the density of the body torn; for this, the velocity of sound, or of *force transmission*, in the given solid, is the limit of the rate at which the rending force can be propagated, from particle to particle. Again, a force will produce rending by impulse, when its velocity

$$V = \frac{\mu}{\phi}$$

μ, being the modulus of force transmission, involved in the former equation, and ϕ that of final extension or compression at rupture; and in this case, the progress of the rent may merely follow on, at the velocity $\frac{\mu}{\phi}$.*

These are the limits of the rate, at which the focal cavity enlarges in any one dimension, by rending; and as the amplitude of the wave impulse, at the instant of its original transmission, depends upon the range of original disturbance, that is, upon the *length of the rent*, or enlargement of the focal cavity, which has already occurred at that instant, and upon the velocity together, (which, if it fall below the latter value of V ceases to generate a wave at all;) so, at the instant the rending or enlargement of the focal cavity commences with sufficient velocity, (tremulous,) waves of extremely small amplitude, begin to be transmitted; their amplitudes rapidly increase up to a maximum and then suddenly diminish to 0.

Such waves of very small amplitude, at the commencement and end, are those of the tremors, and most probably of the sounds; although it is as yet not quite certain, that

* See 'Mallet on the Physical Conditions involved in the Construction of Artillery, Trans. Roy. Irish Acad.,' Vol. xxiii., Part I.

waves of small amplitude, although recognizable as producing sensible movement, and those of very much smaller amplitude, which are only capable of recognition by the ear, have the same rate of transit. The wave of the great shock is the subsequent one of great amplitude, (in proportion,) and which cannot be generated with an amplitude sufficient, to produce the effect of earthquake shock, until after the focal cavity has already been enlarged to a certain amount.

These waves, therefore, *start in succession*, the tremulous waves first, then the shock wave, of large amplitude, and, lastly, the concluding tremulous waves, the sound waves probably accompanying all; and if the velocity of inceptive reuding be sufficient, the sound waves setting out the earliest of all: so that at a distant point of surface, the observer shall *hear* the mutterings of the earthquake *first*, shall *then perceive the tremors* before the shock, *then the great shove of the shock itself*, and, *lastly, the tremors with which it departs along with the sound*. If Mr. Earnshaw's mathematical views of the progression of sound, be adopted, (' Trans. Brit. Ass. 1858 ',) it would follow, that the transit rate for the wave of large amplitude, (the shock,) must be greater than that for either the tremors or the sounds ; and if so, an additional reason is afforded in explanation of the commonly observed fact that the duration of the tremors before and after the shock is often unequal. Mr. Earnshaw's conclusions as to the necessary formation of "breaking waves" where the transit velocities are unequal, have extremely interesting relations with this part of our subject.

The relative times of arrival, at a distant point of observation, however, must be also largely affected, by the form of the focal cavity; for example, let this, as in Fig. 350, be assumed an extensive lamelliform fissure, ff, inclined to the seismic vertical $o\ v$, and sloped *from* the observer, at the point of the earth's surface p; let the rending of the fissure be supposed to commence, from an extremely small

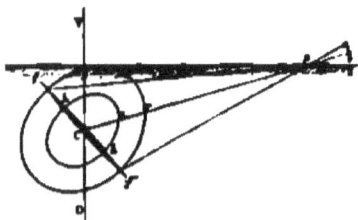

Fig. 350.

cavity at the point c, and for simplicity, assume the medium homogeneous, and that waves of whatever amplitude, have the same rate of transit; then at the instant that the rent commences at c, tremulous waves, and those of sound, will begin to be transmitted, and will reach p in the time $c\ p$, and, so far as the emergent angle of the former can be observed, will emerge with $e = b\ p\ g$.

Let us further suppose that until the fissure has enlarged to the depth $h\ h$, both ways from c, the originating impulse is not sufficient, to generate a wave with the amplitude necessary to produce the effects of shock; then the tremulous waves will have been transmitted to s; *before the wave of shock will have started*; so that the shock will not reach the point p, until after the time $c\ p + c\ s$, and the angle of emergence $b\ p\ g$ will be nearly the same as that of the first tremors.

Moreover, if t and t' equal the time of rending the fissure from c to f and f', the tremulous waves, will continue to start from successive points along the fissure, from c to those limits, and up to the limits of time of $f p + t$, and $f' p + t'$, and will continue emerging, for the time $s \tau$, after the shock, with constantly varying angles between $a p g$, and $e p g$, up to the completion of the cycle of phenomena.

Such were precisely, the circumstances described to me, by all the observers present, at the shock of December, 1857, as those which then occurred. It began everywhere, with tremors; the sounds generally, arrived at the same time; the apparent direction of movement, of the tremulous oscillations, appeared rapidly to change, and still more rapidly to increase in amplitude; then the great *shove* of the destructive shock arrived, in some places rather before, in some a little after, the moment of loudest sound, and it died away suddenly, (*i.e.* with extreme rapidity,) into tremors again, but differing in direction from that of the great shock itself. (Compare Part II. *in locis*.)

To this train of phenomena the exceptions observed, were only at Naples, and in the Terra di Lavoro, where the direction of movement of all the oscillations, (the whole being small,) did not change, and were *all horizontal*, or apparently so; but the exception here, is confirmatory of the truth of the explanation, because, as already explained, the earthquake at Naples, was one only of reflected and refracted waves, transmitted horizontally, or nearly so, from an origin of a totally different character from that of a focal cavity, namely, the axial line, of the St. Angelo range of mountains. Another condition productive of tremulous waves, remains however, to be noticed.

In any case in which a shock is transmitted, from a centre

of impulse *e*, (Fig. 351,) due to the compression of the walls, (of whatever form,) of a focal cavity, in an elastic medium, (which for simplicity we may suppose homogeneous); then besides the primary wave of shock of large amplitude, as in the continuous spherical or ellipsoidal shells, *s s′ s″*, &c., there will be a reflected wave, from the continuous and indefinitely extended mass, of elastic and

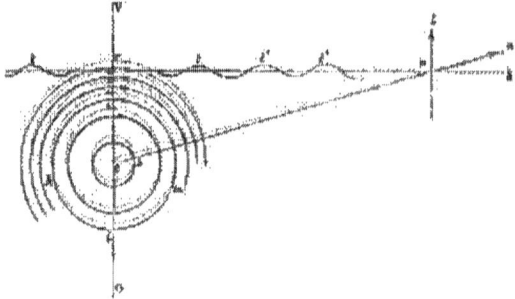

Fig. 351.

resistant material, at *l o*, and below it, given back by the primary or previous compression. This will be delivered, vertically upwards, in the general direction of the seismic vertical *o r*, and divergently upon the surface around it, in the spherical shells, *r r′ r″*, &c., in the dotted lines; and as these emerge at the surface, they will generate, a smaller *transversal* wave, *t t′ t″*, &c., which will be transmitted upon the surface, with an *apparent emergence at every point nearly vertical*, as at *p t*. And these small transversal waves, may reach a distant point of observation *p*, coincident with the shock, or before it, or after it, according to varying conditions, as to depth *e r*, to distance *r p*, and to the form of the focal cavity when not spherical, as supposed in the Figure.

It is highly probable, from the experiments of Wertheim and Breguet, on the linear and transversal vibrations, of stretched iron wire, ('Comptes Rendu,' t. xxxii., p. 293,) in which they found the rate of propagation of the latter, greater than that of the former, in the ratio of 4634 : 3485, that these small surface transversals, will be transmitted from r to p faster than the direct shock can be over an equal distance, and hence the time, during which the tremors may be felt, *before* the shock, be proportionably prolonged.

When to all these circumstances we add, those that heterogeneity of medium must introduce, as somewhat explained in Chaps. IV. and V., there will be no difficulty in explaining the cycle of observed wave phenomena, however complex.

It follows, from what has been stated in the preceding page, that no absolutely single shock, consisting of one clear, sharply defined blow, is physically possible, to an observer situated anywhere out of the centre of impulse.

Wherever the observer may be upon the earth's surface, he must experience a more or less "blurred" and confused shock, even though it were produced by an explosion in itself absolutely instantaneous.

CHAPTER X.

OF THE REITERATION OF THE SHOCK, EXPERIENCED IN SOME LOCALITIES, AND OF ITS CAUSE.

The earthquake of December 16, 1857, consisted, irrespective of tremulous movements, such as those last discussed, of two shocks: the first and more powerful of the two, was felt over the whole area disturbed; the second, which occurred about an hour after the first, was less powerful, however, and limited in its seismal area to a much smaller region than the former.

These two, however, appear to have been, distinct earthquakes, due to separate originating impulses, though from a common originating point, only following each other, with but a brief interval of time; but in some places, as recorded a second shock of considerable intensity, was felt following the first, in rapid succession. In every instance, this second appears to have been a reflected shock, the first, the direct one, and the two differed often very considerably, in wavepath.

The conditions conducing these, will be best explained further on, in treating of the disturbing effects, of local position, &c., upon the shock. In the case of Naples itself, where a distinct moment of pause, was observed, after the occurrence of the first portion of the shock, and then its renewal, it will have occurred to the reader, as due to the *direct wave*, transmitted after refraction, through the S. Angelo range, and to the *transversal vibrations*, propagated from the oscillations of the axial vertical plane of the range itself; the former arriving first, and being the more powerful.

CHAPTER XI.

OF THE ACTUAL DIMENSIONS, FORM, AND SUBTERRANEOUS POSITION OF THE FOCAL CAVITY, AS DEDUCED.

From all that has preceded, in relation to 1st, the form of the isoseismals; 2nd, the horizontal spread, from convergence of the wave-paths, to a small focal area; 3rd, the nature of the sounds heard, at different points, round the focus; and 4th, the tremulous movements; we are enabled to assign, with a very high degree of probability as to correctness, the size, form, and position, of the focal cavity itself.

We have found that (Chap. II.) the vertical dimension of this cavity, could not have exceeded about 5·3 miles, but was most probably limited, to 3 geographical miles. We have also found (Chap. I.) the preponderating numbers of our wave-paths, fall to within an horizontal length of 5 geographical miles, 2½ at either side the focal point. But to the south of this point, we have six wave-paths, (of which five, are nearly parallel, to the major axis, of the meizoseismal and to each other,) which fall, rather above 2 geographical miles, more to the southward, of the 2½ mile circle; viz., those of, Marsica Nuovo, Saponara and its Piano, Tramutola, and Spinosa. These point distinctly to a prolongation of the focal cavity, towards the south and west, to an extent approximately equal to the transverse range of their divergence. Again, on the north of the 2½ mile circle, the extreme of divergence northward of the 2½ mile circle of Laviano, Valva, and Altamura, and the large spread to the northward, of the isoseismals eastward of the great interrupting north and south ridge, between Avigliano and Lauria, *e. g.*, the swelling of the curve, from Ruccino to Monte Peloso; point to an impulse-producing surface, extending northward, within about a mile of Balvano. We therefore come to the conclusion that *the whole horizontal dimension of the focal cavity was about nine geographical miles.*

But to answer the observed conditions, direction of the wave-paths, normal or nearly normal, to the longest, of which within any isoseismal, the surfaces of the walls of the cavity must be; and to answer the observed emergences near the centre, as at Vietri de Potenza, Auletta, Polla, &c.; the horizontal line, joining the north and south ends of the focal cavity, cannot be a right line: the horizontal section, of the fissure or lamelliform cavity, must therefore be a curve, and the only curve that will answer the conditions, is that drawn by a *broad red line or band* on the Maps A and B, between the points marked f and f'. It passes from near Balvano, on the north, close to Vietri di Potenza, Caggiano, and Pertosa, and to the north and west of Polla.

The curve so traced, is one of contrary flexure, and the effects necessarily following, from the concavity and convexity of the surfaces (of impulse,) which it generates with the vertical dimension, will, on careful consideration and comparison with the maps, be found singularly in good accord with the irregularity or distortion of the isoseismals; and with the mutual relations between both; and the physical conditions of surface, &c., operative in their co-determination.

The conditions developed in Chap. V., when applied to the wave-paths, lately referred to, falling to the south of the 2½ mile circle, and the shallowness of focal depth, given (see Diagrams Nos. 1 and 2) by the observed emergences for all the places, very close, to the seismic vertical, and to the north, north-east, and east of it, such as Salvitelle, Auletta, Villa Carusso, &c.; indicate that the *vertical section* of the focal cavity, was also either more or less curved, or, what is much more in accordance with the laws of fracture, was, in its general surface, inclined to the vertical; and, from the seismic vertical, sloped off upwards, towards the N. W., and the contrary way below.

We therefore finally come to this conclusion, that *the focal cavity, when at its full dimensions, was a curved fissure, whose height was three geographical miles, and length along its curve of contrary flexure was nine geographical miles, while its thickness, or third dimension, between wall and wall, was probably very small, but is uncertain.*

The area of the lamelliform fissure, or its height by its length, was therefore 27 geographical miles, and the depth of its central point (nearly) or mean depth of the fissure, —the true focal point, or seismic centre of force, was at 5⅞ geographical miles below the surface. The top edge of the fissure, therefore, did not approach nearer to the surface, than 4¼ geographical miles, while the lower edge reached a depth of at least 7¼ geographical miles below the surface. Whether this were previously an open cavity, which becoming suddenly surcharged with dense steam, had its lateral dimensions suddenly enlarged, and by the impulse of which the wave of shock was generated; or whether a fissure was thus widely rent, where there was nothing before, but perhaps some cavity, at this mean depth and mean central point, which became extended under pressure, along the plane of greatest weakness, in the surrounding formations; we have no means of judging, beyond this, that *the observed tremors indicate rending.* Whether the cavity were pre-existent, or was then at the moment rent, the actual range of movement outwards, of its two great surfaces, (the opposite walls of the fissure,) cannot have exceeded a very small limit, as proved by the small amplitude of the wave of shock, at the places nearest and most exposed to it.

The dimensions thus assigned to the focal fissure, receive very interesting confirmation, from the actually observed duration, (so far as it was observed,) of the tremors that preceded the shock.

The length of the fissure was nine geographical miles (its *extreme* limits, assuming it rent) something more. If the fracture commenced, as we must suppose, at the centre of the length, then the distance it had to run either way, was $4\frac{1}{2}$ geographical miles, $= 27,337$ feet. If the rent occurred at the superior limit of V, as already given, its rate, supposing it to have been all in Apennine limestone, would have been about 3640 feet per second. (See 'First Report on Facts of Earthquakes, Sec. 23rd, Reports Brit. Assoc. 1850.') The *time of rending*, then, would have been $7\frac{1}{2}$ seconds, and this would be the least period of time, during which the tremulous movements would be felt, *previous* to the arrival of the great shock, supposing the latter generated, at the moment the fissure attained its full dimensions. *The least time actually recorded is "six or eight seconds."*

It is improbable, however, that the velocity of rending in

the same medium, should be greater, considerably, than the velocity of actual wave transit in the same. The preceding velocity of 9640 feet per second, being that due to the $\sqrt{e}$, is, as we shall see hereafter, nearly four times as great, as was the actual transit of the wave, in the limestone; and some retardation, more or less, must undoubtedly have arisen, in passing through several miles of rock, more or less shattered, heterogeneous, and discontinuous beforehand, transversely to the line of fracture.

If, therefore, we assume the inferior limit of V, to be equal, only to the transit rate of the shock wave, in the same formation, the duration of the precedent, tremors, would be about $4 \times 8'' = 32''$. The longest observed periods that I have recorded, vary between $30''$ and $40''$.

It is with considerable interest also, that, on referring to our Maps, A and B, and still better, on comparing with the localities, in Zannoni's great map, it will be found, that the curve of contrary flexure, assigned to the form of the fissure, conforms in a remarkable way, to the existing natural lines of surface contour, of the country through which it extends; and to such lines of pre-existent dislocation, as we may predicate, from those, of the valleys, hills, and water-courses. Thus, at its northern extremity, it follows, in part, the lines of the deep valleys, of the rivers Tarno and Landro; crosses the Compostrina ridge, at one of its several transverse depressions, or minor valleys, follows diagonally, the general line of the valley, between Caggiano, and Pertosa; and then to the extreme southern end, strikes right into the deep valley, between the ranges, of Monte Tomaso, and that of the Costa del Castagneto, to the west of Polla.

CHAPTER XII.

OF THE TEMPERATURE OF THE FOCAL CAVITY, AND THE INTENSITY OF THE FORCE THAT ACTED WITHIN IT.

BELIEVING, as I do, that the few facts, supposed to be ascertained, as to subterranean temperature, at a very limited number of distant points, do not warrant any conclusion, such as has been jumped to, from them; that there is a *general increment of temperature*, as we descend from the surface, increasing at *an average rate*, of 1° Fahr. for every 50 or 60 feet additional depth, due to some all-pervading cause. Considering, that the local rates of increase, of subterraneous temperature observed, are due to local action, the nature of which remains yet to be discovered, or at least to be pointed out, and that hence, from the observed depth and temperature at one place, we cannot alone, infer anything, as to the temperature at an equal depth, in another and distant place: and considering, that even admitting the hypothesis of a pervading cause, the discrepancy of the small number of observations, varying as they do, between the wide limits of 1°, for every 30 feet, and 1° for every 90 feet, (*three times* as much,) or even 100 feet, is so wide, that any mean, deduced from such data, must be almost devoid of evidence;—holding such views, I myself attach but slight value, to any deductions that can be drawn, as to the temperature of the focal cavity, by applying to its ascertained depth, the commonly reputed law of increase, of subterranean heat.

It may be interesting, however, to those who give more weight to the common doctrine of Hypogean temperature, to apply it to the case; the rather, as illustrative of the line of reasoning that we should be entitled to follow out, had we the requisite data certain.

There are two deep Artesian wells at Naples, the temperatures given by which, add to the discrepancy and doubt, before sufficient, as to the rate of increase with the depth.

One of these, is at the royal palace in the city; its depth is 1460 feet, and the temperature of the water is 68° Fahr., and taking the mean temperature of the surface soil to be 61° Fahr., this gives an increment, of only 1° Fahr. for 208 feet in depth.

The other one, is at the Largo Vittoria, also in the city; its depth is 009 feet, and its temperature is 71·6° Fahr., say 72°, or 1° for 82·64, or say 83 feet in depth.

These wells are not much more than a mile apart, yet the absolute temperatures differ, and the increments, by more than 2 : 1; both are much below the commonly received mean rate of increase, and these are wells, within ten miles of a volcanic active vent.

This low temperature in both, and great discrepancy between them respectively is traceable, I have no doubt, to the fact, that both are mainly, in tufa beds of vast depth, as porous as a filtering stone, and subjected to great and *variable cooling influences, from the penetration of fresh and of sea water, while the adjacent sources of heat are variable also in a high degree.*

Let us assume, however, that at the focal cavity, the increment is the usual mean, of 1° for each 60 feet of descent; then, at the upper, mean, and lowest levels, of the cavity, we have the corresponding temperatures thus:

	Depth in feet.	Temperature.
Minimum depth	16,705	339·4° Fahr.
Mean depth (seismic focus)	34,930	643·1° ,,
Maximum depth	49,359	883·6° ,,

assuming, as before, the mean temperature of the surface soil, = 61° Fahr.

If the cavity were filled with dense steam, at these respective temperatures, the corresponding pressure upon its walls, would be, from the formula,

$$s = (1 + 0·004\, t)^5$$

t, being reckoned, above 212° Fahr.

	Temperature.	Pressure in Atmospheres.
Minimum depth	339·4°	7·85°
Mean focal depth	643·1°	148·88°
Maximum depth	883·6°	684·11°

In accordance with the law, that vapour can exist, in a vessel whose walls are at different temperatures, at the tension only, due to the *least* temperature of any part; it might be concluded, that the greatest possible pressure within the cavity, would be that due to the temperature, of its uppermost and coolest part; but as the steam must be supposed suddenly admitted to the cavity, in this instance, and may be supposed unlimited in supply; we may conclude that for the instant, it would reach any higher tension, up to the limit of the maximum temperature.

Taking the specific gravity of Apennine limestone, forming, the walls of the cavity, and the whole of its superincumbent mass, = 2·700, and 29·92 inches of mercury, specific gravity 13·57, equaling one atmosphere; it follows that a column of 150·4 inches of the limestone, or of nearly 12·5 feet, will also balance an atmosphere of steam.

Hence, in round numbers, we have the following depths of limestone, necessary to balance the corresponding tensions—

	Tension in Atmospheres.	Depth of Limestone.
Minimum depth	8	100 feet.
Mean focal depth	149	1862 ,,
Maximum depth	684	8550 ,,

We therefore remark, that although the steam pressure, was enough, to lift the enormous column of 8550 feet of limestone, it was not sufficient, by about one-half, to blow up, the weakest portion, of the covering of the cavity, whose least thickness was 16,700 feet below the surface.

The steam tension, of 684 atmospheres, is about one-third that of fired gunpowder, and hence amply sufficient, if either *suddenly* generated, or *suddenly* admitted, to the cavity, to produce the wave of impulse, by the sudden compression, of the walls of the cavity; to which, even the mean tension, would be sufficient.

The pressures upon the walls, due to the preceding tension, are

	Atmosphere's tension.	Tons per square inch.
Minimum depth	8	0·0535
Mean focal depth	149	0·9980
Maximum depth	684	4·5800

so that at the latter pressure — that due to the highest temperature, and lowest portion, of the cavity—*the total accumulated pressure upon its lamellar walls, of 27 geographical square miles in area, would be more than 640,528 millions of tons.*

And yet, it is extremely doubtful, that the temperature of the focal cavity, was not very much higher. The probable superior limit, of temperature, would be that it might be as high, as that of the "foyer" of Vesuvius.

I cannot find, that any professed investigator of volcanoes, has ever thought of making, the very obvious and important experiment, of lowering, with an iron wire a pyrometer, as far as possible, into a crater, in order to get some idea, of its actual temperature, even within a few score yards of its mouth.

When on Vesuvius, on the occasion of this Report, I feel satisfied that I could have so measured the temperature, of the minor mouth, then in powerful action, to the depth of several hundred feet, had I possessed the instrumental means at hand. To this smaller mouth, it was then possible, by wrapping the face in a wet cloth, to approach so near, upon the hard and sharply defined (though thin and dangerous) crust of lava, through which it had broken, as to see its walls, for quite 150 feet down, by estimation. They were glowing hot, to the very lips, although constantly evolving, a torrent of rushing steam, with varying velocity. Accustomed as I have been, by profession, for years, to judge of temperatures in large furnaces, by the eye, I estimated the temperature of this mouth, by the appearance of its heated walls, at the lowest visible depth; they were there, of a pretty bright red, visible in bright winter sunlight overhead. I have no doubt, then, that the temperature of the shaft, at from 300 to 500 feet down, was sufficient to melt copper, or from 1900° to 2000° of Fahr. From the extremely bad conducting power, of the walls, of a volcanic shaft, there is scarcely any loss of heat, from any cause, except its enormous absorption, in the latent heat, of the prodigious volume of *dry steam* which is constantly being evolved. It is *perfectly transparent for several yards above the orifice of the shaft*, and is not only perfectly dry steam, but also super-heated; and although this steam, may be at the mouth very much below the highest temperature of the hottest point, the temperature of the shaft or duct that carries it off will be very nearly at all depths the same, to probably within a very short distance, of the point of greatest incandescence.

In the absence, at present, of better information, we may suppose the temperature of volcanic cavities in this region (where Vesuvius is the most "glaring instance") to be about 2000° Fahr. This would give a superior limit of temperature, for the interior of our seismic focal cavity, $2\frac{1}{3}$ times as great, as the maximum arrived at, by applying the supposed law of hypogeal increment, and would raise the tension, of the contained steam, (admitting that we know anything about the state of water, at such temperatures and pressures,) to much more than that due to fired gunpowder.

The capability of producing an earthquake impulse, depends greatly, however, upon the *suddenness with which the steam is flashed off, and its tension brought to bear upon the walls of the cavity*; and this is not most rapid, at the highest temperature, of the evaporating surface, unless, indeed, intense pressure, by bringing the fluid more completely into contact with the walls of the heated cavity, may modify the effects of the spheroidal state. On the other hand, the experiments of Bontigny and others, indicate, that the *most sudden production possible of steam*, would take place from the walls of a focal cavity, heated to about 500° or 550°, which is but a few degrees below that, of the mean focal depth as ascertained, viz., 582° Fahr.

We may now apply these deductions to some considerations as to the limits of dimension of the wave of shock and the work contained in it.

CHAPTER XIII.

OF THE AMPLITUDE OF THE WAVE AND THE WORK STORED UP IN IT.

Let E F (Fig. 352) be a section vertically, at the earth's surface, o the mean focal point, at the depth $o\,d$, measured

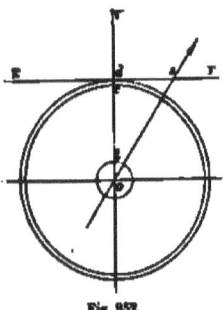

Fig. 352.

upwards upon the seismic vertical o V, and $d\,e$ be the amplitude of the wave, in its path of emergence at e, taken somewhere *near* o V. The wave is originated by the *sudden compression*, of the elastic materials forming the walls of the focal cavity. Admitting the temperature, as just obtained on the commonly-assumed hypogeal increment, we have obtained a measure, of the pressure producing this compression; and if we possessed the coefficient of compression for the material, we should be enabled, to calculate, the volume and amplitude of the wave, upon various hypotheses which might be framed, as to the mode of its origination. For, supposing the compression to originate at a single point o, *the column of least resistance* of the surrounding medium, is the vertical line od, and if the pressure upon the unit of surface, at the focal point, be *unknown*, its greatest limit for the production of a wave, is that, when the elasticity at the base, balances the whole weight of this column, for any increase of pressure beyond that, will lift it bodily. If the pressure at o, be known or assumed, then, if L = the unit of length, of a compressed prism of the material, l = the compression due to the pressure, on the length unit; $\frac{L}{l}$ measures the compressing force, and ot, is the total compression from o, of the entire column od, or $l:ot::L:od$.

And as the compression is supposed equal all round, from the initial point o—

$$0{\cdot}5236 \times (2{,}o\,t)^3 = W,$$

the whole compressed volume, which is equal to *the volume of the wave at a given moment near the instant of starting.*

If we suppose the volume of the wave constant, up to the time it reaches the surface at d, or a point at some small distance as s; then, the volume of the spherical shell, whose exterior radius is od, and interior oc, must equal that of the wave, or

$$0{\cdot}5236 \times (2{,}o\,d)^3 - 0{\cdot}5236 \times (2{,}o\,c)^3 = W,$$

whence, $cd =$ *the wave amplitude on reaching the surface* may be obtained; or if this be observed, the depth of the focus ascertained by the methods we have employed, and the coefficient of compression, be known, then *the total compression may be obtained, and the temperature due to the pressure producing it.* In this way, a new method would present itself, through the medium of seismology, for attempting *the ascertainment of temperatures, at depths that can never be reached experimentally.*

The *vis viva* of the wave, is constant throughout its transit, (assuming elasticity perfect,) and $= \frac{1}{2} M a^2$; M being the mass of material, in any spherical couche, or in simultaneous wave motion, and equal to twice the "work done," in compressing, the originating sphere of impulse, whose radius is $o\,t$. Hence, *we can express, the work of the wave, in foot pounds, and, finally, transmuting the mechanical effort, by the aid of Joules' thermodynamic unit* $(J = 772)$ *into heat; we can determine, the expenditure, of volcanic or hypogeal heat, necessary to the production of the earthquake*; or as there are 11,000,000 foot pounds of absolute dynamic energy, in the combustion of a pound of coal, we can compare the value, of the "shock power," in "cheval vapeurs," or with any other measure of power, we please.

Unfortunately, we are as yet without some of the numerical data necessary, to enable us to attempt putting such a calculation into form.

The only experiments that have been made, upon the compressibility of limestone, are those of Tredgold (' Phil. Mag.,' vol. lvi. p. 290), who deduced the coefficient, by the use of Dr. Young's formulæ, from experiments on flexure, and obtained, for primary limestone, the modulus of elasticity $= 2,520,000$ lbs. for the base of an inch square.

The compression due to each ton pressure upon a prism of a foot long $= L$, is, therefore $= 0.000440$ feet $= l$, a coefficient, probably, somewhat too high for Apennine limestone.

Adopting that coefficient, the compression due to the pressure, of the mean focal depth, and of the maximum depth would be, respectively—

	Pressure.	Compression in feet = c.
Mean f.d. =	0·998 tons =	0·000445 nearly.
Max. f.d. =	4·580 „ =	0·00204

The mean depth $o\,d$, (Diagrams Nos. 1 and 2 emergences) is 35,000 feet in round numbers, and the radius of the sphere of initial compression $o\,t$, due to the pressure of maximum depth = 71·25 feet. This is for *statical* pressure, and as the extension or compression of any elastic body, to which a given force is suddenly and at once applied, is double that due to the same gradually and slowly laid on —so here, the range of compression, for the suddenly-applied steam pressure, is double, or $o\,t = 142·5$ feet, and the volume of the sphere of compression, $= 0·5236 \times 285^3$, and equal to the volume of the wave, or to the spherical shell, whose outer radius is 35,000 feet, and its thickness $d\,c$, which is also equal to the amplitude of the wave.

The actual thickness of the spherical shell, calculated on these data, and on the assumption that the compressing force, emanated from a physical point, at o, at the moment that the wave reached the surface at d; is very small, being only = 0·000787, of a foot.

If, however, upon the same data, we calculate the amplitude, on the assumption, that the impulse was conveyed, (Fig. 353) in directions from the plane of the fissure ff', perpendicular to it, compressing both surfaces in the directions f and f', the compressing force acting to its full extent at $o\,t$, $o\,t'$, and becoming evanescent at f and f', the

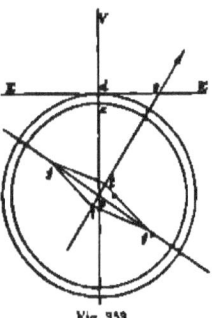

Fig. 353.

extremities of the fissure; and supposing, as already done, (Chap. V.), that the wave of shock, commenced being transmitted, when the lamellar area of the whole focal cavity, had attained half its dimensions; then the amplitude of the wave at d, would be $d\,e = 0.769$ feet, assuming it the same in all directions round o, or about 9 inches. The actual dimensions of amplitude observed at Polla, a place like s, near the seismic vertical $o\,V$, deduced from the widths of masonry fissures was 2·5 inches, being less than the calculated result by 3·6 times. It follows, therefore, either that Tredgold's coefficient of compression, is too great, for the actual material compressed, at the focus of this earthquake, (as it most probably is,) or that the pressure was not that, due to the *maximum* depth, or was due to a smaller coefficient of hypogeal heat increment. If we substitute for it the pressure due to the *mean* focal depth, we shall obtain a result, that does not differ very widely, from the observed amplitude at Polla, and will be still nearer, if we suppose the lamellar form of the focal cavity to be, not rectangular, but circular, or approaching a circle in outline.

These last calculations must only be viewed, in the existing state of our data, as mere illustrations of a method, that a more complete state of experimental knowledge, as to the compressibilities of various rocks, wet and dry, and at different temperatures—some being high—would enable us to make available.

They are sufficient, however, as they stand, to one not unimportant deduction. They disprove at once the assumption very commonly made, and constantly repeated without any attempt to apply measures in test of the validity of the doctrine, that earthquakes are agents of direct permanent elevation of the surface of our globe, *i. e.*, permanent, as contradistinguished from the transient and slight swell of the wave itself, at the moment of the transit of the shock. For it will be obvious that the *amount of elevation possible* from the greatest pressure we can assign, to the momentary force producing the impulse of the wave, is not capable, even right above the focus, of raising the level of the land, by a height, much more than instrumentally appreciable; and there is not the least evidence that any part of even this is permanent. On the contrary, everything tends to the conclusion, that after the passage of the shock, the surface is left again directly, at precisely the same level that it had before. That earthquakes occur along with, and *as part of a train of other circumstances, that do produce permanent elevation* occasionally, and that earthquakes are probably always the signals, that the forces producing elevation are operative, is another matter, with which the erroneous, or loosely expressed view, should not be confounded.

CHAPTER XIV.

OF THE VELOCITY OF TRANSIT OF THE WAVE.

A very common error appears to prevail amongst writers on physical geology and seismology, in either confounding the velocity of transit, *i. e.*, the rate of surface propagation of the wave of shock, with that of the wave itself, *i. e.*, the rate of displacement and replacement of the particles being acted on by the wave, or in supposing them to be necessarily the same; and a want of clearness on this point, has greatly retarded the progress of earthquake investigation. A similar mistake is even found in some treatises on physical geology, in respect to the analogous case of aqueous waves of translation, in which it is assumed, that the enormous transit rate, of the tidal wave of translation upon the deep ocean, may be taken as the measure of its diluvial or drift-producing power.

The ocean tide wave may travel across the deep Atlantic, at the rate of nearly 550 miles per hour, and on reaching soundings, be reduced at the lips of the Irish Channel, to 200 or 175 miles per hour. In the Channel, a further reduction takes place, so that the observed rate of the tide stream is only 2, 3, or 4 miles per hour, and some corresponding decrease in the velocity of the wave particle takes place. As the velocity is proportionate to the amplitude of the wave, for a given depth, and the amplitude depends upon the depth, the analogy is with the wave of light, rather than with that of sound or shock. The similarity, however, is seen in the general equation of elastic wave motion,

$$v = a \cos\left(\frac{2\pi}{\lambda}(x - at)\right)$$

where a, the transit velocity, depends upon the elastic modulus, and may differ to any extent from v: being, in fact, connected only through a^2, the intensity. Geologists must not be surprised, therefore, at finding, (now that the *velocity of transit* and the *velocity of the wave particle* at its maximum *have been both for the first time measured, and for the same shock,*) that they differ enormously from each other; that the velocity of transit is about half that of a cannon shot; but that the velocity of the wave particle (which does the mischief) is not as great as that with which a man reaches the ground when he jumps off a table; and yet that this small velocity is competent to produce all the violent and formidable effects of earthquake, no longer admits of doubt. On the other hand, let any one apply his common sense, to consider what *should be the effect,* if the velocity impressed on solid bodies by the wave, were that of its transit. Take, for instance, the balls of limestone of 1½ foot diameter, projected from the Campanile of Padula monastery (Certosa). If, in place of with a velocity of 11 or 12 feet per second, they had been put in motion with one of 700 or 800 feet per second, which is equal to the velocity of a 13-inch shell on leaving the mortar, in place of falling on the pavement, 40 or 50 feet from where they stood, they would have flown through the air, a mile or two, and so of every other body.

This point would scarcely seem to need prolonged remark, were it not that up to this time, it appears to have been almost universally misconceived; even Humboldt appears never to have formed in his mind any clear conception of the distinction, and Nöggerath and Schmidt, in their excellent accounts of the Rhenish and Hungarian shocks, have apparently equally lost sight of it, as they busy themselves exclusively, with ascertaining exactly, the velocity of transit, and make even no allusion, to the proper velocity of the wave, which, for all purposes of seismodynamics, is the far more important element to determine.

Over the whole wide area of commotion examined, it has been seen, (Part II.) that I was able to obtain only six reliable records of the precise moment of the arrival of the shock, at the same number of localities, viz., at Naples, Vietri di Potenza, Monte Peloso, (D'Errico's station,) Atella, Barielle, and Melfi. These six, however, afford tolerably accordant results, far more so than could have been expected from observations made in a country so backward as to knowledge, and where the accurate public measurement of time—one of the surest indications of advancing civilization—is absolutely unknown. The recorded times, and their reduction to Naples mean time, respectively, are given, for each of the above stations, in their proper places (Part II.). It is only necessary here, therefore, to compare them, with the distances from the seismic vertical, in order to obtain the transit velocities.

Melfi, Vietri di Potenza, and the seismic vertical, close

to Caggiano (see Map A) are almost exactly in one right line. The moment of the occurrence of the first shock at Melfi was $10^h\ 3^m\ 0^s\cdot 0$ Naples mean time, and at Vietri, $9^h\ 59^m\ 16^s\cdot 2$ Naples mean time. Melfi is 24·25 geographical miles from the seismic vertical, and Vietri is two geographical miles from the same. The difference in time between Melfi and Vietri is therefore $= 3^m\ 43^s\cdot 8$, or we may say $3^m\ 44^s$, and the distance between them is 24·25 geographical miles, which gives 9·23 seconds for the time of transit per geographical mile between them, and a transit velocity of 658·2 feet per second.

Vietri di Potenza, being two geographical miles from the seismic vertical, the instant of the occurrence of the shock at that central point, must have been equal to the time at Vietri, less the transit time for the two miles, or,

	h.	m.	s.
	9	59	16·20	Naples mean time at Vietri.
Transit for 2 miles	0	0	18·46
	9	58	57·74	moment of the occurrence of the shock at seismic vertical (Caggiano).

We may therefore take this as the starting-point for all the other determinations, and call it $9^h\ 58^m\ 58^s$ Naples mean time.

The time of the shock at Naples, is given differently by two authorities, both worthy of attention. Signor Fiodo's clock gave it $10^h\ 13^m\ 26^s\cdot 0$ (tempo meridiano), that is the time as per observation of the sun's crossing the meridian. The time, as published in the 'Giornale Reale,' from the Osservatorio, and certified to by Professor Capocci, is $10^h\ 10^m\ 0^s\cdot 0$ Naples mean solar time.

We must reduce the former to the latter.

	h.	m.	s.
Sun's right ascension when on the meridian at Naples, on the 16th December, 1857 . . =	17	36	4·45
Time by Signor Fiodo's clock =	10	13	26·00
	27	49	30·45
Sidereal time at mean noon on that date	17	40	6·91
	10	9	23·54
Acceleration = minus	0	1	39·83
Moment of shock at Naples, according to Signor Fiodo, in Naples mean solar time . . .	10	7	43·71
Which we may call . .	10	7	44

The difference, therefore, between the times noted by him, and at the Observatory, is equal to 2ᵐ 16ˢ. The high probability is, therefore, that Signor Fiodo's clock was stopped by the first tremulous movement, (having been specially prepared by him, that *it should be readily stopped,*) and that the clocks at the Observatory, were stopped by the second which occurred shortly after, with a little interval between, (see Guiscardi, Part II.,) these clocks having been arranged *to go and not to be stopped* by a shock.

We may, however, take the transit time from both data—

	h.	m.	s.
Time of shock at Naples (Fiodo's) .	10	7	44
Time at the seismic vertical . .		9	58 58
Time of transit from the latter to Naples	0	8	46

The distance from the origin (seismic vertical) to Naples, allowing for the change of direction, by refraction, at the Monte St. Angelo range, (but without any allowance for loss of time at the refracting point,) is 68 geographical miles, which gives 7"·735 for the transit rate per geographical mile, and a transit velocity = 781·5 feet per second.

To this we must apply two corrections. 1st. For the loss of time at the refracting point, for which we can only assume probable data, as we know nothing of the change of elasticity, of the limestone, nor of the refracting indices. If we assume a loss of time equivalent to the transit through the axial thickness of the chain, or 2 geographical miles = 15"·47 in time for the retardation at the refracting point; then the 68 miles, with a constant velocity, would have been run over, at a transit rate = 7"·514 per geographical mile, or with a transit velocity = 808·5 feet per second.

2nd. The wave emerged, after refraction from the limestone formations, to the south and S. E. of the St. Angelo range, into the shattered and discontinuous volcanic formation, of the Terra di Lavoro around Naples, and principally into heavy, soft, and very inelastic tufa, (the grand buffer that has saved Naples many a time, from destruction and not the "safety valve" of Vesuvius, as popularly imagined,) which has been ascertained to have a depth of more than 1500 feet beneath Naples, and is probably immensely deeper.

The transit from St. Angelo to Naples, was therefore made at a much slower rate, than that from the (seismic vertical) origin, to the mountain range. We shall be probably very nearly correct if we assume that the transit from the origin to the mountain range beyond Salerno, (40 geographical miles to axis of chain,) was performed at a mean rate, between those from the origin to Monte Peloso, through the flat bedded formations, of the upper limestone and murgic rocks; and from the origin to Atella, chiefly through hard, shattered Apennine limestone, and 4 or 5 miles of volcanic rocks as hereafter to be stated, or

		Feet per Second.
Monte Peloso, transit rate	.	989·4
Atella ,,		759·3
Mean rate .	. .	874·3

At this rate, the total time of transit, from the seismic vertical, to the axis of the chain at Salerno, 45 geographical miles, would require 313″; which leaves 213″ (of the total time = 8′ 46″) for the transit of the remaining 23 miles through the tufa. And, again, deducting the 15″·47 or 16″ for the loss of time, at the point of refraction, we have 197″ nett time, for the transit through the 23 miles of tufa, which gives a transit rate of 8″·6 per geographical mile, and a transit velocity = 706·6 feet per second in that formation, being less than that in the limestone, by 167·7 feet per second. There can be no doubt that a similar correction should be made, for the transit rates, given for Melfi, &c., from the fact that the last six or seven miles of the distance is also through volcanic rocks, though of much greater age, density, hardness, and continuity, at a considerably greater depth than those of the Vesuvian area.

Proceeding now to try the transit rate, by the Naples Observatory time, we find

		h.	m.	s.
Moment of the shock at Naples as stated from the Osservatorio Reale	.	10	10	0
Moment of shock at the seismic vertical	.	9	58	58
Difference	. . .	0	11	2

which, on the 68 miles' total distance between them, gives 9"·735 transit rate per geographical mile = 624·03 feet per second; and applying the same correction as before, for refractive retardation, the transit rate becomes 9"·457 per geographical mile, and the velocity = 642·36 feet per second; and assuming the difference of transit rate, between the limestone and tufa, to be as last obtained; then the transit rate from this observation, in the limestone, would be 642·36 + 167·70 = 810·06 feet per second, or 64 feet per second below that of the preceding determination.

I am therefore disposed to believe, that the Observatory clocks were stopped, by a movement shortly subsequent to that, which arrested Signor Fiodo's; and as we cannot know what the interval was, I reject the Observatory observation, as probably the least correct, and adhere to Fiodo's, as the best time measure we have, at Naples, and, *per se*, essentially a good one.

Monte Peloso is 36 geographical miles from the seismic vertical. At D'Errico's station,

	h.	m.	s.
The moment of shock was in Naples mean time	10	2	39
The time of its occurrence at the seismic vertical . . .	9	58	58
Difference = total time of transit over 36 geographical miles . .	0	3	41

which gives a transit rate of 0·14 per geographical mile, and a transit velocity = 989·4 feet per second. This is the highest velocity obtained, which is what should be expected, inasmuch as more than one-half of the entire distance, is through comparatively level bedded, and little shattered rocks, of elasticity, quite as high as the limestone.

Atella is 21 geographical miles from the seismic vertical—

	h.	m.	s.
The moment of occurrence of the shock as given by the old cathedral clock in Naples mean time	10	1	54
The time of its occurrence at the seismic vertical	9	58	58
Difference = the total time of transit over 21 geographical miles . .	0	2	56

which gives 8"·4 nearly for the transit rate per geographical mile, and a transit velocity = 723·2 feet per second.

Barielle is 24·5 geographical miles from the seismic vertical—

	h.	m.	s.
The moment of occurrence of the shock there, was in Naples mean time	10	2	15
The time of its occurrence at the seismic vertical	9	58	58
Difference = the total time of transit over 24·5 geographical miles .	0	3	17

which gives 8·04" for the transit rate per geographica

mile, and a transit velocity = 755·6 feet per second; differing from the last by only 32·4 feet per second. This strongly corroborates the exactness of both, as the two towns, Atella and Barielle, are both in the same right line with the origin, and only about 3 geographical miles apart, so that the wave-path for both, traversed the same formations.

Collecting our results, we have the transit velocities respectively from the—

Origin to Naples	. . . .	808·5
,,	Salerno (Monte St. Angelo)	874·3
,,	Monte Peloso . . .	989·4
,,	Melfi	658·2
,,	Barielle	755·6
,,	Atella	723·2
Vietri to Melfi	. . . .	658·2
Salerno to Naples	. . . .	706·6

and omitting the second, 658·2 (Vietri to Melfi), which is from the same elements as the first, we obtain a general mean velocity of surface transit in all directions, of 787·97 feet per second.

Such a *general mean*, however, cannot exist in nature, as it must vary, in different directions round the seismic vertical, with differences in continuity and elasticity, &c., of the formations. In fact, looking at the seismic map A, it may be said that, as in a map of marine cotidal lines, the tides are highest, where the cotidal lines are seen to be most crowded, so, here, the transit velocity is seen to be greatest, in those directions in which the coseismal lines are spread out furthest, from the origin.

Partial means having regard to the formation, therefore,

are much more important and true. These, so far as our results admit of them, are—

	Transit Velocity in Feet per Second.
Barielle and Atella, mean transit rate, through highly inclined and shattered, but elastic limestone formations, chiefly with about three miles' volcanic formations at the remote extremity	739·4
Melfi, same line, but about nine miles of volcanic formations, at the remote extremity	658·2
Salerno, through about a mean of the mountainous districts as to formation; upper and lower limestones, some highly inclined, others more flatly bedded, plain of four miles of deep clays, and calcareous districts at the remote extremity	874·3
Naples, through the deep deposits of tufa, and other volcanic products, of the Terra di Lavoro	706·6
Monte Peloso, through about one-half the range, highly inclined and elastic but shattered rocks, chiefly the lower limestones. The remainder, through the less-inclined, flat-bedded tertiaries, of the margie, hard, and more continuous formation	989·4

The extremes are, in round numbers, from 1000 feet per second, in the best transmitting, to 700-feet per second, in the worst transmitting formations.

The whole of the results obtained, accord singularly well, with my own experimental determinations of wave-transit in granite and in sand, ('Report Brit. Assoc., 1851,') which gave the transit rate in dense wet sand, = 825 feet per second, within a mile of the origin; and also correspond remarkably with the mean result, obtained with so much care and accuracy by Schmidt, for the Hungarian shock of 1858, viz., from 700 to 735 feet per second, (French feet); and also with the shock of 26th July, 1855, which gave a transit rate, of from five to seven geographical miles per minute. My highest transit velocity, however, is more than 300 feet per second, below that assigned by Nöggerath, to the Rhenish earthquake of 29th July, 1846, viz., 1370 French feet per second, which is equal to my experimental determination for granite; a difference, however, that we might quite expect, as a high velocity is highly probable, in the hard, elastic, and comparatively unbroken rocks, of the Devonian and Trappean formations, about Coblentz. (Compare also with Table 8, of transit rates, 'Report Brit. Assoc., 1851.')[*]

The velocities that have been here obtained, are those of the transit of the wave *upon the surface*. They are not the same, with the transit velocities in the direct wave-path through the solid materials beneath, from the mean focal point, to each respective station. These distances being greater, than those from the seismic vertical to each station upon the surface, in the proportion of $1 : \cos e$, and the time

---

[*] The results given as part of this Report, also now prove themselves to correspond well, with those experimentally deduced as to transit time, in the rocks at Holyhead. These experiments were incomplete, at the time of penning this Report, and the results had not been calculated and reduced.—(See 'Phil. Trans. for 1861-62.')—R. M., June, 1862.

being constant, the *velocities of* transit *in the wave-paths* will be increased directly as those distances, viz., from the seismic vertical, to each station, and from mean focal point to same, neglecting the time between the focal point and surface, as common to all distances.

The actual distances along the wave-paths, the mean focal depth being 5¾ geographical miles are as follow:

			Geographical miles.
Mean focal point,	to Monte Peloso	.	38·8
,,	,, Salerno	. .	35·0
,,	,, Melfi	. .	27·2
,,	,, Barielle	. .	24·9
,,	,, Atella	. .	21·6

from which the transit period (τ) in the direct path of the wave, may be easily computed.

The greatest velocity we obtained was that for Monte Peloso = 989·4 feet per second on the surface. The velocity for this range, in the direct path of the wave would be, therefore, 1038·5 feet per second; and as the transit velocity for absolutely homogeneous rock of the character of Apennine limestones and murgies, deduced from the $\sqrt{e}$ of the elastic modulus, cannot be taken lower than from 3500 to 5000 feet per second (see 'First Report on Earthquakes, Brit. Assoc. Reports, 1850, sec. 23'), we find that from three-fourths to four-fifths of the full velocity of transit is absorbed or destroyed, by the continual loss of *vis viva*, due to the changes of molecular condition, and the discontinuity of the formations passed through.[*]

[*] A still greater difference, between the theoretic maximum and the actual transit velocity, due to absorption by heterogeneity, has since been experimentally proved by myself, in the old quartz and slate rocks of North Wales. (See 'Phil. Trans., 1861-62.')— R. M.

CHAPTER XV.

OF THE VELOCITY OF THE WAVE PARTICLE AT ITS MAXIMUM, *i. e.* THE VELOCITY PROPER OF THE WAVE OF SHOCK.

The power of the wave of shock, to produce overthrow, depends upon the intensity of the wave, that is, upon its amplitude, and upon the elasticity of the medium in its passing through, conjointly; and as all free displaced bodies, must be displaced to the extent, due to the greatest velocity impressed, at the centre of gravity, the measure of such displacement is always that of the velocity of the wave particle, at its point of maximum. Our ascertained velocities, are therefore those of that maximum velocity, for each separate station.

We have had the following separate determinations, which form three groups: the first being cases, in which the conditions were such, that the true wave velocity was not materially increased, nor the result interfered with, by surface oscillations; the second, where the velocity ascertained, and being in excess of these, is made up of the true wave velocity plus that of the elastic oscillation of the surface, at the displacing point; whether of the whole "colline," as at Saponara, or of any structure, such as a pier or tower; and the third, where it is possible, but not necessary to conclude, that the determination is below the tenth, from some cause.

WAVE VELOCITIES.

Station.	Velocities.	Method of Determination.	Distance from Seismic Vertical.
	Feet per Second.		Geog. Miles.
Polla	12·830 } mean 13·176 13·490	Overthrow and projection	9·45
Padula	12·580 } mean 12·806 13·152	Overthrow and projection	16·45
Cortese di St. Bruno	11·540	Projection	16·50
Moliterno	11·800	Projection	25·50
Viscoglione, near Saponara	11·040	Overthrow	26·00
Tramutola	14·765	Projection	20·00
Potenza	12·255	Fracture and overthrow	15·00
Monticchio	11·757	Projection	21·50
Bariolle	11·504	Overthrow	24·50
Cortese, Vase of Gate, of the Prior's Garden	21·230	Projection	16·50
Saponara	15·627	Fracture and overthrow	25·00
Sarconi	9·780	Projection	26·70

The mean velocity given, by the first group of eleven separate and independent determinations, is 12·366 feet per second. It is a little doubtful, (Part II. *in loc.*) whether the velocity at Tramutola, was not *slightly* increased, by some surface oscillation; reasons of sufficient weight however are assignable from conditions of formation alone for finding a high velocity at that place.

If we omit Tramutola, and deduce a mean velocity from the remaining ten terms, we obtain 12·039 feet per second;

and if we retain both Tramutola and Sarconi, we get 12·107 for the mean velocity in feet per second.

The first, taking all circumstances into account, is the most probable mean, and excepting the two doubtful terms, differs from the highest determination, by only 0·810 feet per second, and from the lowest by 1·326 feet per second.

We shall refer to these differences again, under the next head, Chap. XVI.

The velocity at Sarconi, may either be a really low one, arising from the peculiar circumstances of its position (Part II. *in loc.*), or be defective in amount, as means did not exist for checking it, by a second determination at the same place. Reviewing all the circumstances, I am inclined to conclude that the velocity at Sarconi was really low, but that also, the determination is below th. *....*th by about one foot per second.

The highest velocity of which any measurable evidence was found, was that of the projection of the vase from the pier of the Prior's garden gate, at the Certosa. Of the total velocity here, at least 8 feet per second, is due to the elastic oscillation of the top of the pier itself. Dr. Young has shown (Math. Prin. Nat. Phil. Art. 398) that the time of oscillation of such an elastic prism, will be that of a simple pendulum, whose length is, $L = \dfrac{0.9707 \, h^2}{d, d \, e}$,

h being the height of the vibrating bar, d its thickness in the direction of vibration, and e the elastic modulus expressed in feet; from which the velocity may be calculated when the angle or arc of vibration is known. Unluckily, in this, as in most examples that actually occur in seismic observation, the excursion of the summit of the pier is partly due to elasticity, and partly to small mutual displacements, of the separate blocks of stone; while in the case of an entire isolated steep hill, such as that of Saponara, the irregular form of the vibrating solid, which approaches nearest to that of a cone fixed at its base, as well as the imperfect homogeneity of its materials, and our ignorance of their precise nature, or of whether any or what intestine movements occur at the instant of shock in the interior, defy our obtaining by calculation, the proper velocity of oscillation of the summit, due to the velocity impressed at the centre of gravity, as distinct from that of the shock by any other method than experiment. It will be evident to the mechanician, however, that the elevation, of such an oscillating body, as well as the other conditions upon which L depends, will much affect the combined result, of the proper wave velocity, and that of the oscillation. When L is very great, as it must be, when so great as that of a lofty "colline" of limestone, some hundreds of feet in height, or where it is even that of a mere tower of moderate height, but whose modulus of elasticity, for the whole material, (*i. e.*, the masonry, mortar, and stone, or brick, taken together), is small, then the time of oscillation being long, and the velocity of the summit small therefore, in relation to the time of the wave; the former may add but little to the total velocity deduced from the conjoint effect of both; and, in fact, with a given seismic wave velocity, and given modulus of elasticity of the oscillating mass, a determinate height, and that a very small one in reality, will produce the maximum total velocity.

If we took the true velocity of the seismic wave *alone*, at

Saponara, to be the same as that determined (from unexceptionable data) at Viscolione, in the Piano, only a mile away, it would give the velocity of oscillation of the hill itself of Saponara

$= 15{\cdot}027 - 11{\cdot}042 = 3{\cdot}587$ feet per second;

but Viscolione was on the deep clays of the Piano, Saponara upon the bare limestone rock. The velocity of the wave of shock, therefore, should be taken, from the nearest station also on rock, which was Tramutola, and which would give the velocity of oscillation $= 15{\cdot}267 - 14{\cdot}705 = 0{\cdot}862$ feet per second. Tramutola itself, however, as already stated, had possibly a small surface oscillation; and if we suppose it to have been as much as the last deduced, at Saponara, the final seismic wave velocities will come out, for Tramutola 13·903 feet per second, and for Saponara, the velocity of oscillation of its "colline," $= 1{\cdot}724$ feet per second.

These low velocities of the wave of shock, now for the first time brought within the domain of figures, will, I doubt not, be received with much surprise by most physical geologists. The impression has been universal, from which I was not myself exempt at the period of publication of my first Report ('Reports Brit. Assoc. 1850'), that the velocity of the wave itself, if not as great as its velocity of transit, was, at any rate, very great; and no attempt had been made to correct this fancy, by appeal to observation and to mechanics. It was with quite the same surprise, however, that the low velocity of transit, first indicated by my own experimental determinations by means of gunpowder explosions, was received by physicists, who, twelve years ago, imagined, (myself included,) that the transit rate must be found about that, which theory would indicate from the elastic modulus, but from which it was found to fall short by ⅔-ths or ⅘-ths. Subsequent determinations of the actual transit velocities in nature, by Nöggerath, by Schmidt, and here by myself, have proved the correctness of those first experimentally obtained, transit velocities, and subsequent researches will, I rest assured, equally confirm the generally low velocity of earthquake shock itself, now for the first time announced.

It must not be understood, however, that the velocity of shock in all parts of the world, and from every earthquake, is limited to about 12 or 13 feet per second. And hence an interesting question arises, of what is *the greatest possible velocity of shock that has ever occurred, or may occur.*

We have, curiously enough, one fact recorded on no less authority than that of Humboldt, which enables us to answer this in part.

In the great earthquake of Riobamba, 4th February, 1797, "The explosive movement," he says (Humboldt, Voy. tom. i. p. 317, and Cosmos), "was such, as is produced by the firing of a mine, and the vertical action from below upwards, was most conspicuously displayed near the town of Riobamba, which was totally destroyed, when *the bodies of many of the inhabitants were thrown* upon the hill of La Culla, which rises to the height of several hundred feet at the other side of the Lican torrent." The actual range of vertical projection of these bodies, has been estimated at 100 feet. The velocity due to this height of projection is,

$$V = \sqrt{2 g H} = 80 \text{ feet per second};$$

and this is probably the greatest velocity of shock recorded, or perhaps at present possible upon our earth; it is nearly as great as that with which the body of one who should leap from the top of the Duke of York's column at London, would strike the pavement; and taking the *greatest* velocity that we have ascertained for this earthquake at 15 feet per second, this maximum velocity is $\frac{80}{15} = 5\cdot33$ times greater, than the velocity of our Neapolitan shock.

Admitting, as we must, the identity of the originating cause, (whatever it be,) of the volcano and the earthquake, it should follow that *the relative intensities of earthquakes in different and wide-apart regions, must be proportionate directly to the altitudes above the sea level of the volcanic vents adjacent to or situated in each respectively*—to the *altitudes*, and *not* to the *mass* of the volcanic cones, because the volcanic *effort of ejection* producing these, is counter-balanced and therefore *measured, by the height of the column* of liquid lava, sustained in the volcanic shaft to overflow at its crater lips; as the mercury of the barometer measures the atmospheric pressure, or a steam-boiler gauge, the pressure within it; and the projectile power for stones and lapilli, is subject to the same measure. But the mass, or cube of the altitude, is the proper measure of the *energy and time of its operation*, at the spot, taken together, or of the antiquity of the volcano, for equal energy.

The altitude of Vesuvius, which is the "pressure gauge" for the Neapolitan earthquake region, has varied within a few hundred years, from 4000 feet, down to 3500, in round numbers.

Now the wave velocity, as ascertained for this earthquake, should bear to the altitude of Vesuvius, the same relation that the velocity of the wave at Riobamba, did to the known altitudes, of the volcanic vents of the Andes.

But 5·33 × 4000 feet, is 21,320 feet, and Chimborazo is 21,100 feet in height. Or, taking the lower height of Vesuvius, (and truer one, for the 400 or 500 feet next the summit, is only a tottering and variable *crest of dust*, relatively to the remainder of the mass,) then 5·33 × 3500 = 18,555 feet, which is the height, of a number of the next rank of Andean volcanoes.

Antisana	17,950
Pichincha	17,644
Cotopaxi	17,662
Purace and Sotara nearly	16,000

and Pasto and Tunguragua from 13,000 to 16,000 feet;— an interesting result, viewed in whatever aspect.

No *direct* connection holds, between the velocity of the wave of shock, and the average areas of seismic convulsion, either at the same or in distant regions; for the area depends, not only upon the intensity of the wave, but upon the depth of the mean focal point, in each shock; and this may, and no doubt does, vary much, for even the same region at different times. Hence we find one city only, like Coquimbo in 1820, or but a few clustered near each other, as in the Melfi shock of 1851, may be destroyed, with great violence, *i. e.*, by a wave of high velocity, and yet the whole area of disturbance be very small.

Were the depth of focus always the same, then the area of seismic disturbance, for like formations and configuration of surface, would be a measure proportionate to the total earthquake effort expended in each case, and would also be some function of the velocity of the wave.

We may generally infer from this, that earthquakes like that of Lisbon, which have a *very great area* of sensible disturbance, have also a very deep seismal focus, and also that *the greatest depth of seismal focus within our planet, is probably not greater, than that ascertained for this Neapolitan earthquake, multiplied by the ratio, that the velocity of the Riobamba wave bears, to that of its wave*; or, what is the same thing, by the ratio, of the altitudes, of the volcanoes of the Andes, to that of Vesuvius.

Hence *the greatest probable depth of origin of any earthquake impulse occurring in our planet, is limited to* $5.33 \times 34,930$ *feet, or to* $186,176$ *feet, or* 30.64 *geographical miles*, and therefore only just touches the depth, which upon received notions as to the increment of hypogeal temperature, is supposed to form the upper surface, of the imaginary ocean of liquid lava, of the earth's interior.

One other point remains to be noticed, as to the velocity of the wave: most of our velocities have been deduced from overthrowing, projections, or fractures, produced by the wave in its *first semiphase*, or forward movement; a very few, from those of the *second semiphase*, or contrary one. There is reason to conclude however, that the velocity is not precisely the same, in both semiphases, and is smallest in the second. That this arises from *defect of perfect elasticity*, in the media through which the wave passes, seems highly probable; and this condition affords an additional ground of explanation, of the fact that in fissured buildings, (Part I. *in loco*,) those fissures are generally widest, that are first acted on by the wave. This inequality in velocity in the two semiphases, was first pointed out to me by my friend Professor Haughton, as deducible from the swing of the two chandeliers at Naples, to whom I submitted the facts I had obtained (Part II. *in loco*), in the hope that he might be enabled to deduce from their movements, a measure of the *amplitude* of the wave at Naples. In this aspect, however, the problem (exactly stated) leads to a differential equation, which cannot be integrated, but in the investigation, the difference of velocity in the two semiphases was evolved.

The velocity of the horizontal component, of the wave of shock, (which may be viewed as practically identical with the velocity of the wave, at Naples,) being known, the arc ϕ through which a pendulum will be swung by a *single* undulation of shock, is given by the following expression, or ϕ being given, V can be obtained.

$$V^2 = 2gl(1 - \cos\phi)$$

And if the time between the like points, in the two semiphases, or time of the wave, be very small, compared with the time of vibration due to l, the length of the swinging pendulum, then this velocity will express the *loss of velocity* of the second semiphase as compared with the first one.

Applying this to the Naples chandeliers, we had one 4 feet 5 inches long, and having a certain time of oscillation by trial, (Part II.) from which,

$$l = g \times \frac{T^2}{\pi^2} = 3.25 \text{ feet};$$

then
$$\sin\phi = \frac{105}{1060},$$

and
$$V = 1.02 \text{ feet per second.}$$

In the other pendulum (Lardner's chandelier), 8 feet 9 in. long, &c., we have, in the same way,

$$l = 6.987 \text{ feet.}$$
$$\sin\phi = \frac{11}{105},$$

and
$$V = 1.57 \text{ feet per second.}$$

The results are concordant as nearly as could be expected, from the arcs of oscillation having been only *repeated* for my observation by the *tact* of the two observers, and some weeks after the earthquake, and they show the small difference between the wave velocities in the first and second semiphase.

If a succession of n waves act upon the pendulum, the time of each being small, as compared with that of oscillation, and the arc of oscillation be due to the conjoint action of the whole, then the difference of velocity between the first and second semiphases will be $\frac{V}{n}$. Such was the case at Naples; seven or eight distinct waves, at equal and short intervals, constituted the first movement, according to Guiscardi, and the other most reliable observers. The mean value of V given by the two chandeliers is $= 1\cdot295$ feet per second, and the difference of velocity therefore $= \frac{1\cdot295}{n}$, or $\frac{1\cdot295}{7}$, or $\frac{1\cdot295}{8} = 0\cdot185$ feet per second, for the first, and $= 0\cdot162$ feet per second for the second, number of pulses.

This result gives a difference of velocity, in the first and second semiphases, at most, of less than ⅕th of a foot per second; so that the determinations we have made of wave velocity, are not materially affected, whether they be derived from projections or overthrows, &c. produced by the first semiphase, or by the second; while on the other hand this small difference, in forward and backward velocity, is quite sufficient to account for the observed difference, in fissuring effect upon masonry, of the two semiphases, and so confirms the explanation given of the fact, on other grounds, in Part 1.

A horizontal velocity, as low as even three or four feet per second, is sufficient to fracture some sorts of bad, ill-laid, and ill-cemented, masonry; the above *difference* of velocity in the two semiphases, would be in such an instance, a considerable fraction of the entire fracturing velocity.

To those accustomed only, to estimate force and velocity, by experience and the senses, the low mean velocity assigned in these pages to the earthquake wave, will probably give rise to sensations, of surprise, or of doubt. It may enable the unmathematical reader, therefore, better to estimate tactilely, the effects of a low velocity, to state, that the shock that such a velocity as that of this earthquake wave would communicate to him, if he were standing upon a solid floor, and the wave-path were vertically upwards, would feel the same, as if he had jumped down upon the floor from a height of $3\frac{1}{2}$ feet, alighting upon his heels and with his knees stiffened.

Fifteen feet per second of velocity, is above 10 English miles per hour. Let him imagine to himself what effect would be produced, upon a wall of 1 or 2 feet thick, and 8 or 10 feet high, if built transversely across a railway truck, which, moving along at the rate of 10 miles per hour, was suddenly stopped, by a fixed obstacle; such is quite analogous to the case of a like wall submitted to the shock of a normal wave of the earthquake of December, 1857.

CHAPTER XVI.

OF LOCAL DISTURBING CAUSES PRODUCING ABRUPT PERTURBATIONS OF THE WAVE OF SHOCK.

In the general equation of wave motion

$$V = a \cos\left(\frac{2\pi}{\lambda}(z - at)\right)$$

the velocity of transit a, is constant for a given uniform medium, and the *vis viva* of any particle Δm, whose density is given, is $= \frac{1}{2} \Delta m a^2$ (a^2 being the intensity) for the whole undulation or complete phase, and is also constant.

If the mass of the medium in wave motion, at any moment of the transit, is always the same, the thickness of the successive spherical couches, between similar points of phase, must diminish as r^2 increases, r being the distance from the origin; and the *vis viva* can only remain constant, with a constant velocity in the direction of r, by supposing movement in the ordinates transverse to r, whose range increases as that in r diminishes, and the extinction of the wave in the direction of r, will continually tend towards $\lambda = o$. But the *vis viva* may also be constant, and the extinction of the wave be due to a continually-increasing amplitude, and decreasing wave velocity, as in the analogous case of the widening and flattening of the annular wave upon the surface of still water, as it is transmitted outwards from the point at the centre, whence the impulse emanated. And in such case, the extinction of the wave must depend, upon its velocity falling to the point at which, the molecular constitution of elastic solids is such, as to cease to transmit its movements, further, from particle to particle. Which of those views, or whether either, expresses what actually occurs in nature, I believe physicists have as yet not determined. Nor are the variables, of velocities and amplitudes, which I have been able to obtain in the present case, capable of more than affording a general indication on the subject. The velocities, indeed, have been fixed with a good deal of precision and certainty; but I have been unable to obtain, any better means of approximation to the amplitude, at different points, than those afforded by the width, at the level of the centre of gravity, of fissures, formed through and remaining in, great masses of very inelastic masonry. The obtaining more precise results as to amplitude, remains for the reward of future seismic observers.

On comparing the few cases in which, for the same locality, I was able to obtain, both velocity and amplitude, (the latter approximately,) and choosing such stations only, as are situated nearly in one right line, passing through the seismic vertical—*i. e.*, having a nearly common wave-path, and therefore less exposed to local disturbing causes, (which change both velocity and amplitude often suddenly and without regard to distance from the origin)—comparing such, it will be found, that we have very probable indications, of *increase of amplitude, as the distance from the seismic vertical increases, and also of reduction of wave velocity.* Thus —

Station.	Polla.	la Sala.	Cortona.	Tramutola.	Saponari.
Distance from the seismic vertical, geographical miles	3·45	11·60	10·50	20·60	26·70
Amplitude, in inches	2·5	3·5	4·0	4·5	4·75

There is an obvious increase of amplitude, as some function of the distance directly, but in what precise ratio, it would be useless to inquire, from such mere approximations to accurate measures of the latter.

Again, in the following table, there is apparent an equally distinct tendency to diminished velocity as the distance from the origin increases—

Station.	Polla.	Padula.	Cortona.	Moliterno.	Viaggiano.	Saponari.
Distance from the seismic vertical, geog. miles	3·45	16·45	16·50	25·50	28·00	26·70
Wave velocity, feet per second	13·176	12·886	11·540	11·800	11·040	9·78

Moliterno diverges a little from the law of continual decrease, and Tramutola and Saponara, had they been inserted, would have done so still more, but these both had special causes of increased velocity, as already recorded.

We shall find the same phenomenon presented, if we take another line of wave-path, for example, that nearly north from the seismic vertical, and east of it—

Station.	Potenza.	Monteicchio.	Barile.
Distance from the seismic vertical, geographical miles	15·00	23·50	24·50
Wave velocity	12·255	11·757	11·564

At Naples, in the separate system of reflected and refracted waves, at 68 geographical miles from the seismic vertical, the amplitude was reduced, partly by distance, but also by loss at the reflecting and refracting medium, to not more than 0·5 inch, as derived from the sensations of the best observers questioned by me, while the immunity of the buildings generally from injury proves that the horizontal velocity of the wave there, certainly did not reach 3 feet per second, nor probably *greatly* exceed the highest difference value of V assignable by the swing of the chandeliers.

CHAPTER XVII.

OF THE DECAY OF THE WAVE OF SHOCK AND ITS GRADUAL OR PER SALTUM EXTINCTION.

This will be most conveniently treated of under distinct subsections. In Chap. IV. the great and wide-spread conditions of surface configuration, as affecting the extent of diffusion of the wave of shock, and the forms of the isoseismals, have been already discussed. The present Chapter has reference to some of those conditions of like class, which modify seismic action at particular spots within those great areas, and determine, either reduced or increased earthquake energy, at those localities, or change the directions of its action, and the extent of its propagation in different directions.

> 1st. Local reduction in the intensity of the shock wave, amounting almost to sudden extinction, may be produced by *deep and wide fissures extending transverse to the wave-path*, and filled in with loose or discontinuous or soft materials.

The nature of this action has been explained, as developed upon its largest scale in Chap. IV., and in Part II. *in loc.*, its effects, as remarkably exemplified at Muro and Bella, have been detailed.

This retarding action is capable, of extremely local or

restricted action, as exemplified at St. Arsenio, St. Pietro, and Diano. Indeed, anything that tends to solution or diminution, of continuity between a given extent of surface, and the media at the side whence the wave advances to it, acts *pro tanto* in this way. It must have been the observation of this fact, upon its great scale, but without any clue to its real cause, that gave rise to the ancient belief, which still holds its ground in the minds of the Italians; that caverns or deep pits, wells, or even large vaults, or other hollow substructures, produce more or less immunity from earthquake. Thus Pliny mentions, that the Capitol of ancient Rome, was saved from the effects of earthquake, by the catacombs.

 2nd. Where there are situated along the path of the wave, and transverse (more or less) to it, one or several elevations or ranges of mountains.

At the passage of each such elevation, a portion of the wave is extinguished, as respects its direct path, and places situated *upon the flanks* of the slopes, *remote* from the seismic vertical, receive the effects of the shock with *increased* energy. Places in the *plain beyond* these, in the direction of the wave movement, receive its effects with *reduced* energy.

Places *upon the flanks* of the slopes, *nearest* to the seismic vertical, receive the effects of the shock with *reduced* energy, and in wave-paths differing much, from the direct ones from the focus, and extremely variable in direction, at different near points of surface.

Those *in the plains between the elevations* perceive the directions of shock most nearly in the original wave-paths, mixed with waves of apparently steeper emergence, the nearer they are situated to the bases of the flanks *remote* from the focus. The energy, as evidenced by its effects in each successive valley plain, further from the focus, is found *abruptly reduced*, the moment the intervening ridge has been passed; and when there are many such alternations, the wave of shock becomes rapidly lost and extinguished, and this altogether apart from retardations or reductions, due to discontinuity of formation, or passage through transverse stratification. This will be easily understood from Fig. 354, where o is the mean focal point, $o\ v$ the

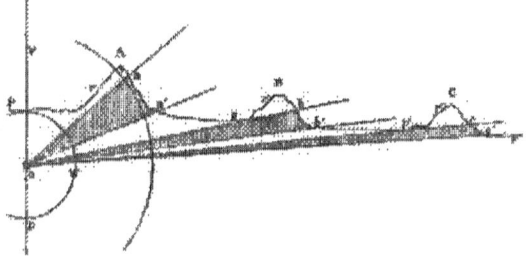

Fig. 354.

seismic vertical, $P p''$ the surface of the earth from which rise three mountain masses in the same right line with o, or three parallel mountain ranges, A, B, C. Of the whole wave P W D, transmitted, the shaded parts are (as respects direct transmission) extinguished at the successive elevations, $a a'$ at A, $b b'$ at B, &c. The places situated upon the flanks $a a'$, $b b'$, &c., being *free-lying surfaces*, are exposed to exalted earthquake action. The places between a' and p, b' and p', &c., suffer less as their distances from o increase; but those on the plain $c'p''$ are abruptly less acted on than those on that $b'p'$; and these, again, abruptly less than in $a'p$; while the places in those plains, nearest to a', b', and c', are exposed to *dispersive* waves, in new wave-paths, due to the breaking up of the direct wave at the flanks $a a'$, $b b'$, &c., and those close to and upon the other flanks r, r', r'', are affected by the direct waves, and by transversals getting more and more nearly vertical, as the distance from o increases.

Several other subordinate complex effects, of similar irregularities of surface will occur to the reader.

These phenomena have found numerous examples in the present earthquake. To such actions, in part produced by the numerous, more or less parallel, chains of mountains, and variously transverse to the wave-paths, were due the alternations of energy, and abrupt reductions of effect, observable all through the districts to the N. W. of the focal centre. Nowhere were these more remarkable, than in the successive valleys between the branch ranges, running towards the south in a north and south direction between Riciliano and Pagano, (Maps A and B); while to similar causes (united with effects due to formation) was due, the comparative immunity of the group of towns, between Brindisi, Tricarico, and Acctura, in the N. E. middle space, between the meizoseismal and first isoseismal curves.

Laviano, Valva, and Oliveto afford examples, of the increased effects, on places situated on *remote* flanks, $a a'$, $b b'$, &c. (Fig. 354); Picerno and Tito, of the disturbances of the wave-paths, by position on the *near* flanks, $r r'$, &c.; while the abrupt loss of energy, (beyond that due to increased distance only,) is well exemplified in the destruction of Tito at the near side, and the comparative safety of Potenza, (within five geographical miles of it in a right line,) at the remote side of the great Apennine.

It would be tedious, however, to go again through many of the facts recorded in Part II., by pointing out their relations in this respect. They will best be studied, the principles once understood being kept in view, and with the Maps A. and B, and Zannoni's great map before the reader.

3rd. Increment of effect, reduplication of shock, and change in the directions of wave-path are produced, locally and abruptly, by dispersive and reflected waves, passed out, along with, or before, or after, the direct wave, from closely adjacent mountain flanks, not transverse, or but obliquely so, to the principal wave-path of the locality.

Of this the most striking examples occur at Potenza, situated, as will be remarked, in a basin-like hollow, with mountain ranges, separated from it and from each other, inflected in various directions close round it. Besides the main shock of the direct wave in the path north, 87·30° E., it was shaken by subordinate shocks, reflected from the flanks of these surrounding mountains, in paths in every azimuth round the horizon.

So also, the chain of cities extending from Melfi south to Atella, not only received the main shock in their respective wave-paths, but as will be seen marked (Map A) had various other wave-paths in different azimuths, yet all pointing out reflected waves, from the east flank of that chain of the Apennines which branching out at St. Fele, ends in Monte Vulture. Montemurro is another remarkable case, where, standing surrounded by a crescent of mountains to the north and west, it will be observed that, besides the main wave-path north 142° E., it is marked with several subordinate ones, *all in directions normal to the flanks of the hills around.* Numerous other examples have been remarked upon, in treating of the facts of the Val di Diano in Part II. It is but just to myself that I should state, that when observing and recording those wave-paths in the country, I had not Zannoni's map with me, nor any other that showed the directions of the mountain ranges with any correctness; and that the beautiful inosculation of cause and effect, as to those perturbations, only showed itself fully, when I was subsequently able to lay down correctly the directions of the mountain ranges, along with the wave-paths.

In the separate system of Naples, the effects of reflection and refraction are developed, on the grand scale already described. Within this area, although the general energy of the shock was so much diminished, examples of local mountain reflection are seen at both sides of the Monte St. Angelo range, and very curiously at Ottajano and Somma; which places, besides the main wave, (after its two refractions at the above range,) in the nearly south to north new wave-path, sustained the subordinate shock, of reflected waves from the N.E. flank of Vesuvius, in a path north 67° E.

Such a reflected shock may, by the accidents of surface configuration, in relation to the seismic vertical and to the place affected, reach the latter before, or after, or along with the main shock, and thus produce two closely-following successive shocks at one spot, differing in direction, though emanating from a single originating impulse, and perhaps only felt as a single shock, at another spot, a few miles away.

Of this, examples were found in the Val di Diano and elsewhere, and are mentioned *in loco*.

    4th. Places situated along the line of mountain ranges, which are also in the line or nearly so of the wave-path, are more or less protected, when situated near sudden enlargements of the mountain mass, and the contrary; and places situated beyond the remote or free-lying *end*, of a mountain range which has gradually or abruptly diminished to the plain, are severely handled.

Just as in a line of ivory balls, the somewhat analogous illustration adduced by Humboldt, where the last (or free lying) ball, is caused to fly off from the others, by the stroke of the moving ball, given to the first, and transmitted through the other. If all the balls be of equal size, all will have equal range of motion, but if the last ball be a large one, in relation to the striking ball, *its* range of motion will be smaller, and if a small one, larger; and this too whether the large or small ball, be at the remote extremity, or be interposed in the range anywhere.

Examples of this *exalted* effect are found, at Spinazzola and Canosa, which received the wave, transmitted from the free-lying northern and eastern extremity, of the great east and west Apennine, branching into furcations at Palazzo (Map A). Saponara, Padula, Lauria, Lagonegro, Sapri, with Ascoli in the extreme north, belong to the same category; while examples of the *reduction* of effect, due to the sudden entrance of the wave to greatly increased masses, have been remarked and the action explained, (Part II.) at various points, but more particularly for the district, between Balvano and Baraggiano.

5th. It is *possible*, as remarked by Humboldt, that *interference* may, though very rarely act as a protecting condition, in diminishing the energy of shock at some local point; but it is certain that places are frequently situated at *nodal* points, where the simultaneous arrival, of the main wave along with a subordinate one, increases the severity of injury, &c.

It is barely within the limits of probability, that two shocks shall arrive at the one spot, with such coincidence in time, that the opposite semiphases of the two respective waves, shall partly or wholly neutralize each other; but it is a different affair, and of much simpler conditions, that two or more separate waves should simultaneously arrive at the one spot, *i. e.*, should overtake or intersect at it.

There is no doubt that this actually did occur at Montemurro, at Marsico Nuovo, and at Vignola, where the conditions producing it will be evident, from Map A; and most probably it took place also, to some extent, at Avigliano, and the cities of the Melfi group, and possibly also at Canosa.

6th. The effects of formation, and of the change from one formation to another; of situation in deep clay plains, or those consisting of loose material, or on solid rock, in locally and suddenly modifying the energy of the shock, and its effects, on towns, &c., have been already made sufficiently clear, and the principles have been elucidated by several examples, in Part II.

Much pains has been devoted by earthquake describers, (Hamilton, Dolomieu, Spallanzani, and others,) to the question whether towns situated upon the plain on loose material, or those on the solid rocks on hill tops, suffered most; and their discussions evince much obscurity of thought, having no guiding principle.

We have in this earthquake, towns such as Saponara and Viggiano, situated upon solid limestone totally prostrated; and we have others, such as Montemurro, to a great extent based upon loose clays, also totally levelled. We have examples of almost complete immunity, in places posited in plains of deep clays, as that of Viscoliona, and in places on solid limestone like Castelluccio, or perched on mountain tops like Petina.

Were the whole of the facts of Part II. discussed with regard to this question, it would be found, that more places were destroyed upon the rock, than upon loose clay or other such foundations, and more upon hills than upon plains; but this would not conduct us to the whole truth, because in all South Italy, there are a great many *more places* upon rock and upon hills, than upon clays and low plains.

Whether it be rock or clay, has, in reality, but a secondary influence. The transit rate, and to a greater or less extent, the velocity and amplitude of the wave will be different; the velocity greater and the amplitude less in the rock, and *vice versâ* in the clays or gravels: but the great differences will be found to arise, not from any molecular properties in the substances, beneath the respective places shaken, but to be caused by the elevation, contour, and form, &c., of the masses, upon which the places are built; and upon their positions in relation to the physical features and deposition of the formations, intervening between them and the focal point.

If a town stand upon a lofty, isolated, rocky eminence,

the oscillation of the eminence, and the vibration of the wave, conspire to its overthrow.

If it stand upon an eminence or table, of loose material, with steep scarps, its fate will be the same, with the added evil, of masses of the loose material being thrown and shed down as at Montemurro along with the ruin of the place.

Two towns may be closely adjacent, the one on a lofty hill, the other low lying in the plain, at its foot, and either may be on the rock, or on the clays; and yet, without a knowledge of what country intervenes, between them and the focal centre, it shall be impossible to discover, to what causes the possible immunity of either one or other, or the destruction of either, or destruction of both alike, shall have been due. The high and loftily situated place is, *cæteris paribus*, likely to suffer most; but the shape of the "colline," as at Castelluccio, may be such with reference to the wave-path, and to what lies between it and the focus, that it may escape; and a place at its foot, like the Taberna D'Urmn, be destroyed.

In a word, the result of my survey, over a wide and varied expanse of earthquake country is, that the grand modifying conditions of local effect are found in—

1st. Physical configuration of surface.
2nd. Physical configuration of formation in depth, such as transverse stratification, &c.
3rd. Elevation, as influencing continuity or isolation from surrounding masses, and admitting or not, of separate mass oscillation.

All these, in relation to the direction of wave-path, at the spot in question; and subordinate to these—

4th. Nature of the material upon which the place stands, and of that, extending from it towards the focal point and in the opposite direction.

ALL these, as to the *actual* effects produced in any *given instance*, being modified by the character, of the buildings, &c., of the place, and by their structural capability of endurance. Future seismic surveys are therefore brought within limits of condition, greatly more simple, than when we imagined that the chief modifying conditions of the effects of the wave, would be found, in the intimate or molecular nature, of the rocky formations deep beneath the surface. These conditions are now shown to be such, as admit of application and deduction, with equal facility and certainty, by the observer who having once understood their principles, will but keep his eyes open.

In such surveys, nothing is so important as good maps, showing with accuracy, the *physical configuration of the surface* of the country. Contoured maps would be of inestimable value, and for the consideration and discussion, of facts obtained in the field, clay models, even of a rude character, if made approximately to scale, would be found to guide the eye, and assist the mind to correct conclusions, upon the apparently complicated phenomena that are often presented to us.

Geological maps, though highly desirable, are less indispensable; the earthquake observer in the field, can generally make out, *en passant*, enough of the geology to enable him to record his facts correctly, with reference to change of formation or boundary.

CHAPTER XVIII.

SECONDARY EFFECTS PRODUCED BY THE PASSAGE OF THE SHOCK.

These, as observed in the present earthquake, have been of three classes—1. Landslips and earth fissures; 2. Rock fissures and shattering falls of rock; 3. Alterations of water courses, which are only a consequence, of one or both of the two former.

Fissures were found formed in the earth, at Auletta, at Brienza, (where a fissure crossed the market-place at the top of the town,) at Carlotta D'Isca, near Bella, at Campostrina Road, at Vietri di Potenza, at Atena, and near Polla. In all these cases, the widths of the lips of the fissure at the surface was small, not exceeding a few inches, (unless when accompanied, as at Carlotta D'Isca, with active landslip,) and the depth was not traceable even when just after the fissure had been opened, beyond a very few feet. The directions of the lengths (which were often considerable) of the fissures, was always more or less transverse to the wave-path, but also always had reference to the slope of the rock, subjacent to the fissured earth; the tendency being for the fissure to run along, more or less parallel to the strike, of the subjacent rock surface. So that, in general, the lengthway of the earth fissure, runs in a direction, which is always, intermediately transverse both to the wave-path and to the slope of the subjacent rock, and very commonly to the slope of the earth's surface itself, which more or less corresponds to that of the rock beneath.

That side of the lips of the fissure, next the descent of the sloping surface is always found lower than the other as due to the original slope of surface.

Upon level ground a fissure in the earth has not been found, unless the earth had one, unsupported or relatively unsupported, side, as on the Campostrina Road and near Polla.

These combined facts, prove beyond question, that earth fissures are not produced by the direct action of the wave of shock, but that they are merely a secondary effect— cases of small and incipient landslips, produced by the shaking downwards of the mass, of earth reposing loosely upon the sloped surface of subjacent rock; or comparatively unsustained in any way at one side, as at Campostrina, where, the earth of the road, resting there upon a sloped surface too, was only upheld by a revetment wall.

It is untrue to nature, to state that, "the wavy nature of the shocks, occasions such *a stretching* of portions of the ground, as sometimes to split it asunder. Hence, amongst the consequences resulting from it, in the earth itself, fissures are the most frequent." (Daubeny, 'Volcanoes,' p. 529, edit. of 1848.) No earthquake wave, with an amplitude not exceeding 6 or 7 inches at the most, could, by possibility, produce any such stretching; nor were this amplitude increased, in the ratio that the intensity of South American earthquakes bears to that of this Neapolitan one, or as 5·33 : 1, say up to 3 feet, (an amplitude not probably reached by any earthquake that has ever occurred in historical time,) could it possibly produce earth fissures of even an inch wide by direct action, whether by stretching or otherwise.

The well-known Jamaica earth fissures, that were said to have opened and closed with the wave, and *bit people in two*, must be regarded as audacious fables; and having now examined a country precisely similar, in all important respects, with Calabria Ultra, I am satisfied, that both the engravings and the descriptions given, in the Historical Account by the Neapolitan Academy of the Earthquake of 1783, of the earth fissures therein produced, and designated constantly by the pompous term "voragines," are gross exaggerations, (as are many other parts of that narrative in other respects); and that many of the instances that they adduce, as "voragines," were really large landslips, the torn surfaces of whose planes of separation they thus name.

What has thus been in the preceding pages adduced as to the amplitude and velocity, of the *greatest possible shock*, points at once to the totally untenable nature, of the hypotheses upon which Messrs. Rogers, have proposed to account for the production of the great successive and parallel undulations, presented by a section transverse to the ranges, of the Appalachian chains.

Earth waves of such magnitude, or of anything at all like it, or resulting in such effects, are purely imaginary.

There is nothing in the facts the Neapolitan Academicians record, of *fissures radiating to or from a central point* incapable of explanation upon the principles above enunciated. If a conoidal mass, of subjacent rock, be covered with deep earth, which is shaken partially down and commences to slip, the slippage will be in lines, radiating downwards the slopes, in all directions from the top, and the fissures must radiate from the top, like the rays of a star, being widest at the centre. Or, fissures with lips of unequal level, may form at different altitudes, in horizontal planes running round the sloping sides; or both such sets of fissures, may intersect each other; dependent upon the angle of slope of the rock, that of repose of the earth, its depth, and other circumstances; but all the phenomena due to mere shaking down and slippage.

Again, if from beneath one portion of a deep plain of earth or sand, the base of whatever sort, be lowered or partially removed, as when the roof of a limestone cavern (like that noticed at Campostrina) may fall in; or when water may be partially withdrawn, from unequally distributed quicksand, beneath, &c.; then, a shallow bowl-like hollow or depression will be produced, and *fissures radiating* from the centre as before, and, as before also, crossed or not by others, tending to the form of concentric circles, may result. This last was just the case described in the Academy Report of the plain of Calabria, about Jerocarne and Rosarno, &c.

The vulgar mind, filled from infancy with superstitions of terror as to "the things under the earth," is seized at once by the notion of these fissures of profound and fathomless depth, with "fire and vapour of smoke" issuing from within their murky abysses, but they should cease to belong to science.

Of actual *landslips* we had examples, at Carlotta D'Isca,

and, far more strikingly, in the bed of the Agri, in the plain of Viggiano, where the great extent of land, shaken and slipped down, into the bed of that torrential river, well illustrates the large scale upon which, these secondary effects may alter and modify, the local features of an earthquake country.

It is to be borne in mind, however, that the magnitude and the superficial extent of such effects, depend but very subordinately, upon the power, or energy of the earthquake, and are mainly dependent upon the conditions of unstable equilibrium presented by great masses of loose material through the configuration of the country. If there be plenty of huge river and other banks, formed of steep masses of clays, &c.; or of great masses of rock, resting upon wet and unctuous beds of shale, or of clays, or suchlike, a very moderate shock, may cause prodigious alteration of surface in this way. Thus it was that the quay of Lisbon slipped with its supporting bank of blue clay, into deep water.

How small a shock, would have been sufficient to have determined the fall of the Rosberg, long before by gravity only, it took place, or would have anticipated and extended, the great landslip at Lyme Regis, as described by Mr. Roberts— how small a vibration would be sufficient, to cause vast masses, of the southern side of the Isle of Wight, to launch into the English Channel, or to fissure the steep slopes of the Hampstead and Highgate hills near London.

Direct *fissuring of rock* by the transit of the wave of shock, is more a physical possibility, than that of earth, yet it remains doubtful if such has ever taken place.

At Arena Bianca, I have recorded the particulars of

fractures or fissures, fresh formed, directly through hard rock, but they were *not due to either bending or stretching of the strata by the roll of the wave itself in transit*; they were still mere secondary effects, due to the *push* at the instant, produced by the wave at the free-lying surface of the hill side, acting upon the enormous mass of clays and shales, &c., behind. The rock there was rent, just as the wall of a water reservoir above ground, might be rent or broken transversely by the pressure from within.

Falls of rock were observed, and upon a very great scale, at Campostrina, Vallone del Raccio, Padula Valley, La Scorza, La Sala, Arena Bianca, and Monticchio, and were recorded in the 'Giornale Reale' as having taken place also at Vesalo, near Laurino, and at Pietra Pertosa. These were all, instances of transverse fracture and separation, at rock joints already existing, and due to inertia.

The occurrence of rock falls, and the scale upon which they are presented, depends more upon the energy of the earthquake, than in the cases of earthslips, but this is also, to a great degree, determined by the physical features of the country. If the rock be, ill-coherent, shattery material, like the cretaceous limestones of the Apennines, larger and more numerous dislodgments will occur, than in a country formed all of bare, rigid, crystalline rocks, and whose surface has been perhaps swept clean, by denudation, from all loose material, upon the elevated points; so also if it be one of steep hillsides, and deep valleys, with slopes often encumbered with boulders, &c., as in the Apennines, great and frequent dislodgments will be found. More numerous falls will take place from rock masses, whose bedding is highly inclined, than from those whose stratification is more nearly or quite level, and the volume generally will be greater of the mass that shall be capable of dislodgement at once. Again, whether, like the Rosberg, it shall slip and launch *en masse* upon a greasy bed, or fall a dislocated chaos, like the great fall of rock at Plürs, (Lyell, 'Geol.,' p. 704,) will much depend upon the direction of the planes of stratification at the place, with regard to the line of the wave-path.

The only instance of a fall of rock observed by me, in which there was actual *fracture*, through any considerable thickness, of previously *sound* and unbroken rock, was in the "aiguille," at the valley to the rear of Padula, where it was broken (like a wall at its base) by transverse action.

This class of secondary effect, is therefore capable of producing its largest developments, in either of two modes. A shock, itself perhaps very moderate, *may induce motion* in a huge mass, which, like the Rosberg, may slide almost as one immense block, and considerable lateral transfer of material, be thus produced *without* great change of elevation, or *with it.* And if the slipped mass, be of clay, &c., by resolution of intestine forces, the pressures at the toe of the talus, may produce *elevations* in parts of the mass, or in other masses of clay, *i. e.*, such phenomena as those recorded by Dolomieu having occurred at Terra Nuova, and Cossolito, &c., in Calabria in 1783.

Or, a shock perhaps equally moderate, passing through an extremely elevated and steep country, of lofty peaks and deep gorges, whose higher regions are bare surfaces of shattery rock, may *bring down by the shake*, millions of separate fragments, great and small, which shall roll and bound down the steeps, and shatter in repose in the lower valleys thousands of feet below their former positions. Hooker's admirable description of the earthquake he experienced in the Sikh Himalaya, is the best instance on record of the latter.

The alterations of water courses, of which such exaggerated notions have been rendered current, by the account of the Calabrian shock of 1783, given by the Neapolitan Academy, reduce themselves, in reality, to the consequences of such slipped masses of earth, or fallen heaps of shattered rock, when precipitated into the beds of running waters.

Thus the masses of rock precipitated at the gorge of Campostrina into the bed of the Tanagro, at first almost completely dammed across its channel; its waters were ponded above the dam, and judging from the masses, in the state in which they were when I examined them some six weeks afterwards, the waters may have reached, perhaps, at some one time, 12 or 15 feet in depth above the dam. The latter was nowhere water-tight, and great leakage took place through the rocky fragments at the *coarser side, nearest the toe.* Partial debacles, also, turned over and gradually removed, more and more of the intruded masses, and after a very moderate time—less than a month—the regimen of the river for ordinary discharge, was re-established, though with a certain amount of change of form of channel at the point. The first great flood would further enlarge this, and soon no trace of change be left.

The turbid discolouration of the waters of the same river issuing from St. Michael's Cave at Pertosa, is a matter quite as simple. The water of the river entering the subterraneau conduit at Polla is in its usual state turbid; and it issues clear or much clearer at the other end. Great enlargements of the tube by caverns, &c., exist therefore, along its length, in which there is but a very feeble velocity; and in this slack water the fine mud of turbidity is deposited, and so the waters pass on clear. The dislodgment of a few masses of stone from the roof or sides of one of these cavernous "settling basins," or the under-water slippage, of one of the soft incoherent beds, of chalky mud in the bottom, would be sufficient to produce turbidity of the issuing water for a long time afterwards, the length of time being greater, as the cubic capacity of the "settling basin" was larger, in proportion to that of the tubular duct leading the water from it. This was also the entire mystery of the discolouration of the springs issuing at La Sala, at Atena, and at Marsico Nuovo. The muddyings alleged to have been observed in some earthquakes, (nothing of the sort was stated to me as respects the present one,) of the water of common draw-wells (dug in the ground) *precedent* to and *forerunning* the shock, are, I believe, mere superstitions, but, at any rate, require further investigation as to the actual fact.

In the case of the great earthslip, into the bed of the Agri, in the Valley of Viggiano, its circumstances, and the mode and rapid progress, of its removal in mud, have been stated in Part II. Its toe, and the mass behind, were not so circumstanced, as to produce upon the occurrence of its descent, an effective dam across the whole river bed to any considerable depth; but had the mere accidents, of the height of the slipped mass at the point, the total volume displaced, the direction of its lateral movement, and the width of the original river course between its steep clay banks, been a little different, a nearly staunch dam would have been at once formed, and the ponded back river would have begun to form a temporary lake. In fact, at hundreds of places, as well as at this one, along some 10 or 15 miles of the river thereabouts, the occurrence of just such a landslip, and of one not much bigger in volume, might have produced a temporary lake of many thousands of acres in water surface, but in almost every case, (probably not one case in a thousand to the contrary,) the lake *could, by no possibility, have been more than temporary*.

As soon as the accumulated waters reach the top of the lowest point of the dam, they begin to cut it through; their action upon loose and ill-compacted earth and stones is rapid, and increasingly so, as the waters enlarge their own channel of overflow, partial slippages from *its* sides soon occur, succeeded by partial debacles, and rapid sweeping down of more of the obstruction; and, at last, nought remains of it but a low, flat, curved-surfaced mud bank or bar, a few inches, perhaps only, above the level of the original stony river bed, and a few hundred feet lower down the stream than where the dam was originally launched into it. Even this mud bank is, in the end, bit by bit carried down to the sea.

The water, while ponded to its full depth, may have sapped the bases and flanks of the temporarily submerged clay banks, at both sides the river course, and partial slippages will then have taken place from them, to be in like manner gradually removed. And thus this secondary effect of earthquake, which looks to the eye so formidable, when the new-born lake of thick turbid water, is first seen covering river and field, wood and crops, homestead, bridge, and church, rushing over its obstructing dam, and sweeping it away, perhaps rolling over it, the bodies of drowned cattle, or even of men, with all sorts of floating wreck; is nothing more, than may occur any day in a similar locality, without any earthquake, nor anything more enduring in its effects, or more capable of permanently changing the face of the country than the accidents of the first great flood in the river.

The only case in which the lake, can possibly become a permanent one, is when two conditions unite, both rare and improbable—

1st. *The dam must*, by accident, precipitate itself so, as to *be absolutely water-tight* from the first moment, for otherwise its final destruction is only a question of time.

2nd. The ordinary and extraordinary discharge of the river, must owing to accidental configuration of surface, of the country at either one or both sides of the river course, abreast of the dam, find a *new and permanent channel of overflow* for the ponded waters, at the level of the permanent surface of the new-made lake, *so that all water shall be diverted permanently from falling over the face of the dam*.

With *both* these conditions, it is just possible, though still highly improbable, that the suddenly-formed dam may stand long enough, to get finally consolidated, and become a permanent water-tight construction of Nature's hand.

Such possibly *may* have been the case with the lakes said to have been formed in Calabria and elsewhere, (but not noticed by or known to the describers); it is, however, much more probable that were examination now made at the sites in Calabria where those lakes are stated to have been formed, all of them would be found to have disappeared long ago.

As the seismic vertical in this earthquake was situated upon land, and not out at sea, *no great sea-wave* or other noticeable disturbance of the sea could have been produced, and no rumour or account of anything of the sort, could be obtained as the result of my inquiries.

I have already fully discussed the facts as to any permanent *elevation of the land*, and shown that they are equally *negative*.

CHAPTER XIX.

CONNECTION WITH METEOROLOGICAL PHENOMENA.

UNDER this head the superstitions of the ignorant, and the ignorance of the learned, leave more to be yet investigated than under any other, although it is one probably of very subordinate importance as respects future scientific "fruit." The only facts worthy of notice, that I was able to obtain, are those recorded of the unusual and diffused light, said to have struck the attention of many, both ignorant and lettered persons, in the region close about the seismic vertical, and for a radius of from five to eight miles round it. I can add nothing to this here, but the observation, that it remains for future discovery whether this may not have been some sort of *earth light*, as Humboldt expresses it, connected with developed electrical tension, produced by the tremendous pressures, amounting to thousands of millions of tons, then rapidly accumulating or suddenly acting on square miles of rock beneath.

The wind was calm, and the stars were not obscured at the moment of shock, and hence not for some time before or after it, as observed by Signor D'Errico. This calm and serenity, appear to have extended over the whole area shaken; it was the same at Naples. The oppressive

CHAPTER XX.

OF THE AFFECTIONS EVIDENCED BY VARIOUS ANIMALS AT THE TIME OF THE SHOCK.

Battista has repeated the observation, made often before, that hogs showed symptoms of uneasiness previous to the shock. All domestic, and many wild animals, evinced the alarmed condition that has been so often recorded. I could not find that any dead birds, shaken to the ground while sleeping on their roosts, had been remarked. I did not, however, press many inquiries under this head, having more than enough of far more important matter on hand.

The only alleged case of nausea felt by human beings at the moment of the shock was that mentioned at Naples, and it appeared to me to have been due to nervous excitement and alarm.

Under this head it may be of some geological interest to notice, that rats and rabbits, though burrowing animals, were killed and entombed by some of the landslips, gripped obviously by the suddenly moved soil before they could escape, and so suffocated. Snakes and torpid lizards were also killed by rock dislocations, facts which rather tend to indicate that *these* animals at least had no premonitions of the coming shock. The isolated occurrence of their organic remains in earthy limestone rock, without any obvious cause of entombment, at some remote future, presents matter for curious consideration.

CHAPTER XXI.

OF THE RELATIONS OF THE SEISMIC FOCI OF THE ITALIAN PENINSULA, AND THE GENERAL RELATIONS OF THE SEISMIC BANDS OF THE MEDITERRANEAN BASIN.

Humboldt has remarked, of the Mexican and South American earthquakes, as well as of those of the United States, that in the course of time, they seem to change their centres of effort, as evidenced by the boundaries of disturbance becoming enlarged in one direction and retracted in the opposite. Such is also the fact in the Italian peninsula. If the Map C be examined, and if the British Association Earthquake Catalogue, or, still better, Perrey's Monograph Catalogue of the Italian Earthquakes, be collated, it will be found *that the locus of their numerous focal centres follows generally the lines of the great ridges of the Apennines*, but the distribution is not uniform. From the toe of Calabria, northward, to the extremity of Gargano, the line of foci is nowhere quite interrupted, along the north and south Apennine, but the seismic centres cluster thickest, round that of the great shock of 1783, (between the Gulfs of St. Euphemia and Squillace); again, between Lagonegro and Melfi; and at the northern end between Foggia and the point of Gargano.

This locus line of foci bifurcates, or rather is crossed,

sense of heat at the moment, so pointedly referred to by Signor D'Errico, does not seem to have been felt elsewhere, so far as my inquiries enable me to judge.

Such oppressive glows have often preluded tornadoes, as in the great cyclone of the British Isles of 1839, when it was felt strongly in the east of Ireland; in this case, there is a traceable connection with the main disturbance; it is difficult to see any as direct with earthquake; but if intense local subterraneous pressure can disturb electrical equilibrium and produce *earth light*, it is not improbable that it may also and more directly produce earth heat.

The tables of the Meteorological Marine Observatory at Naples, which I have given, Part II., prove, that there was disturbance in the amount of rain for a period of several months anterior, as compared with former years; but there was no particular disturbance of rain, of the barometer, or of the magnetometer at the moment, or rather at the times of observation, on the same day. If there really was an emanation of *earth light*, from about the focal region at the time of the shock, analogy with the aurora might induce us to presume that there would also be some disturbance of the magnetometer; such disturbance might not, however, be sufficient to have been observable at Naples, in any case, as that city is at least sixty miles from the circumference of the region within which the earth light was said to have been developed.

Humboldt found that the magnetic needle was not disturbed in any South American shock in which he attended to it. His instruments, however, were not of the delicacy since employed; and it does not follow that, because the results were negative at his stations, disturbance might not by that of the east and west Apennine from Naples and south of it, to Spinazzola on the east, in which the clustering of the focal points again is at Melfi, and about Vesuvius and Naples.

The locus line of foci then follows N. W. from about Melfi, through the line of the Great Majella of the central Apennine, by Campobasso and Sulmone; delivering its greater energies towards the Adriatic, at which side of the central ridge therefore the focal cavities must be situated. About the Lago Fucino there is almost a gap; a considerable space here, right across the peninsula, from the Pontine Marshes to Giulia Nuova and Atri, on the Adriatic, being almost free from shocks, *originating within it*. Northward of this, the locus line of foci divides, one following the eastern, the other the western, great and approximately parallel ridges, of the Apennine. The eastern line includes the band of never-ending shocks, centred along the line, passing through Aquilla, Montereale, Norcia, (of the latest of whose earthquakes, August 1859, Padre Secchi, of Rome, has given so interesting an account,) and Asisi. The western line, is that of the Alban Hills, Rome, Viterbo, and to Orvieto and the Lago Bolseno. Then there comes another breach of continuity, and a wide district about the Lago di Perugia, is almost exempt from shocks *originating within it*. Still northward of this, the Tuscan earthquake regions, follow generally the line of the western ridge of the Apennine; and the eastern line of foci, by Urbino, Rimini, and Ravenna, that of the mountains inland and more or less parallel with these, runs northward, and with several diminutions of intensity as to focal distribution, connects with the seismic system of the Rhetian Alps, and of Hungary.

Generally, therefore, the seismic foci, or *the bands of earthquake disturbance in the Italian peninsula follow the lines of the great mountain ranges*, and accord fully with that great fact, first, I believe, announced in my Report ('Reports Brit. Assoc. of 1858,') and following from the discussion of the earthquake map of the world there produced, as being the law of earthquake distribution over the whole surface of our globe. If we extend the survey wider, as in Map D, to the whole Mediterranean basin, we shall find the southern Italian seismic band, extending westward through Sicily, embracing Malta and Pantellaria; and those submarine seismic regions off the south coast of Sicily, in which, in 1845, the ship 'Victory,' in lat. 36° 40′ 56″ long. 13° 44′ 36″ received a shock from beneath; and running through Gigilli and Algiers, along the Atlas ranges, and finally connecting, with various alternations of intensity, with the Azores. The band that stretches across Italy to Gurgano, crosses the Adriatic, and at Ragusa, (that notorious seismic place,) inosculates with the band that comes down from Hungary, through the mountain ranges of Illyria and Dalmatia; and which, bifurcating near Ragusa, follows the Balkan chain to Constantinople and the western shore of the Euxine; and in its southern branch passing down through Albania, the Ionian Islands, and the Morea, spreads out, and embraces all the volcanic insular mountain tops of the Greek islands. It again bifurcates at Smyrna, (another notorious seismic spot,) one branch (the northern) passing through the mountains of Anatolia, and by Broussa, so sadly and recently known in earthquake story, and on to Sinope, on the south shore of the Euxine, and thence into the southern Caucasus. The southern branch again, passing over Rhodes, and embracing by its fringe Candia, and the whole southern coast of Asia Minor, extends over Cyprus, and joins into the great Syrian earthquake region. The same principle guides this linear distribution throughout; it follows, with variable intensity, the great lines of elevation.

Returning, however, nearer to our own district. Each focal centre, moves in time along the locus line, so that its greatest energy is not recurrent at the very same spot, or not until after a long period. In the last century, the centre of seismic intensity, for that part of the band to which our earthquake belongs, was situated midway between the Gulfs of St. Euphemia and Squillace, in Calabria: it has continued since to move to the northward, and its present centre, is somewhere between the Melfi focus, and that of the earthquake of December, 1857, in fact, somewhere beneath, or north or south of, the great mountain knot of Muro and Bella, (see Maps A and B,) where the north and south, and the east and west Apennine ridges, cross each other.

This slow secular movement of the centre of temporary intensity, along the line of locus, has been noticed by most of the Italian authors, (Grimaldi, Battista, and others,) who have treated of the earthquakes of the south of the peninsula.

During the same interval, to the westward of the Straits of Messina, the centre of temporary intensity, appears to have been moving westward, and seems to be at present nearer to the Palermo end of the island, than to Messina.

These facts distinctly point towards some great conclusions. They indicate that the same forces, whatever they may be, that develop themselves, as volcanic vents, and as earthquakes, are operative *everywhere* along the lines of the seismic bands; that is to say, along the axial lines of nearly all the great mountain ranges upon our globe.

But that the intensity of these forces is greater by much, at some points along these axial lines, than at others; that the intensity remains constant nowhere, but shows itself paramount at certain points, for immense periods of historic time; that it wanes, and again waxes powerful, at the same point, (Vesuvius in volcanoes, Antioch in earthquakes, for example, both long in repose, again long in intense action); and that the points of greatest intensity at any given time, have been found to shift along the axial lines; now most active here, then further on, but slowly moving, and in the same direction, (or expanding in both directions, as Humboldt says of the new Madrid band,) in the same cycle of time.

Can we possibly, with these facts before us, rest in the commonly-received vague notion that volcanic and seismic action have their common origin, in an all-pervading and perfectly uniformly-distributed, planetary temperature, increasing everywhere alike, by a uniform hypogeal increment? Can we remain satisfied with the pompous, but almost empty phrase, (although sanctioned by a Humboldt,) that "they are due to the reaction of the interior of our planet upon its exterior;" if the only meaning that we are to attach to the phrase is, that the reaction is that, of a universal ocean of heated or of molten matter, everywhere to be reached within some certain limit of depth? Do not the facts rather all point towards some cause that has been long present, and is so now, and still in action wherever mountain ranges have been elevated, as well as wherever volcanic vents have thrown or are throwing up, their lines of cones; but whose nature must be such, as is called locally and spasmodically into action, now most energetically at one point, now at another of the same line, but yet is never exhausted at any?

The discovery of the real nature of this cause will be the key to all true knowledge, both of volcanic action, which is only its symptom, and of all the forces that have produced, and do produce, the elevations, or, to speak more correctly, the changes of level of the surface, of our own and that of other planets. Earthquakes, then, demand to be regarded, not as themselves agents of permanent elevation of the land, which they cannot be at all, and with respect to which, even the greatest volcanic efforts (accumulated cones) upon our globe, are mere skin-deep phenomena. We must regard seismic and volcanic phenomena as both unequal effects and local evidences of a wide-spread, and constantly, but unequally acting, yet always active force, resulting in elevation; which is not evidenced indifferently all over the surface of the globe, but is mainly confined to broad bands conforming to its mountain ranges.

CHAPTER XXII.

RETROSPECTS AND CONCLUDING WORDS.

The method of seismic investigation in this Report developed, indicates, that it is now in our power, more or less, to trace back, wherever we can find buildings or ruins, fissured or overthrown by ancient earthquakes, the seismic centres from which these have emanated, in epochs even lost perhaps to history.

In the ancient churches of Southern Italy, that nine centuries ago were founded by Lombard or Norman bands, in the massive walls of the Coliseum, the arches of the Campagna, the shattered columns of the Forum, we can still ascertain the direction, in which the shocks were delivered, and even approach to measure the forces, by which, while England was receiving its first Norman lords, these churches were ruined, and centuries before that, and the edifices of the Imperial city, were overturned and destroyed. We can, therefore, in Italy, perhaps still more perfectly in Mexico and elsewhere, even yet, more or less recover the ancient fluctuations of position, of these centres of seismic intensity, and compare the intensity itself in past historic and at the present time.

It is, therefore, no longer true to say (if it ever were so) with Humboldt, that " these waves of succussion can be measured as to their direction and force, but *can in no way*

be investigated, in the intimate nature of their alternations and periodical intumescences." ('Cosmos,' vol. i., p. 214.)

Had this Report not already so very far exceeded the length which I had originally projected for it, some deductions of a practically constructive character, as to the proper *methods of structure for safe houses and other edifices in earthquake countries* resulting from my opportunities of observation in this research, coupled with previous professional knowledge, would have been not unsuitable, especially to our nation, the mother of so many colonies in earthquake regions.

I must reserve such for some other opportunity, however, merely stating here my conviction, that the evils of the earthquake, like all others incident to man's estate, may be diminished, or even nullified, by the exercise of his informed faculties and energies, by his application of forethought and knowledge, to subjugate this, as every other apparent evil of his estate, by skill and labour.

The earthquake is, therefore, but the subject of superstition, when viewed or denounced as a curse or a judgment; it is as much the operation of one part of a beneficent machinery, as "seedtime and harvest."

All human difficulties, to be dealt with, must be understood: were understanding and skill applied to the future construction of houses and cities in Southern Italy, few, if any, human lives need ever be again lost by earthquakes; which there must recur, in their "times and seasons." In some degree this has been seen by Italian writers, and Colosimo, in his little account of the Calabrian shock of 1832, points out some of the conditions that should be structurally observed.

In conclusion, I have to return my thanks to the former President, the Lord Wrottesley, to the Council, and Officers of the Royal Society, and more particularly to my much-respected friend General Sabine, then Treasurer and now President, for that assistance and co-operation, from the outset, without which this investigation could never have been accomplished.

To my distinguished friends, Sir Roderick I. Murchison, Bart., and Sir Charles Lyell, for their assistance in laying the objects of the proposed expedition before the Council of the Royal Society, and for valuable letters to influential persons abroad. To Cardinal Wiseman for his most useful encyclical letter; and to the Lords of the Admiralty for chronometers placed at my disposal.

To several friends resident at Naples, both English and Italian, I am indebted for advice and assistance, not the less important because too multifarious to specify, but to none more than to Signor Guiscuardi.

Most of all, however, are my thanks personally due to my friend Dr. Thomas Romney Robinson, Astronomer, of Armagh, the weight of whose authority gave the first impulse to my expedition; to Mr. Edmondson, Assistant Astronomer of Armagh Observatory, for instructions as to the best practical methods of correcting my magnetic bearings, and for checking all the reductions of my barometric measurements; and lastly, (but very far from least,) to my friend Professor Haughton, Fellow of Trinity College, Dublin, for the series of formulæ that have been the working tools of my research.

INDEX.

Abnormal wave, what so called, i. 31.
Abnormal wave, inferences from, i. 64.
Adhesion and cohesion-cements, i. 45.
Agri and Moglia, beds of the rivers, i. 424.
Agropoli, shock at, i. 239.
Alburno, Monte, range of, i. 245.
Amalfi, quay at, examined with reference to change of level, i. 226; shock at, alarmingly felt, i. 229; no noise at, i. 220.
Amplitude of the wave, and the work stored up in it, ii. 316.
Amplitudes observed and calculated, ii. 320.
Angle of emergence, and the seismic vertical, i. 11, 18.
Angle, abnormal, found, i. 61; for greatest overthrow, i. 112; of intersection, i. 327.
Animals, affections evidenced by, at the time of the shock, ii. 377.
Apertures in walls, effects of, i. 110.
Appalachian chain, ranges of the elevation of the, ii. 364.
Apsæ, effects of shock on, i. 87.
Arabia, Signor, best account of the Melfi earthquake of 1851 by, ii. 174.
Arches, steep emergence acting on large, i. 119.
Architectural structures, conditions of earthquake action upon, i. 25.
Architecture, general style of, in the kingdom of Naples, i. 25; loss of life and limb attributable to imperfections in, not inevitable in earthquake, i. 94.
Arch keystones worked up, example of, at Padula, i. 300.

Areas of the isoseismals, ii. 255; within which sounds heard, ii. 287.
Aritello, Valley of the, erosion in the, ii. 80; prodigious rate of denudation, ii. 81.
Artesian wells, temperature of, at Naples, ii. 311.
Atella, ancient town of, ii. 86; wave-path at, ii. 86; Lombardic church at, ii. 86; moment of shock at, ii. 87; chiesetta of St. Johanes at, ii. 88; ancient silver shrines of St. Johanes, ii. 89; relations of the calcareous and volcanic rocks near, ii. 90.
Atena, position of, i. 321; streets of, choked with rubbish of fallen buildings, i. 324; difference of effect of same shock on well and ill constructed buildings at, i. 325; fissure above, i. 328.
Auletta, good illustration of one class of fracture at, i. 73; evidences of overthrow at, i. 253; house near, i. 258; condition of, i. 260; earth fissures at, i. 253; fissure at, due to a great earthslip, i. 264; Port Cochère, on the military road, Villa Caruso, near, i. 245; view of the great valley from, i. 272.
Avigliano, position of, ii. 82; filthy condition of, ii. 82; shock at, ii. 83; castello at, ii. 83; Chiesa Madre at, ii. 83.
Azimuths of primary and secondary shocks at Certosa, difference in, i. 387.

Barille, position of, ii. 106; severe injuries at, ii. 106; church of St. Nicolo at, ii. 106; palazzo of Prince

2 c 2

Torvils at, ii. 106; reflected waves and earthquake echo at, ii. 107; heavy wall outside the town of, far out of plumb il. 107; wave velocity at, ii. 108; wave amplitude at, ii. 110; the syndico's watch at, ii. 110; movement of shock at, ii. 111.

Barragiano, view of, ii. 51.

Basilicata, the earthquake of, Dec. 16, 1857 (Appendix), account of, ii. 176—108.

Bella, situation of, ii. 122; injuries not severe at, ii. 123; great earth fissures three miles from, ii. 130.

Bella and Muro, effects of the chasm on, ii. 128; immunity of, ii. 129.

Bench-marks, letter on establishment of, as is level of the land, submitted to (late) Neapolitan Government, ii. 149; proposal to fix (Appendix No. 4), ii. 231.

Brickwork, flexibility of, i. 91.

Brienza, view of, in the distance, ii. 34; severe injuries at, ii. 34.

Buildings, observations on square, long, rectangular, i. 49; conditions as to form and structure in, which modify the effects of shocks, i. 91; of various forms considered, i. 95; effects due to flexibility and elasticity of the materials in, i. 91; unsymmetric, involve unsymmetrical phenomena of dissolution, i. 98; effect of shock upon, the fourth modifying condition, i. 102, 110; hollow square, i. 129; hollow round, i. 130; various forms of, i. 143, 145.

Buompietri, grand elliptic staircase at the Cistercian Monastery of St. Lorenzo, Padula, designed by, still uninjured, i. 374.

Buttresses, effects of shock on, i. 88.

CALABRITA, few symptoms of injury at, ii. 140.

Calore, subterranean deposits of the, i. 241; gorge of the, i. 285; cataracts of the, i. 300, 301; fissures at the, i. 327.

Canino, or chimney-hood, at the Palazzo Palmieri, important deductions from, i. 307—311.

Campanelli, Canonico Il Padre, testimony of, regarding shock at Rionero, ii. 93.

Campanilies, effects of shock on, i. 87.

Campostrino, great fall of rock at, damming up the river course, i. 285; in-fallen roof of great duct at, i. 280; rool fissures near, i. 288.

Capri, island of, shock scarcely perceived at, i. 279; escape of, and cause, ii. 266.

Capua, shock felt, but no mischief done at, ii. 160.

Caputo, Taberna of, cutting a way through snow near, ii. 121; elevation of, ii. 122.

Cardinal building, what so called, i. 35.

Cardinal buildings and normal shock, i. 38, 39.

Carlotta, earth fissures of, proved to be landslips, ii. 131; compared with phenomena of 1783, ii. 132.

Carpineto, Monte, i. 253.

Caruso, Monte, intense cold on, ii. 84.

Caruso, Villa, at Anletta, i. 208; arched gateway of, heavily fissured, i. 270.

Casa Communale at Pertosa, wave-path and emergence from, i. 270.

Castellucio, site and exterior of, irregular and narrow streets of, i. 30; mediæval character of, i. 250; cause of its immunity from injury, i. 262.

Cataldo, remarkable debouchure of, ii. 133.

Certosa, the, de St. Lorenzo, magnificent monastery, near Padula, graceful hospitality at, i. 369; ruin of described i. 370; monument to St. Bruno at, i. 370; specialities observed at, i. 376; the church at, i. 372; the refectory at, i. 372; the great square and garden of, i. 373; few of the walls or roofs of, actually prostrate, but everywhere fissured, dislocated, and tottering, i. 373; grand elliptic staircase of, only part uninjured, i. 374; first deductions from facts, double shock at, i. 376; the chimney at, i. 380; mechanics of the tilting and twisting of objects at,

i. 377; difference in azimuths of primary and secondary shocks at, i. 347; final deduction as to both shocks at, i. 390; further observations on, i. 391; gables of refectory at, i. 392; amplitude of the wave deduced at, i. 394; vase in Prior's garden at, i. 394; thrown chimney caps at, i. 395; return to the, ii. 31; striking features of the prolongation of the limestone mountains northwards, and end-on-ciders of the beds near, ii. 32.

Chiesa d'Incoronata, the shock at the, i. 272.

Chiesa Madre at Militerno, i. 409.

Chiesa Madre at Tramutola, fissures in, ii. 23; statues of St. Leonardo in, ii. 24; figure of St. Michael in, ii. 25.

Chimney at the monastery of St. Lorenzo (the Certosa), near Padula, oscillation of the, i. 380.

Coefficients of fracture, tables of, i. 143—154.

Cohesion and adhesion—cements, i. 45.

Cohesion and adhesion, i. 154.

Columns, effects of shock on, i. 87.

Columns overturned, i. 121.

Configuration, effects of the physical, of the surface, and the formation beneath it, upon the progress of the wave, ii. 258.

Croce, Monte, snowed up on, ii. 118; grand scenery between, and Laviano, ii. 136.

Curves, cause of the flattening of the cosinusals to the extreme south-east, ii. 279.

Cylindric vaulting, i. 114.

Data for determining the velocities and directions of shocks given by fractured walls and overthrown objects, i. 8.

Deaths from earthquake, estimate of, ii. 164; mostly preventible by proper care in the construction of houses, ii. 164.

Decay of the wave considered, nature of, ii. 349.

Deductions and conclusions, general, Part III., ii. 333.

Depth of focus of earthquake, first approximate calculation of the, ii. 15.

Depths, local, remarkable result of comparison of, ii. 343.

D'Errico's, Signor, document, shock at Monteforme, ii. 74.

Determinants, first class of, fracture in rectangular buildings as evidences of wave-path, i. 83; second class of, objects overturned or projected by shock, i. 124.

Diagonal fissures, i. 118.

Diano, view of the town of, i. 105; Vallone di, formation of, i. 319; geology of, i. 320; town of, little injury from the shock at, i. 329; cause of its immunity explained, i. 330.

Diano, great plain of, no permanent change of level discoverable, though certainly perceptible, if any, on the, ii. 33; enormous erosive action by winter floods on the, ii. 33.

Disasters of the earthquake, synoptic table of, in the district of Sala, ii. 161.

Disintegration, result of direction of fracture, i. 63.

Dislocation combines fracture and overthrow, i. 112.

Distortion of the isoseismals, actual cause of, ii. 275.

Divergence of wave-paths approximately equal to the horizontal dimension of the focal cavity, G. 246.

Duchessa, La, post-house, first prostrate walls seen at, i. 246; indications at, conflicting with those at Naples, i. 247; sounds at, i. 248.

Earth-light, probable nature of, ii. 375.

Earthquake, the, at Naples, Dec. 16, 1857, the author receives authority of the Royal Society to make scientific investigations connected with, i. 1; to be investigated by means of its phenomena or effects, i. 6.

Earthquake phenomena, questions for inquiry and methods of observations of, i. 5; entirely new mode of examining, based on the proposition that the disturbances and dislocations of solid objects, observed with reference to direction and range of disturbance, and to mechanical conditions in play, must afford the means of tracing back from these effects the directions, velocities, &c., of the movements or forces that caused them, i. 8.

Earthquake of Dec. 1857, preceded by several minor shocks, i. 201; lying wonders about the, i. 280.

Earthquake night, an, ii. 7.

Earthquake, first approximate calculation of the depth of focus of, ii. 45; synoptic table of disasters of the, in the district of Sala, ii. 161; meteorology and its relations to, ii. 165; peturbations of rain-fall in relation to, ii. 168, 169; suggestions as to probable convection, ii. 170, 171; modifications of, in dry countries, ii. 172; historic confirmations of, ii. 174; of Dec. 16, 1857, translation of all the notices on the, in the 'Giornale del Regno delle due Sicilie,' ii. 213—230.

Earthquakes, action upon architectural structures, i. 26; of ancient Rome, i. 115; dates of Italian, i. 82; since the commencement of the twelfth century, i. 200.

Earthquakes not agents of permanent elevation, ii. 321; not necessarily fatal, and not curves, ii. 323.

Earth's surface, effects at the, ii. 208.

Eboli, synclinal beds of limestone developed upon the grandest scale near, i. 237; buildings of the Locanda di Vozzi at, i. 240, 241; wave-path at, i. 242; church at, i. 243; evening with Signor Palmieri at, i. 244; limestone breccia near, i. 244; return to, after completing entire circle round the earthquake focus, ii. 140.

Elasticity of materials in buildings, effects due to, i. 91.

Elastic wave of shock, i. 10.

Elevation, earthquakes not agents for permanent, ii. 321.

Emergence, shocks of vertical or nearly vertical, effects on rectangular buildings, i. 78; sleep, acting on large arches, i. 119; nearly vertical, i. 124.

Emergence, angle of, obtained, i. 157, 164.

Emergences, determined at Villa Caruso, i. 249; stations for, ii. 249, 250.

Evidences fitted for observation, i. 13.

Extraneous support in relation to bodies projected, i. 17.

Factors for coefficients, table of, i. 161.

Falls, nodes of, i. 110.

Fino, Don Andrea del, entombment of, alive, ii. 7.

Florio's, Signor, regulator clock, how affected like, ii. 6, i. 213.

Fissures, in buildings not overthrown, the short anchor, as respects direction of wave-path, to the seismologist, i. 24; widths of, deductions drawn from, i. 40—42; differences of, at opposite ends, i. 47; peculiarity of, i. 60; eight main, alternately wide and narrow, often observable in a rectangular building exposed to an abnormal wave, i. 82; diagonal, i. 118; deep, filled up, effects of, ii. 265; in the earth are initial landslips, ii. 363; radiating; formation of, in the earth, ii. 365; rock, ii. 366.

Fissures and mountains, effects of, ii. 361.

Flexibility of materials in buildings, effects due to, i. 91.

Floors and roofs, relations of, i. 102.

Floors, forces in the plane of, and transverse to same, i. 105.

Floors over each other, i. 106; fissures in, valuable indices, i. 109; observation of, only secured to that of the walls, i. 160; at Palazzo Palmieri, i. 336.

Focal cavity, depth of, found, ii. 251; various forms of the, ii. 260; inclined, ii. 270; dimension of, ii. 289; approximation to form and size of, ii. 292; probable dimensions, form, and subterraneous position of, deduced, ii. 304; temperature of the, and intensity of the force that acted within it, ii. 309.

Focus of wave-path, inland, reiterated proofs of, i. 216.

INDEX.

Form, first indications of the, i. 316;
depth of, of earthquake, first approximate calculation of the, ii. 15; mean and extreme depth of, below the surface, ii. 248.
Fossli, clock at, ii. 153; immunity of place from injury attributed to the 'abundance of springs,' ii. 153.
Force, hypogeal, nature of, ii. 383.
Forces, oblique, i. 133.
Forces, effects of, in regular bodies, i. 20, 21.
Forms and areas of the metaseismal and kemeismal curves, and the position of the seismic vertical therein, ii. 252; conditions affecting, ii. 258.
Formulæ of bodies overturned or fractured, i. 124—146; referring to Cap. D, i. 155.
Fractures, in rectangular buildings as evidence of wave-path, i. 33; and velocity, relation of, i. 43; usually follow joints, i. 44; in rectangular buildings—subnormal shock, i. 52; remarks on direction of, i. 52; relations of, at opposite ends, i. 57; rectangular buildings, abnormal shock, i. 59; in rectangular buildings, abnormal shock, i. 59; direction of, in rectangular buildings by sub-abnormal shock, i. 95; over windows, i. 117; at base, normal wave, i. 140; overturning and projection, i. 146; tables of coefficients for, i. 149—154; in walls occur at joints, i. 150; of beds of hard rock, first example of, i. 405.

Gantoliano, great basin plain, of volcanic filling, ii. 162.
Geology, physical, investigation of earthquake phenomena, probably one of the most fruitful applications of mathematics to, i. 0.
Geology, its features in the country shaken, i. 101; of kingdom of Naples very little known, i. 108; of the Fiume Lago Maurzo, i. 403; section over the, i. 403.
'Giornale del Regno delle due Sicilie,' translation of all the notices in, respect-

ing earthquake of Dec. 16, 1857, ii. 213—230.
Gravity acting with vertical shock, remarks on, i. 70; centre of, within and without the base, i. 125.
Gravina's, Duc di, taberna, ii. 126.
Grellier, Monsieur, photographs of more important points of earthquake country produced by, ii. 148.
Ground, effects of form of the, i. 101.
Giuscuardi, Signor, services rendered by, i. 4; ii. 388; account by, of the earthquake, i. 211.

Haughton, Rev. Samuel, F.R.S., equations furnished by, i. 9; ii. 386.
Heat, hypogeal, producing greatest shock, ii. 315.
Historic configurations of earthquakes, ii. 174.
History of the Melfi earthquake, August 14, 1851, translation of report of Palmieri and Scacchi on the, ii. 197—212.
Hoar-frost, unusual form of, ii. 80.
Humboldt, remarks on observation of, that in South America the tendency of earthquake is continually to enlarge its circle of action round a given focus, ii. 155.
Hypogeal force, nature of, ii. 383.
Hypogeal temperature, deductions from assumed increase, ii. 313.
Hypsometric determinations by barometer at various places, i. 259.
Hypsometric elevations about Auletta, i. 259.

Inclined beds, relation to conformable, ii. 263.
Intersection, angle of, i. 317.
Isoseismals, references to, on maps, ii. 253; forces of the, ii. 254; areas of, ii. 255; of great shocks compared, ii. 256; application to the actual form of the, ii. 273; actual causes of distortion of the, ii. 275; causes of their great extension towards the south-east, ii. 277.
Italy, Southern, structure of buildings in, i. 20, 21; general appearance of the

ancient towns in, i. 28, 70; provincial towns in, i. 80, 31.
Itry, position of, ii. 153.

JAMAICA shock, ii. 364.
Joints, fractures usually follow, i. 44.

KILLED and wounded, return of, in communes of the province of Basilicata, ii. 162.

LA CAVA, traces of the earthquake at, i. 231.
Laviersna, entrance of the valley of the, i. 424; lignite beds of the, i. 431.
Lakes, temporary, explanation of formation of, ii. 371.
Lando and Torno, valleys of the, ii. 38.
Landslip, great, and fissure in the plane of Mattine, near Viggiano, ii. 15.
Landslips, initial, all fissures are, ii. 363.
Landslips, great, ii. 360.
Lardner, Dr., account by, of the earthquake Dec. 16, i. 210.
La Sala, changed character of the limestone near, i. 333; road to, i. 334; extent of, i. 335; structures at, more or less fissured, but few actually demolished, i. 335; house of the Notto Intendente, i. 336; pictures and probable at Internienzis, i. 338, 339; table and lamps of secretary to Sotto Intendente, i. 341, 312; church of, i. 343; fall of church tower, i. 344; church bells at, i. 345; angle of emergence inferred at, i. 346; wave-path prior. lations at, i. 347; good observation of the sun at, ii. 32.
Laviano, grand scenery near, ii. 135; position of, ii. 136; Palazzo Carmine at, ii. 137; experience of occupiers of the palazzo, ii. 138; mysterious light heard of at, ii. 139; shock and sound at, ii. 139.
Level, changes of, accompanying earthquake, i. 217; any deductions from, whether of elevation or of depression, not to be depended upon, i. 219; permanent changes of, examination round

the coast as to, i. 225; no evidence of, i. 227.
Lictl, Palazzo (Naples), fissures at, i. 207.
Limestone and clays, wave transits through, i. 385.
Limestone masonry, effects due to, i. 98.
Limestone, nummulitic and hipparite, i. 180.
Local effect, grand modifying conditions of, ii. 300.
Lupino, scarcely any damage done at, i. 249.
L, values of the coefficient, i. 149.

MAGNETIC declination at Anletta, observations to determine local, i. 269; declinations near Salvitello, ii. 34; relations, ii. 378.
Maldo, Valley of the, slipping rocks in the, ii. 134.
Mancini, Padre Vincenzio, information derived from, i. 274.
Maorno, Lago, a dreary pool, i. 406.
Maps, reference to braciamala on, ii. 253; goal, necessity of, ii. 301.
Maps.—Seismic map A, with wavepaths and isoseismal curves.—Report to Royal Society of London: map B, showing the physical features of the Neapolitan earthquake of December 16, 1857. — Approximate comparison of seismal areas, map C.—Comparative map, D, of the seismic lands of the Mediterranean, vol. ii. 379. Earthquake of December 16, 1857: Map E. —No. 1. Diagram of observed maxima and minima wave emergences, and resulting depth of focus. No. 2. Diagram of mean wave emergences, and deduced mean local depth, vol. ii. 248, 253.
Marine observatory, Naples, meteorological tables of the, ii. 166, 167.
Marli, sub-Apennine, i. 168.
Marsico Nuovo, situation of, ii. 20; original fissures in produced by the twisting movements, transferred quite round the walls, by transverse vibrations, i. 87.

INDEX.

Mediterranean, seismic zone of the, i. 200; seismic bands of the, ii. 372.
Meizoseismal and isoseismal curves, forms and areas of, ii. 252.
Melfi, situation and elevation of, ii. 113; the shock of 1851 and 1857 at, ii. 114; church of Monticelli at, ii. 115; exact time of shock at, ii. 116; sounds at, ii. 116.
Melfi earthquake of 1851, report of Professors Palmieri and Scacchi upon, i. 173.
Meteorology and its relations to earthquake, ii. 105.
Meteorological phenomena, connection with, ii. 374.
Michael, St., Monastery of. See Monticchio.
Models, clay, utility of, ii. 361.
Modulus of dynamic cohesion, i. 141.
Moglia, geology of the, i. 414.
Moglia and Agri, the beds of, i. 423.
Mola, position of, ii. 152; shock at, ii. 152.
Moliterno, position of, i. 408; thriving condition of, i. 408; the Chiesa Madre, i. 409; the Castello, i. 409; Chiesa della Rosario at, i. 410; direction of wave at, i. 410.
Monteferro, Signor D'Errico's account of shock at, ii. 74; moment of the shock at, ii. 77.
Montemurro, journey to, i. 429; arrival at, ii. 1; night at, ii. 2; author's narrow escape at, ii. 3; position of, ii. 5; the whole town one vast heap of rubbish, ii. 6; Palazzo of Don Andrea del Fino, ii. 6; lower of the great monastery of St. Dominies at, ii. 9; general wave-path at, ii. 9; conditions of destruction, ii. 10; column and cross enInjured at, ii. 10; compared to Oppido in the Calabrian earthquake of 1783, ii. 11.
Montemao, no lives lost south of, i. 400; position of, i. 400.
Monticchio, monastery of, ii. 100; wave velocity at, ii. 101; statements of the monks at, ii. 102; elevation of, ii. 103; map declination, ii. 103.

Morano, Signor, hospitality of, and valuable information derived from, ii. 17; house of, ii. 19.
Mountain chains, direction of the, i. 183; and valleys how affecting transmission of shock, ii. 261; refraction of shock wave in, ii. 262.
Mountains and valley fissures, effects of, ii. 352.
Mountains, adjacent, effects of, ii. 354.
Mountain enlargement or depression, sudden, effects of, ii. 357.
Muro, view of, ii. 51; strange atmospheric light and noises at, ii. 124; prodigious 'illuvione' at, ii. 125.
Muro and the Maddo, levels of the, ii. 127.
Muro and Bella, effects of the chasm on, ii. 128; immensity of, ii. 129.

Naples, general style of architecture in the kingdom of, i. 25; course of observation decided upon at, i. 202; official notice of the shock at, i. 203; visit to the observatory at, i. 204; alarm in, at the shock Dec. 1857, i. 208; evocations of those at, i. 209; collections of wave-path at, i. 216; the shock at, merely a reflected and refracted one, i. 216; return to, ii. 147; stoppage of the clock belonging to the self-acting anemometer of the marine observatory by shock of Dec. 16, ii. 147; rare books and pamphlets on earthquakes at, ii. 149; how the shock reached, ii. 281; chandeliers, measure difference of velocity in semiphases at, ii. 345; small amplitude at, ii. 350.
Nature of overthrow with resistance, i. 14, 15.
Neapolitan statistics, ii. 160.
Nodal points, places frequently situated at, ii. 357.
Nomad life, fascination of, ii. 140.
Nomenclature adopted in reference to the directions in azimuth and emergence of the earth-wave, relative to those of walls, buildings, or other objects affected by it, i. 31.

394   INDEX.

Normal shock and cardinal buildings, i. 32, 33.
Normal wave transit, what so called, i. 35.
Nummulitic and hippurite limestone, i. 167.

Objects overturned, second class of desideminants, i. 124.
Oliveto, large old monastery of "Zoccolanto" at, ii. 142; no second shock at, ii. 144; volcanic lakes near, ii. 144.
Ordinal building, what so called, i. 35.
Oscillation, remarks on, i. 10; of chimney-stack of the Certosa near Padula, i. 390, 393.
Osservatorio, Capo di Monte (Naples), fissures at the, 205.
Ovoideo, pass over shoulder south of Monte della Vojara, so called, i. 421.
Overthrow, nature of, with resistance, i. 14, 15.
Overthrow and projection, i. 16.
Overthrown objects solid, i. 124.
Overturned bodies, formulæ of, i. 124—143.

PADULA, site of, i. 50; parished position of, exposed transverse effect of earthquake shocks, i. 30; position of, i. 350; large fissures near, i. 351; aiguille of rock overthrown near, i. 352; transit of two shocks crossing obliquely at, i. 354; Palazzo Romani at, i. 355; Il Croce Romani, i. 356; velocity that would have overthrown il Croce, i. 357; overthrown column in Palazzo Romani at, i. 359; velocity of shock deduced from the column, i. 361; overthrown vases, i. 362; corresponding velocity deduced, i. 364; arch keystones worked up, i. 366; the Certosa de St. Lorenzo monastery near, i. 389.
Palagonica's, Padre, testimony respecting shock at Potenza, ii. 62.
Palmieri, Professor, visited by author at Naples, i. 4; report by, on earthquake of August 14, 1851, i. 171; Signor P., erroneous conclusion of, as to change of level of the land, i. 226.

Palmieri, Palazzo, at Polla, examination of, i. 202, 203; angle of emergence and velocity determined at, i. 211.
Palmieri and Scacchi's report on Melfi earthquake of August 14, 1851, ii. 197—212.
Pausillipo, fissures in tufa at, i. 213.
Paterna church, good illustrations of class of fracture at, i. 74.
Paterno, geology of country near, ii. 28; severe injuries at, ii. 29; alleged fall of rock at, for the most part fabulous, ii. 29; sulphurous springs at, ii. 29.
Perrey, Professor, conferred with, at Dijon, i. 2.
Pertosa, church at, well-developed case of normal phenomena in the, i. 43; destruction at, i. 273; severe loss of life at, i. 273; surviving inhabitants at, i. 274; English charities at, i. 274; direction of shock at, i. 275; emergence sleep, i. 276; second shock felt at, i. 277; sound heard before the shock, i. 272; geology of the valley at, i. 242.
Pesina, cause of immunity from injury, i. 302.
Petrosa, Il Vallone, geological evidences of violent dislocation and elevation at all sides in the mountain formation strikingly grand in, i. 250.
Phenomena presented by the effects of earthquakes resolved into problems of three classes, and all amenable to mechanical treatment, i. 22, 32; analysis of, i. 97; luminous, in the sky or air, on night of the earthquake, i. 323; possible nature of, i. 324; illustrations of, ii. 272; meteorological connection with, ii. 274.
Physical features of the country shaken, i. 101.
Piserno, church at, relations of roofing exemplified in a, i. 111; position of, ii. 50; indication of wave-path at, ii. 51.
Plains, the great, i. 164.
Pestum, the plains from Salerno to, no visible sign of earthquake throughout, i. 235; fawn-coloured aqueous tufa found beneath, i. 235; driftwood of com-

mon traditions of earthquakes having
desolated, i. 237; direction of shock
there, i. 238.

Polla, a part of, dislocation through enormously thick, ill-filled mortar joints in, i. 93; direction of shock exemplified in a street in, i. 90; fissure on the road near, i. 288; position of, i. 291; destruction and terrors at, i. 292, 293; and its neighbourhood, observations at, i. 294; monastery of St. Claire at, i. 295; Madonna of Loretto at, i. 296; St. Dominico, i. 297; heavy dislocated and inclined fissures in arched wall of monastery of St. Dominico, i. 298; views of isolated sluice-house fissured at, i. 299; Palazzo Palmieri at, i. 302; angles of emergence and velocity determined at, i. 311—315; sounds and time at, i. 317; road from, i. 321.

Population, Neapolitan statistics of, ii. 160, 161.

Portella, shock at, ii. 156.

Potenza, arrival at, ii. 56; extent of and traffic at, ii. 57; destruction at, ii. 57; grotesque appearance of theatre converted into lodgings, ii. 57; intense cold at, ii. 57; position of, ii. 57; geology of, ii. 58; effects of shock at, ii. 59; political prisoners at, ii. 59; diminished action of shock, compared with Montemurro, ii. 59; intendenzia at, ii. 60; Casa Communale at, ii. 60; church of St. Angelo at, ii. 61; Collegio di Jesuiti at, ii. 61; observations at the collegio, ii. 62; tower of St. Carlo at, ii. 64; Magazine del Summano, ii. 65; direction of wave-path at, ii. 65; street-lamps and Don Dominico's house, ii. 66; Chiesa Madre at, ii. 67; the campanile at, ii. 68; cathedral at, ii. 69; images and paintings, ii. 70; wave-path and direction determined by cathedral at, ii. 71; noises at, ii. 72; supposed heat at, ii. 72; no strange lights at, ii. 72.

Problems, particular, i. 138, 142.

Projection, seismical laws of, i. 16; and overthrow, i. 16.

Projected bodies or structures, i. 155.

RAINFALL, perturbation of, in relation to earthquake, ii. 168, 169; suggestions as to probable connection, ii. 170, 171; modifications, ii. 172.

Rapolla, position of, ii. 112; little injury at, ii. 112; wave-path at, ii. 112.

Rectangular buildings, fractures in, as evidence of wave-path, i. 33; normal shock, 38, 39; subnormal shock, i. 52; abnormal shock, i. 69; sub-abnormal shock, i. 69; shocks of vertical or nearly vertical emergence, effects on, i. 75.

Reflection and refraction, ii. 350.

Refraction in mountain chains, ii. 242.

Reiteration of the shock in same localities, and its cause, ii. 322.

Relations of seismal area and depth, ii. 257; to conformable inclined beds, ii. 263; to incoherent formations, ii. 264; of the seismic foci of the Italian peninsula, and the general relations of the seismic bands of the Mediterranean basin, ii. 378.

Retrospects and concluding words, ii. 384.

Rhodes, severe shock felt at, on day preceding the earthquake of December, 1857, i. 242.

Riotorto, position of, ii. 91; picturesque appearance of inhabitants, ii. 91; examination of, ii. 92; wave-path at, ii. 92.

Rivers, changes of channels, ii. 369; courses, great, ii. 164; falls of the great, i. 169; courses of, i. 171; turbidity of, ii. 369.

Rock, first example of actual fracture of beds of, i. 405; falls of, ii. 367.

"Rombo," at Moliterno, said by every one to have been heard, i. 412.

Rome, Ancient, earthquakes of, i. 115; ancient earthquake effects at, ii. 157.

Roofs and floors, relations of, i. 102.

Roofs, groined and domed, i. 112; vaulted, i. 113; construction of, in Neapolitan kingdom, i. 111.

Roofing, relations of, i. 110.

Rossi, Achille Antonio, Storia del Tremoti di Calabria, negli 1835, 1836, ii. 114.

Royal Society, the author receives authority of the, to proceed to Naples for the purpose of making scientific investigations connected with the earthquake, December 10, 1857, L. 1.

Ruined cities, first sight of, L. 80; apparent confusion of, only superficial, L. 38; first aspect of, L. 86.

SALARA, sediments of the river, near Pæstum, L. 236.

Salerno, shock at, not sufficient to throw down furniture, L. 232; abundance of large measurable fissures at, L. 232; the Intendenzia and cathedral at, L. 233; the tribunale at, L. 234.

Salvitelle, magnetic declinations near, ii. 34; indications of steep emergence of wave at, ii. 35.

Santa Dominica, Montemurro, remarkable example of form of fracture seen at, L. 69.

Saponara, position of, L. 418; remains of the Castello Uffiliarti at, L. 418; awful character of desolation at, L. 419; utter destruction of, due to the movement of its hill-site, L. 420; velocity of shock calculated, and of the oscillation of the hill, L. 423; destruction too absolute to render it conceivable that it will be rebuilt, L. 424; objects that may hereafter be exhumed from beneath its ruins in relation to geology, L. 425; velocity of the shock in the adjacent plain calculated, L. 427.

Saracena, Castel, shock felt at, from north-west to south-east, or 135° E. of north, L. 429.

Sarconi, situation of, L. 413; ancient church at, L. 415; church bell, L. 415; wave amplitude at, L. 415; little to be learned at, L. 417.

Sasano, little injury from the earthquake at, L. 308.

Satriano, Il Torre di, view of, from summits above Tito, ii. 54; ruins of ancient town near, ii. 55; probable result of examination of these old ruins, ii. 55.

"Sbalza," nature of the, i. 108.

Scacchi, Professor, visited by author, at Naples, L. 4; report by, on earthquake of August 14, 1851, i. 178.

Schmidt's, Dr. Julius, method of computing transit velocity, L. 122.

Sciarra, descent by the, L. 407.

Secchi, Padre, opinion of, that the shock had been instrumentally sensible as far as Rome, ii. 150.

Secular movements, ii. 381.

Seismic inquiry of two distinct orders, i. 6.

Seismic vertical and angle of emergence, L. 11, 18; region, extent of, from Rome to Otranto, and from Gargano to Reggio, L. 109; area under observation, bounded by a line eastward from Bermoneta, at head of the Pontine Marshes, to Foggia in Capitanata, and thence to the Adriatic, L. 197; vertical, superficial position of the, ii. 235; Map A, ii. 230; area and depth, relations of, ii. 257.

Seismology, recent origin of this branch of science, L. 5; method of inquiry into, L. 5, 9.

Seismometer, Professor Palmieri's, at the Observatory upon Vesuvius, affected by shock, L. 212.

Semiphases, both, L. 138.

Serapis, temple of, evidence at the, as to change of level, L. 218; new views as to change of level at, L. 221; foundation of, moving slowly downward, L. 223.

Serra Mandrane, pass of the, glorious sunset view from the, ii. 29; probable abnormal declination at, ii. 30.

Sesse, position of, ii. 152; shock at, loud enough to awaken all the people, ii. 152.

Shock, elastic wave of, L. 10; normal, L. 24, 39; abnormal, fractures in rectangular buildings by, L. 49; sub-abnormal, direction of fracture in rectangular buildings by, L. 65; effects of five principal conditions as to form and structure in buildings which modify the, L. 91; second class of conditions modifying effects of, L. 96; third modifying condition, L. 101; fourth modifying condition, L. 102; fifth modifying condition, i. 110; mountain chains and valleys affecting the transmission of, ii. 261; sounds attending, ii. 286; tremulous movements that preceded and followed the, ii. 295—297; reflected wave in every, ii. 300; no single, possible, ii. 301; heat producing greatest, ii. 315; decay of the wave of, and its gradual or per saltum extinction, ii. 331; secondary effects produced by the passage of the, ii. 302; affections evidenced by animals at the time of the, ii. 371.

Shocks of vertical or nearly vertical emergence, effects on rectangular buildings, i. 75; double, as the Certosa, near Padula, i. 373, 378; difference in time between, i. 384; sporadic, close before and after the great shock of December, ii. 158; great, inessentials of, compared, ii. 256.

Solid cubic block, i. 126.
Solid parallelopiped, i. 129.
Sorrento, earthquake at, October 12, 1856, i. 201.
Sorrento to Amalfi, direction of wave-path at, i. 229.
Sounds attending the shock, ii. 280; area of, ii. 287; varied with position, ii. 288.
Sounds and shock, relations of, ii. 214.
Sperlonga, position of, ii. 154; no evidence of earthquake at, ii. 155.
Spinosa, not much as to reward the time and labour of ascent, i. 429.
St. Michael's Cave, near Pertosa, corroborative proof of the steepness of emergence of the wave at, i. 281; geology of the valley at, i. 282.
Subabnormal wave, easy method of finding the path of a, i. 71.
Subabnormal wave, what so called, i. 35.
Subnormal wave, inferences from, i. 58.
Summits, effects of towns perched on, i. 201.
Surface, statistics of, in Neapolitan kingdom, ii. 160.

TABLES of coefficients for fractures, i. 149—154; of factors for coefficient I_c, i. 151; second ditto, i. 152; of values, i. 153.

Tanagro, higher stream of, now called Calore, i. 283.
Telegraphic communication between Naples and earthquake district, how cut off, i. 289.
Temperature of the focal cavity, and the intensity of the force that acted within it, ii. 309; of artesian wells at Naples, ii. 311; hypogeal deductions from assumed increase of, ii. 313.
Tenements della Madonna Campostrino, remarkable fissures in the, i. 289; wave-path at, i. 289.
Termoino, shock at, ii. 154; all trace of the earthquake about thirty miles from, finally lost, ii. 155.
Terra di Lavoro, physical conformation of, ii. 151.
Thermometer, earthquake wave becomes one, for inaccessible depths, ii. 310.
Time, interval of, between the double shocks at Padula, i. 381, 384; of tremors and of reading compared, ii. 308.
Tito, position of, ii. 52; loss of life at, ii. 52; severe injuries at, ii. 52; old church of St. Antonio at, ii. 52; Chiesa Madre at, ii. 53; cross at, ii. 53.
Topo, il, di Moto, ii. 81.
Towers, cylindric, effects of shock on, i. 86; high, effects of shock on, i. 98.
Towns, position of, i. 172; high or low, on rock or on clay, effects of shock on, ii. 358.
Trumpisole, arrival at, ii. 17; situation of, ii. 18; wave-path at, ii. 19; Casa Marotta at, ii. 21; greater velocity of earth-wave at, than in limestone districts, ii. 21; the Chiesa Madre at, ii. 23; statue of St. Leonardo at, ii. 24; Chiesa dell' Rosario at, ii. 25; general wave-path at, ii. 26; noise during and after shock at, ii. 27.
Transit motion, direction of, inferred, in the case of a cardinal building and abnormal wave, i. 64.
Transit velocity of the wave form, i.

121; of secondary importance as respects seismometry viewed as a branch of physical geology, i. 123; deduced, ii. 325, 326, 329, 334; Schmidt and Niemeyth's calculations and results, i. 324—334.

Transverse shake, a minor, evidence of, at Arcos Diauna, i. 401.

Trigonometric solution, advantage of, i. 69.

Trinita, Chiesa della, a mile south of La Sala, injury done to, i. 849.

Troglodytes, Prince Doria's, ii. 85.

Tufa over limestones, i. 170.

Tufa, remarkable erosion of the, on Monte Vulture, ii. 96.

Turbidity of rivers, ii. 36.

Turno and Landro, Valleys of the, ii. 86.

Twisting strains not "vorticose," i. 78.

Twisting and tilting of objects at the Certosa, near Padula, i. 377.

VAL DI DIANO, general aspect of, i. 168.

Valleys, connection of, i. 171.

Valva, state of, ii. 142; magnetic declination at, ii. 142; ancient fissures at, ii. 143.

Vastento, source of the, ii. 57.

Vaulted roofs, i. 113.

Vaulting, cylindric, i. 114.

Velocities of transit, of particle, i. 12.

Velocity and fracture, relation of, i. 43.

Velocity, transit, of the wave form, i. 121; angle of, obtained, i. 157; geometrically, i. 158; of projectile may be less than wave, i. 159; of transition of the wave of shock through the limestone country near Padula, calculated, i. 344; of first shock deduced from bell of Campanile (the Certosa), i. 380; greatest, of reading rock, ii. 296; of transit of the wave, ii. 322.

Velocity, transit, deduced, ii. 325, 328, 329, 334.

Velocity, proper, of the wave of shock, ii. 335.

Velocity of oscillation of Nojeasara Colline approximated, ii. 338.

Velocity found compared with sensation, ii. 340.

Vertical, seismic, a perficial position of the, ii. 235; position of the, in the meizoseismal and isoseismal curves, ii. 252.

Vesuvius, examination of the courses of several ancient and recent lava currents, ii. 148.

Vesuvius crater, actual bent of, ii. 314.

Vibrating particle, movements of the, i. 76.

Vietri, effects of shock at, in the highest degree complicated, i. 232.

Vietri di Potenza, situation of, ii. 37; monument at, ii. 39; emergence and direction fixed for, ii. 40; house of Signor Pescarum, ii. 42; Communal Campanile, ii. 43; bells of the campanile, ii. 43; great steepness of emergence of wave at, ii. 44; shock severely felt at, ii. 46; sounds at, ii. 46; calculation of moment of shock at, ii. 47; no confirmation as to light on night of the shock, ii. 48.

Viggiano, position of, ii. 13; free from contact of other hills, ii. 13; severe suffering at, ii. 13; great landslip near, ii. 15.

Volcanic lakes near Oliveto, ii. 144.

"Voragine" near Itella, proved to be landslips, ii. 130.

Vulture, Monte, view of, near Rionero, ii. 92; a ride round, ii. 96; rain torrents descending from, ii. 90; impressive forest scenery of, ii. 98; descent of, into the once innermost bowl of a volcano, now full of every leafy beauty, ii. 98.

Vulture district, volcanic phenomena developed in the, on a scale of grandeur to which Vesuvius is insignificant, ii. 117.

WALLS, opposite, effects produced on, i. 50, 51; line of pressure in, i. 66; overthrown by force of an abnormal wave, observations on, i. 63; effects of apertures in, i. 116; effects of the three classes of, i. 103.

Wave, resilience conspiring with, i. 102.

Wave form, transit velocity of the, i. 121.
Wave of refraction and refraction, ii. 280; proof of, ii. 282.
Wave, reflected, occurs in every shock, ii. 300.
Wave amplitude and volume, ii. 317.
Wave, earthquake, becomes a thermometer for inaccessible depths, ii. 319.
Wave, velocity of transit of the, ii. 322.
Wave of shock, velocity proper of the, ii. 833.
Wave-particle, velocities discussed, ib. 377; new method of comparing, ii. 341.
Wave of shock, local disturbing causes producing abrupt perturbations of the, ii. 347.
Wave, abrupt reduction of the, ii. 853.
Wave-path, first class of determinants—fractures in rectangular buildings as evidences of, i. 33; in reference to buildings, i. 34; inferred, in the case of a cardinal building and abnormal wave, i. 64; radiation of, from Caggiano, ii. 227; general tabulation of, ii. 234—241; convergence of, ii. 242—215; divergence of, approximately equal to the focal cavity horizontally, ii. 246.
Wave transit, direction of, discovered in buildings similarly placed, i. 37; through limestone and clays, i. 385.
Wedges detached, i. 68; severed off, i. 131; from quoins, i. 132.
Windows, fractures over, i. 117.
Wiseman, Cardinal, value of encyclical letter by, i. 2; ii. 388.

" Zoccolante," large old monastery of, at Oliveto, ii. 143.

www.ingramcontent.com/pod-product-compliance
Lightning Source LLC
Chambersburg PA
CBHW020539300426
44111CB00008B/726